MARGUERITE IKNAYAN

The Concave Mirror

From Imitation to Expression in French Esthetic Theory 1800-1830

STANFORD FRENCH AND ITALIAN STUDIES 30 · ANMA LIBRI

THE CONCAVE MIRROR

FROM IMITATION TO EXPRESSION
IN FRENCH ESTHETIC THEORY 1800-1830

STANFORD FRENCH AND ITALIAN STUDIES

volume XXX

ANMA LIBRI

THE CONCAVE MIRROR

FROM IMITATION TO EXPRESSION
IN FRENCH ESTHETIC THEORY 1800-1830

MARGUERITE IKNAYAN

1983

ANMA LIBRI

Stanford French and Italian Studies is a collection of scholarly publications devoted to the study of French and Italian literature and language, culture and civilization. Occasionally it will allow itself excursions into related Romance areas.

Stanford French and Italian Studies will publish books, monographs, and collections of articles centering around a common theme, and is open also to scholars associated with academic institutions other than Stanford.

The collection is published for the Department of French and Italian, Stanford University by Anma Libri.

© 1983 by ANMA Libri & Co.
P.O. Box 876, Saratoga, Calif. 95071
All rights reserved.
LC 83-71053
ISBN 0-915838-07-9
Printed in the United States of America.

Contents

Introduction

This book studies the evolution of one aspect of esthetic theory in France between 1800 and 1830, the relation between the artist and the world outside him, in particular the natural world. It was inspired in part by a reading of M. H. Abrams' *The Mirror and the Lamp*, which examines poetic theory during the Romantic period in England and to some extent Germany; Tzvetan Todorov's *Théories du symbole*, which I read as my own work was nearing completion, includes chapters on Neoclassic and Romantic esthetics in Germany. But neither Abrams nor Todorov deals with French writing on the subject after 1800. It is not surprising that the English and German theorists should have received attention, since their works furnish a concentrated richness of esthetic concepts which are more scattered and less fully developed in French writings of the early nineteenth century. But for devotees of French cultural history a lacuna remains to be filled.

Concentration on the rapport between the artist and the universe pushes to the periphery other aspects of esthetics such as the nature of beauty, form in the arts, the psychology of creation and of esthetic experience, and relationships between the artist and the spectator/listener/reader; they are dealt with briefly on occasion.

The decision to include other arts besides literature was prompted in part by my personal interest in the arts in general, but more so by my curiosity to see how the principles of representation and expression in the arts evolved in the early nineteenth century and whether the various arts participated in these changes in the same way. Moreover, literary theory of this period, especially the polemics between *classiques* and *romantiques* has been extensively studied, whereas general esthetic theory has not.

1

I have, however, concentrated on certain arts and eliminated others except for brief mention. The visual arts include primarily painting and sculpture; in literature I have concentrated on poetry. To keep this study within feasible limits I have excluded any systematic examination of the theory of drama, the original mimetic art as expounded by Aristotle. In any case, dramatic theory has been thoroughly investigated by others. The path through the relationships between the arts is strewn with pitfalls, but it is legitimate to study the history of the concepts of those relationships, in a period that begins by subscribing to the principle of *ut pictura poesis* and ends with an invitation from Sainte-Beuve to join "la fraternité des arts." Etienne Souriau points out that even in the twentieth century, estheticians who are not artists have a tendency to apply the criteria of one art, usually poetry, to all arts.[1] In 1800 the axiom that art imitates nature does not primarily refer to drama; the emphasis has shifted mainly to the visual arts, which are at the center of esthetic theory.

Since my approach is that of a literary or art historian, or more precisely a historian of ideas, I have dipped into many sources of the late eighteenth and early nineteenth centuries, books, periodicals, and published lectures of a wide range of writers from famous to obscure. While the best-known and most important ones receive the most attention, it is essential to take them all into consideration to attempt to define a climate of opinion. At the same time, those who wrote most extensively on the arts, such as Quatremère de Quincy and Stendhal, are not here studied as throughly as is possible in the separate studies their importance warrants. I have made little attempt to draw upon the creative works for expressions of theory: I have not, for example, examined Lamartine's poetry but have limited myself to a few statements of a theoretical nature made by the poet. There are two chronological divisions: chapters 1 to 5 deal with the period between 1800 and 1815 to 1820, chapters 7 to 10 deal with the 1820s, and they are connected by chapter 6, dealing with the years 1815 to 1820, which mark the end of the domination of Neoclassicism.

Much of the material presented here is familiar to students of the period; my investigations have not been exhaustive; but by combining various elements I can perhaps shed some new light on the attitudes of the time or show more clearly what we already believe to be true.

---

[1] *La Correspondance des arts*, 2nd ed. (Paris: Flammarion, 1969), p. 11.

1. Imitation (I)

At the beginning of the nineteenth century the most widely accepted axiom in Western esthetic theory was that art imitates nature. On one hand art imitates men and their actions, said Aristotle, and on the other the sensible universe. This principle, which descended from antiquity through the Renaissance, would not lose its hold until the rise of modernism.

Most theorists in 1800 looked back half a century for the basic statement of the mimetic doctrine to Charles Batteux's *Les Beaux-arts réduits à un même principe* (1746). The fine arts, those whose object was pleasure, included music, poetry, painting, sculpture, and dance, and their common principle was imitation. Models for all works of art must be taken from nature; even monsters must be made of parts drawn from nature. "Le Génie qui travaille pour plaire, ne doit donc, ni ne peut sortir des bornes de la nature même. Sa fonction consiste, non à imaginer ce qui ne peut être, mais à trouver ce qui est."[1] All nature is the artist's realm: "La nature, c'est-à-dire tout ce qui est, ou ce que nous concevons aisément comme possible, voilà le prototype ou le modèle des arts"(p. 33). The limits of this nature are quite wide, since they include not only the verisimilar but the mythological. The natural model, says Batteux, may be drawn from four different worlds: 1) the existing world, of which we are a part (e.g., Socrates depicted by Aristophanes), 2) the historical world (the Horatii), 3) the fabulous

---

[1] *Les Beaux-arts réduits à un même principe* (Paris, 1883; rpt. Geneva: Slatkine, 1969), pp. 31-32. In this and in subsequent quotations I have taken the liberty of modernizing the spelling.

world filled with gods and heroes (Medea), and 4) the ideal or possible world from which our imagination may draw individuals and characterize them (Tartuffe). The beings of this last world seem to be given, as are the others, to exist already as in a world of archetypes where the artist has only to go look for them. The artist does not create his subjects, he finds them. "Inventer dans les arts, ce n'est point donner l'être à un objet, c'est le reconnaître où il est" (p. 32).

Batteux devotes most of his attention to literary genres and very little to the plastic arts, though the latter are at the very center of the doctrine. On one hand, he recognizes that the plastic arts and literature differ in some ways, chiefly in that perfection in painting depends only in its resemblance to reality, whereas poetry lives on fictions (p. 330). On the other hand, he tells us that poetry and painting are so much alike in their imitation of *la belle nature* (see below, pp. 13-14, 27, 28) that what is said of one can be applied to the other. Their elements correspond: thus the drawing and color of painting have their counterparts in the story (*fable*) and the versifying of poetry.

This close parallel between the two arts is at the base of a corollary to the doctrine of imitation, that of *ut pictura poesis*, whose name came from Horace but which had been developed in the Renaissance and remained a reigning principle between the mid-sixteenth and mid-eighteenth centuries.[2] It insisted on the fundamental identity of poetry and painting; both were imitations. It encouraged description and picturesque effects in poetry, but its principal effect was seen in painting. From its inception it was interpreted as the elevation of painting, a manual art, to the dignity accorded to poetry as a liberal art by giving it moral, affective, and intellectual content. The function of painting thus ennobled was to represent human action in its higher forms. This conception was the basis of the hierarchy among types of painting: the most prestigious was history painting, dealing with historical, mythological, religious, or literary subjects, after it portrait painting, then in lower rank landscape, genre painting, and still life. Neoclassical landscape painters could ennoble their paintings by including human figures and portraying historical or mythological subjects; some even included words in their paintings.

Réflexions sur la poésie et la peinture (1719) of Du Bos was one of the first works to examine carefully the meaning of *ut pictura poesis*. On

---

[2] For a complete exposition of this doctrine see Rensselaer Lee, "*Ut pictura poesis*: The Humanist Theory of Painting," *Art Bulletin*, 12 (1940), 197-269. Also published in book form (New York: Norton, 1967).

studying the two arts, Du Bos found that they differ in many ways, and his remarks on the immobility and instantaneousness of the visibly perceived versus the duration and emotional expression of poetry prefigure Lessing. However, it is taken for granted that both are imitations, and Du Bos studies the power of an imitation in either art to move the spectator.

Batteux was still very influential in 1800 and the idea that the arts are imitated from nature generally accepted, but there was some disagreement as to which arts were to be included. Sometimes arts were classified according to the degree of imitation, and painting always came first, especially landscape and genre painting; at the same time, portraits and history painting required their own particular accuracy. Painting's greater range of means and resources, its elements of perspective, chiaroscuro, and especially color gave it its pre-eminent place as an imitative art.[3] Sculpture ranked second, for all its three dimensions; it was the art most closely identified with ideal beauty, as we shall see.

Architecture was not usually considered an *art d'imitation*; Batteux did not include it, and Père André, following tradition, based it on principles of geometry.[4] But the two outstanding writers of the early nineteenth century diverge from this view, thus making a definite break with the classical style. In a famous passage in *Le Génie du Christianisme* Chateaubriand proclaims the natural sources and inspiration for architecture:

> Les forêts ont été les premiers temples de la divinité, et les hommes ont pris dans les forêts la première idée de l'architecture. Cet art a donc dû varier selon les climats. Les Grecs ont tourné l'élégante colonne corinthienne avec son chapiteau de feuilles sur le mode du palmier. Les énormes piliers du style égyptien représentent le sycomore, le figuier oriental, le bananier et la plupart des arbres gigantesques de l'Afrique et de l'Asie.[5]

Here Chateaubriand goes back to the primitive principle whereby architecture echoes the natural setting in which it is placed.

A few years later Mme de Staël sees in nature an inspiration for architecture, as well as for painting and music. In a passage that recalls

---

[3] See Fabre d'Olivet, *La Musique*, 2nd ed. (Paris: Chacornac, 1910), pp. 84-85.
[4] *Essai sur le beau*, in *Oeuvres philosophiques* (1843; rpt. Geneva: Slatkine, 1969), p. 15.
[5] *Le Génie du christianisme* (Paris: Flammarion, 1948), Pt. III, Bk. i, Ch. 8. Subsequent references to this work will be indicated in abbreviated form and will refer to Part, Book, and Chapter, respectively.

not only *Le Génie du christianisme* but also the prologue of *Atala*, nature inspires art and also recalls it: "Les beaux-arts ont aussi leur type dans la nature, et ce luxe de l'existence est plus soigné par elle encore que l'existence même: la symétrie des formes dans le règne végétal et minéral a servi de modèle aux architectes, et le reflet des objets et des couleurs dans l'onde donne l'idée des illusions de la peinture; le vent, dont le murmure se prolonge sous les feuilles tremblantes, nous révèle la musique."[6] Such are her thoughts on contemplating nature; when it comes to imitation as an esthetic doctrine, she will adopt a different point of view.

Among literary genres, descriptive and dramatic poetry imitate most closely; the epic is also sometimes mentioned. The novel, though it is commonly said to be the genre which best reflects society, is seldom mentioned in theoretical works before 1820, since it has not yet found its place among the traditional literary categories.

Descriptive poetry is the one poetic invention of Neoclassicism, born around the middle of the eighteenth century, when poetry was at a low ebb, but falling into decline after 1800.[7] It was subject to considerable unfavorable criticism from its inception on charges of poor composition, artificiality, and monotony, and this critical attitude is accentuated after 1800. Of the commentators of the first decade of the century whom I have read, Chateaubriand is the only one who speaks favorably of the genre. In *Le Génie du christianisme* he ascribes its origin to the influence of Christianity. (In fact, it was naturalist and materialist in origin.) Antiquity had neither landscape painting nor descriptive poetry, he claims, but nature was transformed in man's eyes by the Christian religion, and as soon as the Apostles began to preach the Gospel, descriptive poetry appeared. In France, Louis Racine was the founder of the genre, in which Delille has recently excelled (II.iv.1, 2, 3). Chateaubriand's praise for this genre is at odds with his own practice in natural description, constrained as he is by the thesis of his work, and his descriptions of the *solitudes* of nature as transformed by the new religion belie his Neoclassical professions of faith.

---

[6] *De l'Allemagne*, Pt. IV, Ch. 9; Pange-Balayé ed. (Paris: Hachette, 1958-1960), V, 179-80. Subsequent references to this work will be indicated in abbreviated form and will refer to Part, Chapter, Volume, and page number, respectively.

[7] For a detailed study of the genre see Edouard Guitton, *Jacques Delille (1738-1813) et le poème de la nature en France de 1750 à 1820* (Paris: Klincksieck, 1974).

Other critics, of the most diverse tendencies, either have strong qualifications about the genre or reject it completely. Marie-Joseph Chénier, who believes that arts should be kept separate, attacks Delille's poetry as interminably boring.[8] The *Débats* critic, Dussault, voices the common opinion that no poem should be entirely composed of description: "... les descriptions ne sont, par leur nature, que des ornements qui doivent servir à embellir et à parer un fonds plus solide qu'elle."[9] However, he does approve of poetic prose, and the poets who have used the material that natural history has to offer are Buffon, Rousseau, Bernardin de Saint-Pierre, and Chateaubriand; their works contain more real poetry than all the descriptive poems of the last sixty years.[10]

What critics increasingly miss is a lyric or emotional element. Fauriel's remarks on this score are particularly trenchant. When a poet describes material objects, says he, he is appealing not to our emotions but to our curiosity to know. Objects and phenomena of inanimate nature can have poetic interest only to the extent that they involve our feelings. In any case, no absolutely and purely descriptive poetry is possible; what passes for such is a bastard composition floating between the domains of science and art and in reality a corruption of both.[11] According to the young Guizot, the descriptive poet must paint nature faithfully and from direct personal knowledge, but the genre is cold if he does not mingle with his descriptions the sensations they awaken and the analogies they bring to mind.[12] An anonymous critic of the *Archives Littéraires* calls upon the poet to arouse the reader's feelings or ideas. A painter needs only to depict faithfully; his scene will strike our senses as reality would. The poet does not have these means: he cannot paint forms and colors with sounds. "Il n'imite pas l'objet, il ne fait qu'en réveiller l'image ou l'idée."[13] The effect of painting may stop with the senses; poetry must strike the senses only to penetrate into the soul.

[8] "Essai sur le principe des arts," *Oeuvres diverses et inédites* (Bruxelles: Weissenbruch, 1816), pp. 99-100.

[9] *Annales Littéraires* (Paris: Maradan et Lenormant, 1818-1824), I, 356. The article, which deals with *Atala*, dates from 1802.

[10] *Ibid.*, II, 564-68, quoted by Guitton, p. 530.

[11] "Réflexions primaires" to his translation of Baggesen, *La Parthénéide* (Paris: Treuttel-Würtz, 1810), pp. lxxx-lxxxii.

[12] *Archives Littéraires*, 15 (1807), 261. See also 17: 260.

[13] "Réflexion sur la poésie descriptive," 10 (1806), 310.

So poetry comes to be looked upon as imitative only in the broadest sense. Works of Bernardin de Saint-Pierre and Chateaubriand, which are more evocative, are not cited as examples of imitation. The move of poetry away from the description of purely visual effects marks an important stage in the weakening of the doctrine of *ut pictura poesis*.

Music was included among the *arts d'imitation* to an extent that is surprising to the modern reader, yet even in Batteux's own time the principle was brought into question or qualified. The response depended to a large extent upon the breadth of meaning one wished to give to the word "imitation." Batteux recognized two kinds of music: one which imitates unfeeling sounds (corresponding to landscape painting) and the other which expresses animate sounds, i.e., the human voice (corresponding to paintings of human beings). Though both kinds are characterized as imitations, the second is an imitation of a personal expression. In the first type Batteux calls for faithful reproduction of physical phenomena by the musician as well as the painter: "... il est partout, et constamment soumis à la comparaison qu'on fait de lui à la Nature. S'il peint un orage, un ruisseau, un zéphir, ses tons sont dans la Nature, il ne peut les prendre que là."[14]

Many others admitted this double meaning of imitation, though when we speak of music as an imitation of voice and/or speech, or spontaneous cries or of declamation, as Rousseau, Diderot, or Grétry did, we are moving into the domain of expression. For Grétry, who bases his theory on declamation, music is tied to words, in song, and instrumental music is an imitation of the human voice: "... il est pour la musique un principe certain, le seul par lequel le musicien puisse appliquer à son art, et sans arbitraire, les sons de la nature: il consiste à retracer toutes les inflexions de la parole, comme le principe de la peinture et de la sculpture consiste à tracer les formes, les contours et les couleurs des êtres animés ou inanimés."[15] Diderot places a similar idea in the mouth of Rameau's nephew. When *Moi* asks, "Quel est le modèle du musicien quand il fait un chant?" *Lui* replies, "C'est la déclamation si le modèle est vivant et pensant; c'est le bruit, si le modèle est inanimé. Il faut considérer la déclamation comme une ligne, et le chant comme une autre ligne qui serpenterait sur la

---

[14]   Batteux, p. 356.
[15]   *Mémoires* (Paris: Imprimerie de la République, An V), III, 251.

première."[16] A symphony is to singing what singing is to real declamation, he says somewhat later, that is, an imitation at one degree further removed.

Some were opposed to the imitation of natural sounds in music. Grétry thought that physical effects like rain, hail, or birdsong gave a pitiful effect.[17] Chabanon insisted that music was much less imitative than the visual arts or poetry, but he recognized that composers had for a long time effectively imitated certain natural sounds such as stormy seas and running brooks, for which tried and true procedures existed. This is the kind of music that is the closest to imitation. Rather than repeat these well-known devices, says Chabanon, why not write, for example, a sweet, calm melody to suggest a lovey countryside?[18] Here Chabanon has hit upon the solution proposed by most commentators from Rousseau on: in his *Discours sur l'origine des langues* Jean-Jacques says of the musician's art: "... il ne représentera pas directement les choses, mais il excitera dans l'âme les mêmes sentiments qu'on éprouve en les voyant" (Ch. 16). The goal has moved from an objective imitation to a subjective reaction. Grétry too recommends what he calls an indirect imitation: instead of rendering objects directly, the composer should express the sensation which they give to him.[19]

It is commonly accepted that in addition to these two kinds of imitative music, there is also non-imitative music, or "musique vague." Of this kind of music we shall speak in chapter 3. There is a division between chamber or symphonic music and opera. As Chabanon points out, what makes us smile in a concert hall may be eminently suitable at the opera.[20] In general, however, imitative music is not associated with opera so much as with orchestral effects. The debate concerning music with or without words, or orchestral versus vocal music, looms large at this time, and we shall touch upon it later (pp. 58-61).

The beginning of the nineteenth century shows no great change in these diverse opinions, though there are signs that at least the term "imitation" is falling into disuse. The Abbé Morellet, who had some years earlier written briefly on imitative music (*Réflexions sur la musique dramatique*, 1771), makes the usual distinction between physical

[16] *Oeuvres* (Paris: Bibliothèque de la Pléiade, 1946), p. 481.

[17] *Mémoires*, I, 35-36.

[18] Michel Chabanon, *De la musique considérée en elle-même et dans ses rapports avec la parole, les langues, et le théâtre* (Paris: Pissot, 1785), p. 58.

[19] Grétry, III, 264.

[20] *De la musique*, p. 63.

objects and emotions as objects of imitation but cannot differentiate between imitation and expression in music. For his purpose, "exprimer" and "peindre" are synonyms. He takes into account different degrees of imitation but points out that it cannot and should not be as exact as some would like: "... elle doit même être imparfaite, et différente de la nature par quelque côté, sous peine de perdre une partie de ses droits sur notre âme,..."[21] But he does expound at some length on procedures for imitating, or rather suggesting, phenomena other than sounds, such as high sounds for elevated objects and deep sounds for low ones, diminishing sustained sounds to indicate flight (*fuite*), twittering high instruments to indicate sunrise. The resulting sounds may not be resemblances, he admits, but they certainly are analogies. When music depicts impressions made on other senses than hearing, it is a metaphorical language, says Morellet, who was an early believer in synesthesia.

Le Génie du christianisme contains both conventional statements and new *aperçus* on music. When Chateaubriand says, "... la musique, considérée comme art, est imitation de la nature" (III.i.1), he seems to be repeating a trite formula, but he invests it with a new meaning in the following pages, ringing new changes on *Coeli enarrant gloriam Dei*. Nature herself sings the praises of the Creator:

> ... il n'y a rien de plus religieux que les cantiques que chantent, avec les vents, les chênes et les roseaux du désert. Ainsi le musicien qui veut suivre la religion dans ses rapports est obligé d'apprendre l'imitation des harmonies de la solitude. Il faut qu'il connaisse les sons que rendent les arbres et les eaux; il faut qu'il ait entendu le bruit du vent dans les cloîtres, et ces murmures qui règnent dans les temples gothiques, dans l'herbe des cimetières, et dans les souterrains des morts.

Such "imitation" seems rather the suggestiveness of religious association and the need of communicating a feeling of awe. However, in his famous parallel between the forest and the Gothic cathedral, Chateaubriand is specific about imitative music for religious effect: "L'architecte chrétien, non content de bâtir des forêts, a voulu, pour ainsi dire, en imiter les murmures; et, au moyen de l'orgue et du bronze suspendu, il a attaché au temple gothique jusqu'au bruit des vents et des tonnerres, qui roule dans la profondeur des bois" (III.i.8).

---

[21] "De l'expression en musique," *Archives Littéraires*, 6 (1805), 168.

Mme de Staël does not care for imitative music such as Haydn's *The Creation* or *The Seasons*; representing the creation of light by a sudden blast of music is, to her thinking, nothing but "un jeu factice."[22] On the other hand, certain harmonies can remind us of the marvels of nature; the key, again, is to produce the same effect on the listener: "Les ressemblances réelles des beaux-arts entre eux et des beaux-arts avec la nature dépendent des sentiments du même genre qu'ils excitent dans notre âme par des moyens divers" (*loc. cit.*). For Mme de Staël, imitation and expression are at opposite poles, and imitative music is to be excluded from consideration.

Other commentators of this period whom I have read add little that is new but do seem to indicate a gradual turning away from imitation. Joseph Droz makes the usual division between the two kinds of music, pointing out that there is no imitation or "truth" in a symphony, but after all, no doctrine of beauty can apply to all the arts.[23] Castil-Blaze uses the term "picturesque" for what others call "imitative." Some people condemn this music, but in many cases, says he, it is successful and quite charming.[24]

According to Stendhal, music can imitate nature in two ways, *imitation physique* and *imitation sentimentale*.[25] Direct physical imitation is briefly amusing but soon bores the listener; but Stendhal does not reject physical imitation if it is properly done: "En musique, la meilleure des imitations est peut-être celle qui ne fait qu'indiquer l'objet dont il est question, qui nous le montre à travers un nuage, qui se garde bien de nous rendre avec une exactitude scrupuleuse la nature telle qu'elle est: cette espèce d'imitation est ce qu'il y a de mieux dans le genre descriptif."[26] In this way music observes the principle that all arts should have "un certain degré de fausseté." Echoing Rousseau like so many others, Stendhal recommends a musical solution that will be affectively analogous for the receptive listener: "Il faut que l'imitation produise l'effet qui serait occasionné par l'objet imité, s'il nous frappait dans ces moments heureux de sensibilité et de bonheur

---

[22] *De l'Allemagne* (II.32; III.379).

[23] *Etudes sur le beau dans les arts* (Paris: Renouard, 1815), p. 26.

[24] *De l'opéra en France* (Paris: Janet et Cotelle, 1820), I, 143-144.

[25] *Vies de Haydn, de Mozart et de Métastase*, ed. del Litto and Abravanel (Geneva: 1910), p. 179. Unless otherwise indicated, all subsequent page references will be taken from this edition of Stendhal's works.

[26] *Ibid.*, p. 180.

qui donnent naissance aux passions."[27] This is the other kind of imitation, *l'imitation sentimentale*, which "ne retrace pas les choses, mais les sentiments qu'elles inspirent." Stendhal also uses the words "pittoresque" and "expressive" to indicate the essential division, terms which smack slightly less than "imitation" of eighteenth-century convention and have the additional advantage of clarity. He cites Haydn's *The Creation* as exemplar of the first type, and *Don Giovanni* and *Il matrimonio segreto* as the finest examples of the second.

Other attacks on music as imitation came from opposing directions. An interesting and untypical remark comes from A. J. Morel, a mathematics professor and music lover, in his *Principe acoustique nouveau et universel de la théorie musicale*. He detaches music from the emotional as well as from the picturesque and bases it on sensation; the effect of music, says he, depends on its perception by the ear: "... dans des compositions de ce genre, ce n'est pas la *nature* que l'on imite,... l'on obtient le beau en observant par quelle marche, et au moyen de quels ressorts l'art se met en harmonie avec la nature; ce mot signifie *organisation physique* de l'oreille."[28]

When an illuminist considers music, he also deals the principle of imitation a heavy blow. If music imitates, says Fabre d'Olivet, it imitates intellectual beauty; the model is in the composer's soul.[29] We have reached the other end of the spectrum from Batteux and Diderot, from imitation and declamation. But from the beginning, music critics and theorists are more interested in other properties of music, especially its expressiveness, as we shall see in chapter 3.

The term "arts d'imitation," when referring to the visual arts, as it usually does, encompasses such a wide variety of degrees that it comes to mean simply representational art. At one extreme is photographic realism, which is the closest imitation, understood in a narrow sense. This would be the kind of painting produced by following the method recommended by Leonardo da Vinci: hold up a glass in front of a natural site, then paint on the glass what you see through it. This method posits the beauty of the natural site and the passage

---

[27] *Ibid.*, p. 181. See also his letter to Félix Faure of 2 October 1812, quoted by G. Blin in *Stendhal et les problèmes du roman*, p. 30.

[28] Alexandre-Jean Morel, *Principe acoustique nouveau et universel de la théorie musicale, ou Musique expliquée* (Paris: Bachelier, 1816), p. 362.

[29] *La Musique*, pp. 86-87.

of that beauty into the work of art through exact reproduction of appearances.

The questions of what to imitate and how to imitate it are dealt with by Batteux in his theory of *la belle nature*, which was, he said, the fundamental principle of the arts. Technical skill is obviously important, and Batteux even recommends *trompe-l'oeil*, (Pt. III, Sec. 2) though, as André Fontaine points out, it was generally frowned upon by the mid-eighteenth century.[30] Such a complete illusion was not considered necessary to communicate the beauty of the subject. The goal of imitation is to please (Batteux) or to awaken the passions (Du Bos).

The choice of what to imitate was of primary importance, since though nature is on the whole beautiful, some places and some people are more beautiful than others. Artistic beauty derives from natural beauty and is dependent on it, hence a fine subject will give a fine picture or poem. According to Du Bos, a painter should choose for his painting a subject that would move the spectator if he saw it in reality, and the spectator's response to the painting will be the same as to the original subject, but diminished in intensity.[31] How the choice of subject is to be made is not revealed, and Diderot, in his *Essai sur les sourds et muets* complains that Batteux does not explain what "la belle nature" is. Diderot differs from Batteux on some other important points: he does not believe that all the arts imitate in the same way, and he distinguishes between esthetic beauty and natural beauty, but his writings on art were not known or not read by critics of 1800 (his *Salons* were first published in book form in 1818-1819). Batteux and Du Bos remained the most influential writers on esthetics, along with Père André.

If the artist had difficulty finding a sufficiently beautiful subject, he might have recourse to the method of choosing elements from various places or features from various persons ("beautés de détail") and composing them into a more nearly perfect whole, as the ancient Greek artist Zeuxis was said to have combined separate traits from several beautiful women to make his portrait of Helen. This is still presumably depiction of "la belle nature" which Batteux recommends to the artist:

Tous ses efforts durent nécessairement se réduire à faire un choix des plus belles parties de la Nature, pour en former un tout exquis, qui

[30] *Les Doctrines d'art en France de Poussin à Diderot* (Laurens, 1909), p. 204.
[31] *Réflexions sur la poésie et sur la peinture*, 7th ed. (Paris: Pissot, 1770), Pt. I, Sec. 3.

fût plus parfait que la Nature elle-même, sans cependant cesser d'être naturel... si les arts sont imitateurs de la Nature, ce doit être une imitation sage et éclairée qui ne la copie pas servilement; mais qui choisissant les objets et les traits, les présente avec toute la perfection dont ils sont susceptibles: en un mot, une imitation, où on voit la Nature, non telle qu'elle est en elle-même, mais telle qu'elle peut être, et qu'on peut la concevoir par l'esprit. (Batteux, Pt. I, Ch. I, 3).

This is now a much more qualified imitation, which has taken a considerable step away from Leonardo's glass.

At the beginning of the nineteenth century, the critics who leaned toward naturalism were in the minority, as against the larger group of partisans of the ideal in art, who derived their beliefs largely from the Classical revival of the late eighteenth century, the writings of Winckelmann, and a return to Platonism as represented in *L'Essai sur le beau* of Père André. Both these broad tendencies are still within the domain of imitation, as most critics see it, and the lines between them are not always clearly drawn.

Those painters and critics who favored a relatively close imitation of sensible reality placed emphasis on the *vrai*, the *naïf*, the particular, and opposed the use of allegory. For them, the end of art was pleasure, and in painting line was less important than color and especially chiaroscuro. Casting aside the Academic prejudice in favor of history painting, they welcomed all genres, in particular landscape, portrait, and genre painting, which were the most popular with the public. The landscape painting they practiced or enjoyed usually depicted rural settings, or nature as it is, according to the classification of Valenciennes and Roger de Piles before him. (The other type was heroic landscape, or *paysage historique*, nature as it ought to be.)[32] They admired Dutch and Flemish painting, and some of them broke through the conventional strictures on subject matter sufficiently to praise the genre scenes which offended others by their "vérité triviale." Nature was to be modified only minimally, as the artist perceived it. In their theorizing critics seldom considered the fact that no two people see things in exactly the same way, and that in addition to individual differences, artists' perceptions of nature vary from one period to

[32] P.H. Valenciennes, *Eléments de la perspective pratique*, 1820 ed., pp. 307-08; quoted by Albert Boime, *The Academy and French Painting in the Nineteenth Century* (London and New York: Phaidon, 1971), pp. 134-36.

another. Nor did they deal, except rarely, with the technical impossibility of reproducing in pigment what the eye perceives; as Stendhal says, the artist does not have the sun on his palette,[33] and even *trompe-l'oeil* requires the complicity of the spectator.

Early nineteenth-century texts yield many passages reflecting traditional attitudes. Ingres sometimes sounds like a defender of *trompe-l'oeil*: "L'art n'est jamais à un si haut degré de perfection que lorsqu'il ressemble si fort à la nature qu'on peut le prendre pour la nature elle-même."[34] He proclaims the superiority of nature over art like the most ardent realist:

> C'est dans la nature qu'on peut trouver cette beauté qui fait le grand objet de la peinture; c'est là qu'on doit la chercher, nulle part ailleurs. Il est aussi impossible de se former l'idée d'une beauté à part, d'une beauté supérieure à celle qu'offre la nature, qu'il l'est de concevoir un sixième sens.[35]

The method of assembling "beautés de détail" (or "la nature choisie") is very much alive; it is, says Ingres, the only way the artist can hope to surpass the beauty of nature:

> On doit se rappeler que les parties qui composent la plus parfaite statue ne peuvent jamais, chacune en particulier, surpasser la nature et qu'il nous est impossible d'élever nos idées au-delà des beautés de ses ouvrages. Tout ce que nous pouvons faire, c'est de pouvoir en opérer l'assemblage. A parler strictement, les statues grecques ne surpassent la nature que parce qu'on y a rassemblé toutes les parties que la nature réunit bien rarement dans un même sujet. L'artiste qui procède ainsi est admis dans le sanctuaire de la nature.

Nicolas Ponce, who expounds the same idea, proposes for it the term "vrai idéal": beauty exists in nature and only in nature, though perfection perhaps not.[36] The name for this eclectic method, which Emeric-David also uses, is well chosen, for, as Benoît points out, it is idealist in its ends and realist in its means.[37]

---

[33] *Histoire de la peinture en Italie*, I, 136.
[34] Henri Delaborde, *Ingres* (Paris: Plon, 1870), pp. 116-17.
[35] *Ibid.*, p. 113.
[36] *Mélanges sur les beaux-arts* (Paris: Leblanc, 1826), p. 179. The text dates from 1806. The expression "vrai idéal" originally came from Barthélemy's *Le Voyage d'Anacharsis*.
[37] François Benoît, *L'Art français sous la Révolution et l'Empire* (Paris: L.-Henry May, 1897), p. 30.

According to the naturalists, the artist strives to achieve both beauty and truth (a particular truth) in his work, but of these two, beauty is perhaps not the supreme value. It is fidelity to nature, says Emeric-David, the art historian and critic, that gives a work lasting appeal: "... malgré les modes et les systèmes, une figure plaira dans tous les temps, lors même que les formes n'en auront pas été habilement choisies, quand elle sera vraie, quand elle nous offrira une imitation simple, mais parfaite de la nature."[38] He agrees with the idealists that nature rarely creates perfect beings, but she makes others attractive to us by arousing our love and pity. The artist will in turn move the spectator more by rendering the subject faithfully than by beautifying it: "Sans la vérité il n'y a pas de beauté; sans la vérité il n'y a pas d'expression: avec la vérité toute seule, on arrive au coeur et on le pénètre" (p. 234). An imperfection found in nature is more appealing than cold Classic perfection, says Ballanche:

> Une tête parfaitement belle et régulière, sans aucun défaut, est une tête qui rentre dans le beau idéal: mais à cette tête céleste, angélique, faites un petit signe, un léger pli sur le satin de la peau, ou, comme dit Gessner, une légère coupure; et cette tête, sans cesser d'être belle, aura un caractère de vérité; elle ressemblera plus à un visage humain; on l'admirera moins, mais on l'aimera davantage.[39]

It is the painter David, innately realist for all his severe and heroic Classicism, who most clearly states the value of a faithful rendering of nature. Study the great masters, he advised his pupils, "et puis reviens devant le modèle, oublie les maîtres et copie la nature comme tu copierais un tableau, sans science, sans idée faite d'avance, avec naïveté, et tu seras tout étonné d'avoir bien fait..." He again emphasizes naïveté in another piece of advice, where the stress on the innocent eye prefigures impressionism: "Il faut oublier tout ce que vous savez, et tâcher d'arriver devant la nature comme un enfant qui ne sait rien..."[40] You paint what you see, not what you know. Such precepts no doubt underlie his own great realist works, though these are certainly more than "slavish copies."

---

[38] *Recherches sur l'art statuaire* (Paris: Nyon aîné, An XII-1805), p. 231.
[39] P.S. Ballanche, *Du sentiment considéré dans ses rapporte avec la littérature et les arts* (Lyon: Ballanche et Barret; Paris: Calixte Volland, An IX-1801), p. 221.
[40] As reported by E.J. Delécluze, a former pupil of David, in *Louis David, son école et son temps* (Paris: Didier, 1855), pp. 55, 57.

As Benoît points out, naturalistic painters or critics often had specific moral or political aims, seeking to edify their public and support the liberal cause. A case in point is Amaury Duval, art critic for the republican *Décade Philosophique*, whose reviews often set forth naturalistic criteria in painting. He insists that landscape painters work on the site of their subject, in the woods, on the streets, and that portrait painters study different physical types of all classes. A portrait which he praises could be set beside "nos bons auteurs Flamands."[41] The touchstone is, and for many years will continue to be, the critic's attitude toward Dutch and Flemish realistic painting. Its counterpart in novels, long minute description of details of everyday life, is praised by Petitain and Duval. The latter points out the parallel here: "[Les Allemands] sont en littérature ce que sont en peinture les maîtres de l'école flamande: ont-ils à représenter des buveurs de bière? Ils décrivent la table vacillante, la vieille cruche écornée, le bonnet sale et posé de travers de l'un des buveurs, sa pipe, sa tabatière, le chat qui dort sur le table etc., etc."[42] On the whole, the *Décade* critics approved what J. Kitchin calls "un réalisme équilibré et réconfortant" in fiction.[43] Duval himself is not consistent and sometimes calls for more ideal beauty in portraits, especially on grounds of moral edification. But the partisans of naturalism are aware that most spectators are likely to be attracted by a faithful reproduction of the model, and it is to a broad public that they wish to appeal. By attracting and moving the spectator or reader, a work will become morally useful. To quote Duval again, "Ces tableaux si vrais de la nature laissent dans l'esprit des impressions durables."

Ingres, who wished the spectator of his paintings to respond as if he were standing before nature itself, realizes, like Batteux and Du Bos, that the exact copy is not the most convincing representation of reality, and he calls upon the Classic principle of verisimilitude: "En matière du vrai, j'aime mieux qu'on soit un peu au-delà, quelque risque que l'on coure, car, je le sais, le vrai peut n'être pas vraisemblable. Bien souvent il ne faut pour cela que l'épaisseur d'un cheveu."[44]

---

[41] 30 vend. An V, p. 151.
[42] 20 mess. An IX, p. 91.
[43] Joanna Kitchin, *Un Journal "philosophique": La Décade (1794-1807)* (Paris: Minard, Lettres Modernes, 1965), p. 257.
[44] Delaborde, p. 116.

Quatremère de Quincy, the chief defender of the ideal, from whom we shall shortly hear at greater length, characteristically frowns on naturalistic landscape painting: "Cette prétention mesquine et rétrécie qu'ont eue les paysagistes de représenter fidèlement des sites donnés, et de faire ce qu'on appelle un portrait de la nature, n'était pas en usage alors [17th century], et il faut dire que rien n'a plus contribué à éteindre le génie et l'invention poétique dans le paysage."[45] It is a different kind of landscape and a more poetic kind of illusion that enchant him as he observes the effect of the sun's rays in a painting by Claude Lorrain:

> Que dis-je! la toile a disparu; c'est la vaste surface de la mer, tantôt argentée par les purs effets de l'aube matinale, tantôt dorée par l'embrasement pompeux de l'astre du jour... On ne voit pas ses tableaux; on y est, on en respire l'air, on est enveloppé de leur atmosphère; leurs impressions se confondent avec celles de la nature...[46]

It must be pointed out that this is not Quatremère's habitual response; he usually remains outside the picture, fully conscious that he is contemplating a work of art.

Emeric-David is the chief defender of realism during the Empire, and his debate with Quatremère de Quincy, chief of the idealists, served to sharpen the issues.[47] Though the arguments in favor of exact imitation had long centered on painting, Emeric-David shifted it to sculpture and in particular ancient Greek sculpture, as current artistic preoccupations demanded. The new interest in Classical archeology, nurtured in the late eighteenth century by the writings of Mengs and especially Winckelmann, had turned esthetic theory as well as artistic activity in a different direction. (Lessing's *Laocoon*, translated by Charles Vanderbourg, was published in France in 1802, but was relatively unknown during the years immediately following.) Discussions about art and beauty moved into the realm of the history of art. The traditional speculations about poetry and painting were

---

[45] "Essai historique sur l'art du paysage," *Archives Littéraires de l'Europe*, 10 (1806), 207-08.

[46] *Ibid.*, p. 204.

[47] This controversy has been related many times, starting with Victor Cousin in *Du vrai, du beau et du bien*; see also R. Schneider, *L'Esthétique classique de Quatremère de Quincy*, F. Benoît, *L'Art français sous la Révolution et l'Empire*, and Albert Cassagne, *La Doctrine de l'art pour l'art en France*.

in the early years of the century somewhat overshadowed by theorizing about ideal beauty, based on Greek sculpture. The exemplar of this much discussed ideal beauty was the Apollo Belvedere, which could be seen in the Louvre between 1800 and 1815. The ancient Greeks achieved ideal beauty in their works as no modern artists have, said the idealists, and we should look to them for guidance.

Emeric-David, along with his fellow realists, admired Greek sculpture as much as the idealists but saw it with different eyes. His *Recherches sur l'art statuaire* (1805) was submitted in the *concours* of the Institut concerning the causes of perfection in antique sculpture, and it won first prize. It is at the same time a scholarly study on sculpture and an argument in favor of naturalism in art, conducted on Quatremère's own territory. What the Greeks valued first, said Emeric-David, was truth in imitation, and then beauty of form.[48] Habitual mental states were visible in outward appearances, and the Greeks esteemed outward signs of a firm character. An exact imitation was then the best means of achieving an effective, and affecting, expression of character.

Emeric-David included among the principal artistic means the choice and harmonizing of forms, and the choice and expression of mental states, but the one indispensable means was true imitation: "Imiter, c'est l'art; imiter ce qui est beau, après l'avoir choisi, c'est l'art éclairé des lumières du goût; imiter ce qui est beau, grand et expressif tout-à-la-fois, c'est l'art guidé par le goût et par la philosophie: mais imiter enfin, imiter avec fidelité, c'est l'art dans son essence même." In his discussion of genius he maintains that for the Greeks the word meant a talent for imitation. Genius does not create anything, says he; "Il s'approprie les faits; il les combine; il saisit les rapports prochains, les rapports éloignés; il choisit; il imite; il ne va point au-delà."[49] Great artists and writers were geniuses because they had the talent to see in physical nature the true color and form of objects, and in moral nature (i.e., in people depicted in literary works) the quality of mental states, and then imitated them with a truthfulness rivaling nature itself.

Emeric-David opposes the idea that true beauty has its origin in a region of incorporeal ideas, as Winckelmann had recently preached, or in God's bosom, as Malebranche had believed; these are realms

---

[48] *Recherches*, p. 43.
[49] *Ibid.*, pp. 236, 263.

too far away from our earthly organism. He also rejects the idea that the artist finds his model of beauty within himself; this seems to place the artist's genius above nature, but is in reality cruelly discouraging. The questions he poses to show the fallacy of Winckelmann's theories, reveal his own sensualist point of view. Would nature condemn man to have the idea of beauty, always seek it and never find it? If it is not perceptible to our senses, how did it come into our mind? What is it? If an artist were sufficiently superior to humanity to be able to conceive of supernatural beauty, how could he be sure that forms beautiful to him are also beautiful to others? The Greeks would never have understood the term "beau idéal," he continues; since *idée* comes from *eido* (I see), it would have meant for them "le beau visible." Even if we believe that external models existed in the divine intelligence before their creation, an artist could not rise to the level of this first exemplar in order to imitate it. God created man's form in imitation of an uncreated model, but the artist imitates God's work; he copies a copy and makes an imitation at the second degree. Thus Emeric-David accepts (at least for the sake of argument) what Plato says in the *Republic*, Book X, about the inability of the artist to rise above appearances to depict a higher truth, but rather than deploring these limitations and trying to break through them, he simply divorces them from art. The thoughts of Plato and Malebranche rise above the terrestrial sphere, says he, and hence are apart from the realm of the arts.

Though Emeric-David placed great emphasis on faithful representation of a living model, he did not take an extreme position and was much more nuanced than Quatremère de Quincy was willing to concede; he pointed out the importance of a wise choice of subject and combination of parts, he valued the beauty of forms or expressiveness, and acknowledged that Greek sculptors were guided by canons, which they had formulated after long and careful observation. Even so, he maintained, Greek statues are an imitation of nature; if they seem to surpass nature, it is because they are so beautifully proportioned, with all parts in harmony.

2. Imitation (II)

For a statement of the opposite position we shall draw chiefly upon Quatremère de Quincy, the most articulate and prolific of the idealist critics.[1] Quatremère owes little to Batteux or other French writers; he stems principally from Winckelmann, most of whose views on the art of antiquity he adopted (Victor Cousin called him the the French Winckelmann), along with others drawn from a wide variety of sources, ancient, Germanic, and others.[2]

---

[1] We can give here only a brief résumé of some of Quatremère's ideas, as set forth in some of his many theoretical and historical works. The longest and most detailed study of Quatremère is René Schneider's *L'Esthétique classique chez Quatremère de Quincy* (Paris: Hachette, 1910); François Benoît in his *L'Art français sous la Révolution et l'Empire* sums up the idealist position in sculpture and painting and gives some special attention to Quatremère. Both these writers stress his Academic and anti-Romantic side. But he was more varied in his opinions than either indicates, and his *Considérations morales sur la destination des ouvrages de l'art* (Paris: Crapelet, 1815) contains some interesting material sometimes at variance with his more pro-Classic utterances made elsewhere. One may also note a slight broadening of his views between his *Essai sur l'Idéal dans ses applications pratiques aux ouevres de l'imitation propre aux arts du dessin* (Paris: Adrien Leclerc, 1837), most of which was originally written in 1805, and *Essai sur la nature, le but et les moyens de l'imitation dans les beaux-arts* (Paris: J. Didot l'aîné, 1823). These works will hereafter be abbreviated *L'Idéal* and *L'Imitation*, respectively. René Canat even calls him Romantic (*L'Hellénisme des romantiques* [Paris: Didier, 1951], I, 110), and Esther Unger in a 1959 article (*Modern Language Quarterly*, 20:355-59) sees him not as a retrograde partisan of Classicism but as an innovator whose idealism announced the later triumph of subjectivism in art. Such a divergence of views reveals not only the complexity and variety of his thought but the difficulty of defining what is Classic or Romantic.

[2] For a comprehensive list of Quatremère's sources see R. Schneider, pp. 75-92.

Quatremère's retort to Emeric-David was first published as a series of three articles in *Les Archives Littéraires de l'Europe* in 1805, which in modified form made up part of his book *Essai sur l'idéal* (1837). In his multitudinous publications through a long and productive career, his conception of imitation remained basically the same and the definition of the ideal that he gave in 1805, he still subscribes to shortly before his death. Like Winckelmann, he sees ancient Greek sculpture as the epitome of ideal beauty, but for him the principles by which the Greeks achieved pre-eminence are very much alive and should be followed in his own time. A combative personality, he never ceases castigating artists of the realist persuasion, whether they be called "l'Ecole du modèle" in the early 1800s or "romantique" later.

According to Quatremère, a naturalistic imitation is too dependent on a chance model. Even supposing a model of perfect beauty, which he hardly believes possible, a too faithful imitation will give the illusion of reality, an illegitimate illusion that replaces appearance. *Trompe-l'oeil* is devoid of esthetic pleasure, it is not true imitation. "Imiter dans les beaux-arts, c'est produire la ressemblance d'une chose, mais dans une autre chose qui en devient l'image."[3] An image (which he also calls a metaphor) is an incomplete resemblance, not an identical representation. The artist gets his inspiration not from the object but from the very act of imitation, and pleasure for the artist and the spectator depends on the distance between the model and the image, and the act of comparing the two. The spectator receives pleasure which he would not get from the object precisely because it is an image, rather than the real thing. The pleasure of true or legitimate illusion comes from the spectator's mind, which completes the work of art.[4] No art can equal nature in its life and movement[5]; each art has its own limitations within which the artist must work, and he will do well not only to stay within them but to exploit the limitations as well as the possibilities of his medium. Quatremère wished always to be aware that he was looking not at flesh but at marble or at pigment on canvas.

In his 1805 articles he undertakes to clarify by metaphysical (the word is his) analysis the meaning of the term "ideal" which, he says, has been ill defined. His explanation bears a strong resemblance to

---

[3] *L'Imitation*, p. 3.
[4] *L'Imitation*, p. 22; *L'Idéal*, p. 307.
[5] *Considérations morales*, p. 61.

the Aristotelian normative ideal but takes off from there in the direction of metaphysical idealism. Nature works on too vast a scale to give attention to each individual, says Quatremère; it is perfect in its principle and in its whole, but has neglected the perfecting of details. As a result, complete beauty is never found in an individual, but art takes up the challenge. "Il la tira du vague abstrait où elle était visible et cachée tout à la fois. Il la réduisit en méthode; son analyse produisit le beau complet de l'individu qu'en vain on demanderait à la nature. Le résultat de ce procédé de l'art dans la génération de ses ouvrages, est ce que nous appelons idéal."[6] The artist does not imitate the model directly, but he consults it; the model is only the means, not the end of imitation. The artist studies its physical aspects, but beyond that he contemplates the intellectual model which he can see only with his mind's eye. This is how Phidias worked, said Cicero (as quoted by Quatremère), to make his statues of the gods. In response to Emeric-David's argument that "idea" originally means "I see," Quatremère counters that it means principally "voir par l'esprit." The artist must make himself a model which he will then depict; this is what Phidias did. "Cette beauté avait son type au fond de son âme; et ce type ne peut exister que là." The inner model confronts the living model and regulates it, correcting its irregularities and its faults. Then the artist has become a creator.

At the end of the first article Quatremère sums up: "Le mot *idéal*, joint au mot *beau*, exprime... cette beauté que l'art sans doute rend visible, mais plus particulièrement à l'âme, à l'entendement, au sentiment et aux yeux de l'esprit, qu'à l'organe matériel; il exprime cette beauté dont aucun modèle isolé ne peut être le type, dont aucun individu ne peut fournir l'image complète, et à laquelle l'artiste n'arrive que par la puissance d'*idéer*."[7]

An exact representation of a beautiful object may give pleasure, but Quatremère characterizes this pleasure as "sensual" and "material." The artist of the ideal has a higher aim, intellectual and moral, which is the enriching of our spirit and insight into the unknown. He seeks to discover and impart what is at the heart of reality, the essence of things, God's intentions in his creation, he says in the later edition. "Imiter la nature, c'est étudier l'homme dans les lois de l'espèce humaine... c'est rendre sensible par l'ouvrage de l'imitation les volontés

---

[6] *Archives Littéraires de l'Europe*, 6 (1805), 391.
[7] *Ibid.*, 6:396-404.

de l'action du Créateur; c'est en opérer, en développer les effets et
les intentions, sur la conformation la plus parfaite de la créature."[8]

The inner model ("modèle imaginatif") from which the artist will
try to produce his work is freely formed in his mind, "au gré de son
imagination,"[9] but it has a solid foundation in long philosophical and
scientific study: "... une science qui a pour objet d'interroger et de
connaître les causes générales de la conformation de l'homme, de
scruter les principes de l'organisation des êtres, de la fin à laquelle
la nature a destiné chaque partie du corps, et des moyens par lesquels se produisent les effets qui entrent dans les desseins du
créateur..." Whether the artist consults one model or more, there will
always be a point of comparison, "la règle du beau et du vrai,"[10] which
the artist will have drawn from study, from existing art works, or from
a multitude of parallels and observations. In the end, the process remains in the mysterious realm of the formation of ideas and in taste,
and varies according to individual differences in ways of seeing, judging, and feeling. Canons of physical features such as those set up by
the Greeks can be of some aid, but what makes beauty is the moral
harmony of the whole. In contradiction to the then widely accepted
view that idealized art evolved historically from realistic art,
Quatremère insists that the ideal style preceded the individual style
as the hieroglyphic preceded the image.[11]

The work of art in which the inner conception is embodied, the
archetypal representation, will be a generalized form, "indéterminée,"
of an abstract simplicity, in which no individual being can be recognized. Detail is eliminated, and the simplicity of line, which
Quatremère calls "geometric," is intended to show an inner structure
common to all. To generalize is to abridge, not to diminish but to
intensify, to concentrate the most into the least volume. Art is a concave mirror, says Quatremère, not a *verre á facettes*.[12] (The French expression of the period was "un miroir concentrique." We shall meet
this comparison often.)

The ideal in its acceptation of generalization and search for a type
is not limited to beauty: there is also a "laideur idéale," even an "horrible

---

[8] *L'Idéal*, p. 46.
[9] *Archives Littéraires*, 7:14.
[10] *Ibid*, 7:20, 22.
[11] *Ibid.*, 7:316. Modern art historians confirm this: see E.H. Gombrich, *Art and Illusion* (New York: Pantheon, 1960), p. 118.
[12] *L'Imitation*, p. 280.

idéal,"[13] which by their generalized presentation will interest us rather than repel us, as a naturalistic rendition would. But Quatremère does not assign an important place to ugliness; the emphasis remains strongly on the *beau idéal*, since ugliness often consists of a deformation (in original creation, or by illness or old age) or deviation from the norm, an individual rather than a type.

To generalization, the first method of ideal imitation, Quatremère in later work adds a second, transposition or metaphor. Metaphorical composition is suitable for subjects from other times and places. In painting it may involve changes in form, physiognomy, and proportion; hence metaphor means metamorphosis.[14] The artist may change natural forms in various ways: in the drawing of individual figures, in combination of figures and representation of action, the enlarging and beautifying of a heroic subject, the use of nudes, costumes, symbols, allegory. Quatremère cautions against the use of new symbols, which like any new language will be unintelligible. An accepted conventional system of signs has evolved over the years and is understood by cultivated people (the others do not matter).[15] A violin cannot replace a lyre, for example, as a symbol of musical genius and harmony. The use of these devices will vary according to the type of art: history painting is less metaphorical than allegory or fiction, and its means of representation are more subject to the principle of verisimilitude. Allegory and symbol are more suitable to sculpture.

Quatremère distinguishes symbolic composition as that in which things are represented not by their image but by abridged signs of their idea, which are hieroglyphics:

> A le prendre dans le sens philosophique, l'imitation symbolique, par le pouvoir qu'elle a de nous faire saisir l'idée d'un objet sous le signe d'un autre, est l'imitation (à proprement parler) la plus idéale de toutes. Elle est celle qui exerce le plus la faculté de percevoir par l'imagination. Elle est celle qui, considérée sous son aspect matériel, occupe le point le plus opposé à celui de l'imagination positive ou identique.[16]

It is the highest type of composition in the realm of the ideal, the one that most changes the visible nature of objects. It is usually associated

---

[13] *L'Idéal*, p. 34.
[14] *L'Imitation*, pp. 327; 350-51.
[15] *L'Idéal*, pp. 217-41.
[16] *L'Idéal*, pp. 272-73.

with allegorical figures, which would often be meaningless without symbolic attributes.

Though idealists place greater emphasis on formal beauty than the naturalists, their principal object is finally not intrinsic beauty but the connection with the idea.[17] Too much verisimilitude in a symbolic figure will distract from its true object, for a work of art must first of all be intelligible.

In his early work on the Ideal, Quatremère de Quincy deals with other arts briefly by implication. Not until later, in his *L'Imitation* (1823) does he extend his doctrine to literature. He is more aware of differences than of likeness between the arts; he argues against the *mélange des genres*, wishing to keep the arts distinct in their means though alike in their basic principles. This is especially clear in this book, which is an anti-Romantic polemic. But literature and the visual arts have this in common: the most ideal and poetic compositions of literature, like those of the fine arts, differ from other literature not by being less true, in a positive sense, but by manifesting a different truth: "Celles en effet qui sembleraient dénaturer le plus la fidélité des faits et l'image des personnes, (par exemple dans les compositions épiques ou dramatiques) ne font cependant qu'échanger une sorte de vérité contre une autre."[18] Racine's Britannicus is as true as Tacitus's: the dramatic character's truth is an abstract truth which expresses not things and facts, but principles and causes.

Quatremère de Quincy's writings are important, even indispensable, for an understanding of the idealist position, for he was the first to attempt to set up a rigorous system at the dawn of the Romantic movement. Unlike most others, he thinks questions out and explains them fully; the theory of the ideal, says he, can be explained only to the intelligence by rational analysis. He admits that reasoning has its limits and does not minimize the role of the imagination and of the emotions in the creation and the appreciation of art. However, he does not approve of emotional and imaginative theories, because, says he, they teach us to feel, not to know.[19] Imagination and intellect are not in conflict; they are both contrasted with the senses, and the term "moral" often serves the same function, to designate what is opposed to the material or sensual. Quatremère remained active and

[17]   *L'Idéal*, p. 275.
[18]   *L'Idéal*, p. 165.
[19]   *L'Imitation*, pp, 251-53.

influential through all the period we are studying, but particularly during the Empire. He was a sculptor and remained especially attached to sculpture. Though he temporarily relented from the rigidity of his views on seeing the Elgin marbles, he in general remained faithful to his belief in the ideal. The *Archives Littéraires* articles were read with profit by both Stendhal, who adopted some of his views but rejected others, and by Victor Cousin, who named Quatremère along with Chateaubriand and Mme de Staël as one who rehabilitated spiritualism at the beginning of the century.

The important creative artists of the time left little critical writing and exercized influence through their works or the instruction they gave their pupils. The lessons David learned from archeology were somewhat different from Quatremère's; we know, for example, that he thought that for the ancient Greeks an idea exists more by the form it takes in the work of art than in the idea itself: "Donner une apparence, une forme parfaite à sa pensée, c'est être artiste; on ne l'est que par là..."[20]

As we have seen the most articulate defenders of opposing viewpoints attenuate their positions, so a number of critics and theorists support now one, now the other principle or take an intermediate position. They sometimes acknowledge that part of their disagreement may come from inprecise use of conventional vocabulary. Both sides can claim "la belle nature" since elements are taken from nature, but they are combined in new ways and usually modified by the artist. For Nicolas Ponce, "le bel antique" was the same as "la belle nature."[21] When Emeric-David spoke of the Greek canons, he emphasized the fact that they were established after long and careful observation of individual forms. Ponce too leans toward naturalism, but he concedes that some may see these canons as ideal beauty; if so, says he, we are not so far apart.

Aside from the *Décade* writers, the principal *Idéologues* occasionally deal with these questions; Cabanis, Fauriel, and Ginguené made interesting contributions to literary criticism and history, and Maine de Biran made some acute comments on the arts. In his "Lettre à M. T. — [Thurot] sur les poèmes d'Homère" Cabanis leaves open the widest possibilities relative to the individuality of the artist, his aims,

---

[20] Delécluze, *Louis David*, p. 62.
[21] *Mélanges sur les beaux-arts*, p. 177 (written 1806).

his subject, the genre, and the audience to which it is directed.[22] Starting with Homer, whom he especially praises for having individualized his tableaux, he indicates chronological development of our way of seeing nature, emphasizing the differences in mentality of men of different periods. He sees in art an imitation of nature — but modified:

> ... soit que les arts peignent des objets physiques extérieurs, soit qu'ils pénètrent dans le sein de l'âme humaine, pour y surprendre les idées et les affections morales, soit qu'ils rappellent des actions, des événements et des discours réels ou supposés, c'est toujours la nature qu'ils imitent; et, lors même qu'ils s'élancent dans les régions de l'inconnu, ils n'imaginent et ne retracent ce que personne n'a jamais pu voir ni sentir, que d'aprés ce que l'homme voit et sent tous les jours.[23]

The Greeks at an early stage, he goes on, adopted the principle of imitation of nature but soon saw that in order to make their work pleasing they would have to make a choice among objects and not imitate exactly: "Le principe général fut donc modifié, et les arts eurent dès lors pour but *l'imitation de la belle nature*, que l'enthousiasme des Grecs appela le *beau* par excellence, et que nous nommons le *beau idéal*." Cabanis like so many others pronounces himself against *trompe-l'oeil*: "le plaisir du spectateur ne peut commencer qu'au moment où cesse ce dernier degré d'illusion."[24]

In *Influence de l'habitude* Maine de Biran stresses the relativity of beauty and ugliness according to what we are accustomed to seeing.

> ... observons, quant aux habitudes, que nos idées de *beauté* ne sont point, comme on dit, *archétypes*, mais calquées sur certaines impressions choisies d'abord parmi celles qui nous sont le plus familières: l'imagination réunit ces idées, en forme différents groupes plus ou moins fixes; lorsqu'un objet vient ensuite frapper les sens, il est comparé au groupe, au modèle idéal qui lui correspond, et jugé beau ou non, selon qu'il a plus de qualités analogues ou contraires à ce modèle...
>
> Puisque ce prototype que nous nommons *beau idéal* se compose d'abord des impressions de nos sens, il doit varier avec tout ce qui les occasionne, comme les climats, les lieux, les coutumes, les degrés de sensibilité des nations et des individus.[25]

---

[22] *Oeuvres* (Paris: Bossange, Didot, 1823-1825), V, 307.

[23] *Ibid.*, V, 310-11.

[24] *Ibid.*, V, 312.

[25] *Influence de l'habitude sur la faculté de penser*, in *Oeuvres*, ed. Pierre Tisserand (Paris: Alcan, 1922), II, 145-47. Subsequent passages quoted here come from pp. 146-48 of this volume.

Though denying the existence of an archetype of beauty in the usual sense, Maine de Biran recognizes two kinds of models for judging both nature and art: "l'un idéal, modèle de perfection; l'autre formé des impressions familières." An object may appear beautiful compared to the second model, says he, though imperfect according to the first; he thus distinguishes between beauty, judged by the second model, and perfection, judged by the first. "Observons que le modèle abstrait auquel nous rapportons nos idées pour les ranger dans telle classe diffère du modèle sensible qui nous les fait trouver beaux ou laids. Ce dernier est une image; l'autre une sorte de mesure qui n'a pas d'existence hors du langage."

Even if an artistic genius is drawn out beyond the realm of real objects into an imaginary world where his creative powers operate freely, he goes on, habit will necessarily draw him back into the depiction of familiar reality: "... cette belle nature qu'il conçoit, qu'il paraît deviner, n'est encore que la copie embellie de celle qui frappa ses premiers regards, et donna l'impulsion à sa sensibilité naissante."

Man imitates nature in many ways, some useful, some artistic; architecture combines the two, whereas painting and music belong to the artistic realm. As an example of a useful imitation of nature in building, Maine de Biran cites the form of aquatic birds applied to the hull of a ship; an artistic aim is shown when the proportions of a tree trunk are given to columns.

Maine de Biran distinguishes between the arts according to the degree to which they appeal to the senses and to the imagination:

> La musique s'adresse tout à la fois à l'imagination et aux sens, et dans un degré plus éminent; l'architecture et la sculpture s'adressent plus exclusivement aux sens et parlent à l'imagination précisément parce que leur langage est plus déterminé. De là il suit que les arts tels que la peinture, et surtout la musique ne produisent point leurs grands effets, comme arts imitatifs; c'est là la moindre cause du charme qui leur est attaché. Lorsque l'artiste ne vise qu'à l'imitation absolue de quelque objet par les couleurs ou les sons, mieux il réussit, moins il laisse faire à l'imagination.

In another passage he contrasts music and poetry, which appeal to the ear and the imagination, with painting, which appeals to the eye and which he treats as more purely imitative. "Ce n'est jamais l'objet même que la musique et la poésie peuvent représenter d'une façon sensible et directe. Tout le mystère de leurs procédés consiste à réveiller le plus vivement et le plus agréablement possible une impression analogue à celle qu'eût excitée la présence même de l'objet et c'est par cette impression que l'objet même se trouve rappelé."[26]

Guizot's judicious commentaries on painting show him leaning toward naturalism, but he too with reservations. While conceding that modern artists may properly imitate objects that are not perfectly beautiful, especially in painting, they should use this freedom with moderation: thus he would have Girodet make his Arabs less ugly and his dragoon more noble in *La Revolte du Caire*.[27] He also recognizes that some artists, such as Gros, force their talent if they try to beautify their real models, but gives preference to Girodet's portrait of Chateaubriand because the artist has added the "sentiment du grandiose" to the "sentiment de la nature."[28]

Joseph Droz is another theoretician whose mind is open to a broad appeal and multiple approaches to the arts, though he too sets limits. His often ambiguous use of the words "truth" and "beauty" show some confusion and hesitation between the broadminded and the strictly Neoclassic; each principle limits the other. At the same time, he insists that, except in the case of music, "la vérité, plus ou moins fidèle, plus ou moins ornée, est toujours une des sources du beau dans les arts."[29] "Plus ou moins fidèle, plus ou moins ornée": Droz is a true middle-of-the-roader. A kind of instinct, says he, makes us wish to know the truth; truth has an attraction for our soul, so the recognition of truth in a work of art is the most spontaneous basic response. He recognizes various kinds of truth and of imitation: "la vérité particulière" of portraits and historical scenes, which is hard to reconcile with beauty, and "la vérité de convention" of opera, tragedy and nudity in sculpture, as well as a higher general truth; he accepts naive as well as ideal imitation.[30]

In his early works that deal with artistic matters, Chateaubriand does not depart from the ideas prevailing in his time. His early "Lettre sur l'art du dessin dans les paysages" (1795) is closer to Rousseau than to Winckelmann; he admires the portrait and the landscape, is

---

[26]   *Ibid.*, II, 129.

[27]   *Etudes sur les beaux-arts en général* (Paris: Didier, 1852), p. 18 (Salon de 1810).

[28]   *Ibid.*, p. 24. We shall deal with the continuation of this commentary in the next chapter.

[29]   Droz, p. 48.

[30]   *Ibid.*, pp. 39-47.

more likely to individualize than generalize, and, as we would expect, places emphasis on emotional response to the natural landscape. He gives the traditional approval to the erudite artist, recommending that a landscape painter always start with direct observation of nature (though the actual painting is done in the studio); it would be useful for him to study botany, for a knowledge of plant structures will enable him to paint authentic and convincing vegetation. It is essential that a landscapist know what is behind appearances, just as the portrait painter should make a study of human passions. However, this deeper knowledge is less metaphysical than emotional: "Le paysage a sa partie morale et intellectuelle comme le portrait; il faut qu'il parle aussi, et qu'à travers l'exécution matérielle on éprouve ou les rêveries ou les sentiments que font naître les différents sites."[31]

Le Génie du christianisme, despite its Christian orientation, expounds an esthetic closer to the Neoclassic than the earlier work. Or perhaps we should say because of its Christian orientation, for here religion simply replaces the rationalism of Quatremère de Quincy. (Even Quatremère spoke of a desire for the limitless.) The principles are similar and the vocabulary combines the Neoclassic with the religious: in the Christian Andromaque we see "la nature corrigée, la nature plus belle, la nature évangélique" (II.ii.6). Chateaubriand recognizes the spiritual quality of ancient sculpture: "D'où naît cette magie des anciens, et pourquoi une Vénus de Praxitèle toute nue charme-t-elle plus notre esprit que nos regards? C'est qu'il y a un beau idéal qui touche plus à l'âme qu'à la matière" (II.ii.3). However, Praxiteles and Homer represent an intermediate stage between primitive times and modern societies, and the *beau idéal* has continued to develop in Christian nations. Gradually, artists learned not to show everything in their pictures, but to choose, beautify, and arrange:

> Ce premier pas fait, ils virent encore qu'il fallait *choisir*; ensuite que la chose choisie était susceptible d'une forme plus belle, ou d'un plus bel effet dans telle ou telle position.
>
> Toujours *cachant* et *choisissant*, *retranchant* ou *ajoutant*, ils se trouvèrent peu à peu dans les formes qui n'étaient plus naturelles, mais qui étaient plus parfaites que la nature: les artistes appelèrent ces formes le *beau idéal*. (II.ii.11)

The *beau idéal* is either moral or physical, and one is as necessary to art as the other. The principles for the two are the same: the weaknesses

---

[31] *Oeuvres complètes* (Bruxelles: Weissenbruch, 1829), I, 830.

of men's souls should be hidden as well as those of their bodies. Only men, not animals, can thus be shown more nearly perfect than in nature. It is this *beau idéal moral* which distinguishes Christian societies: "C'est que le christianisme a fourni, dés sa naissance, le *beau idéal moral* ou le *beau idéal des caractères*, et que le polythéisme n'a pu donner cet avantage au chantre d'Ilion." But even the *beau idéal physique* is enhanced under Christianity, for the two kinds of ideal beauty are necessarily linked, and the more noble soul will be manifest through the matter which clothes it. Classical ideal beauty converges with and is enriched by the Christian ideal of perfection.

> ... la religion chrétienne, étant d'une nature spirituelle et mystique, fournit à la peinture un *beau idéal* plus parfait et plus divin que celui qui naît d'un culte matériel;... corrigeant la laideur des passions, ou les combattant avec force, elle donne des tons plus sublimes à la figure humaine et fait mieux sentir l'âme dans les muscles, et les liens de la matière;... (III.i.3)

In addition, the Christian religion has furnished "des sujets plus beaux, plus riches, plus dramatiques, plus touchants" than mythological subjects (III.i.3). By destroying the mythological allegory of the ancients, it has brought us closer to nature and inspired us to depict it in its true character in two new art forms, landscape painting and descriptive poetry.

The notebooks and other writings of Joseph Joubert do not yield a systematic esthetics but reveal consistent attitudes in tune with his Platonism. He is thus inclined in the opposite direction from the Aristotelian mimetic and from the conventional patterns of the time. The ideal is for Joubert a mental conception, to be seen by the imagination, and his views, though nuanced and even ambiguous, give the preference to the representation of an idea: "Ce qui est vraiment beau est ce qui ressemble à son idée."[32] The impulse is always inner, from thought or even from the dream. "Tout est né de quelque songe; même le monde, qui est né d'une idée de Dieu."[33] The parallel between man and God as creator, which recurs in Joubert's work, sets

---

[32] *Carnets*, 2 vols., ed. Beaunier (Paris: Gallimard, 1938), I, 214. For fuller discussion of this and other aspects of Joubert's esthetics, see Patricia A. Ward, *Joseph Joubert and the Critical Tradition* (Geneva: Droz, 1980), particularly Ch. 4, "The Arts and Their Interrelationship."

[33] *Carnets*, II, 699; see Ward, p. 79.

him apart from those who, like Quatremère, included creation in imitation. "L'art (dit-on), l'art. C'est bien quelque chose, que l'art si (comme on l'a fort bien dit) 'la nature est l'art de Dieu,' *ars Dei in materia.* L'art est aussi une nature qui vient de l'homme..."³⁴ When Joubert speaks of imitation, it is an imitation of the conception in the author's mind, not of external reality. "De l'imitation. — Les anciens et Platon lui-même n'ont jamais bien connu comment il devait être l'objet de l'art; les modernes encore moins. Chacun aime à voir reproduit ce qu'il pense, ce qu'il cherche, ce qu'il estime beau, ce qu'il conçoit."³⁵

The matter of art may come from external reality or from the realm of the mind; they mingle in the artist's imagination: "Le monde intellectuel ou intelligible, est celui que voient les esprits et que, pour ainsi dire voit Dieu. Le monde idéal est celui que les poètes imaginent et composent en mélant ensemble ce qu'ils connaissent du monde terrestre et ce qu'ils connaissent du monde intellectuel."³⁶ In reference to the outer world, Joubert prefers to speak of "representation" rather than "imitation" in the visual arts, and he uses the verb "exprimer" in a way that prefigures the writers of the 1820s: "Tout artiste est, ne peut et ne veut être qu'un peintre de portraits. Son ambition et son mérite sont d'exprimer fidèlement ce qui est ou ce qu'il imagine. Quand sa pensée ressemble à son objet et son ouvrage à sa pensée, il fait un ouvrage excellent..."³⁷ The resemblance achieved by such expression is a perfect correspondence between object, thought, and work. In some cases art may transform the original perception or physical impulse, bringing it onto a higher plane of beauty: "En effet, la musique et la danse ont assujetti à l'ordre et à la mesure ce qu'il y a de plus immodéré et de plus excessif par sa nature, les sauts et les cris."³⁸

Joubert also touches upon the question of how the artist is to paint the idea of an object. He bases his depiction on the real object but not in order to give an appearance of reality. "Le vrai commun, ou purement réel, ne peut être l'objet des arts. L'illusion sur un fond vrai, voilà le secret des beaux-arts."³⁹ The illusion which Joubert seeks in

---

³⁴ *Ibid.*, II, 865, 19 Oct. 1817.
³⁵ *Ibid.*, I, 450, 6 June 1804.
³⁶ *Ibid.*, II, 566.
³⁷ *Ibid.*, I, 117.
³⁸ *Ibid.*, I, 450 (continuation of passage quoted above).
³⁹ *Pensées et lettres*, 2 vols., ed. Dumay (Paris: Grasset, 1954), I, 173.

art takes into account the fact that phenomena can be known to us only through our senses. It is an integral part of reality and of our perception of it, adding to it a quality of charm.[40] But he sometimes seems to hesitate between illusion and the "fond vrai": "Si, dans les peintures, la ressemblance est réelle pour les yeux ou si elle ne l'est que pour l'esprit et ne résulte pas du jugement encore plus que de la vue."[41] The predominance of depiction for the mind is more easily distinguished in writing:

> Ce qui peint à l'esprit et non pas ce qui peint aux yeux. Par exemple, *rouge* peint aux yeux, l'*incarnation de la rose* peint à l'esprit, parce que cette dénomination a en effet passé par l'esprit et s'est comme teinte de sa réflexion. Ce n'est donc pas tant d'après nature que d'après l'âme qu'il faut peindre.[42]

At other moments Joubert comes closer to the conventional doctrine of the *beau idéal*, physical or moral: "De celui qui peint trop vivement le mal, on dit qu'il exagère. Et de celui qui peint trop vivement le bien, on dit qu'il embellit. Or qui embellit perfectionne mais ne dénature pas. Qui exagère déforme."[43] All things tend toward perfection and toward beauty, and so it should be in art. "L'art n'est que naturel perfectionné."[44] There is no place for ideal ugliness here.

Joubert is the most important French Platonist of the early nineteenth century and in his observations on esthetics one of the most interesting writers of his generation. However, the influence of Platonism in the years following will not come from these notebooks, unavailable to the public, but through Victor Cousin's lectures and his translation of Plato's works.

Ballanche, in his early book *Du sentiment*, sings the praises of *le sentiment*, Jean-Jacques Rousseau, and the return to nature. It is feeling (*le sentiment*) which is at the source of all that is good and true, and genius (or talent) is the faculty of perceiving what elements of nature should enter into ideal beauty. It is difficult to define Ballanche's viewpoint; though he sometimes seems to lean toward naturalism (see quote

[40] See Ward, *Joseph Joubert*, pp. 110-12, on Joubert's conception of illusion.
[41] *Carnets*, I, 396, 29 Aug. 1803.
[42] *Ibid.*, II, 551, 28 April 1806.
[43] *Ibid.*, II, 632, 9 Dec. 1807.
[44] *Ibid.*, I, 419, 11 Dec. 1803.

above, p. 16), he theorizes that the Platonic world commonly called ideal, is real. Man, who has his place on the border between two worlds, belongs to earth by his body and to heaven by his intelligence. God has placed in us an ideal model of perfection which constantly escapes our desires, and the principle of ideal perfection in the *arts d'imitation* is the same as that of ideal perfection in the moral sphere. The ideal is within us, and the work of art is conceived and nurtured there:

> Avant qu'un artiste exécute un ouvrage, il le conçoit dans sa pensée il s'isole de toute sensation extérieure; il se retire au-dedans de lui-même, et il voit ce Jupiter olympique, cet Apollon de Belvédère, cette Vénus de Médicis, cette Psyché de Canove, qui doivent faire l'admiration de tous les siècles: le chef-d'oeuvre est dans sa tête avec l'attitude, les attributs, les grâces, la majesté, avec toutes les perfections enfin dont jamais l'oeuvre de ses mains ne pourra approcher.[45]

Hence true beauty remains invisible; the work is only an imperfect reflection of it, and the artist is never satisfied with what he has executed.

In his later book *Essai sur les institutions sociales* (1818) Ballanche again goes far beyond the traditional idea of the mimetic. The subjectivity of the artist transforms the model and communicates its individuality:

> L'imitation de la nature consiste à faire éprouver aux autres l'impression reçue par le spectacle de la nature. En effet, un site, ainsi que chaque homme en particulier, est marqué d'un trait distinctif, porte un ensemble qu'on pourrait appeler physiognomonique, et qui le signale entre tous. [This sounds like Chateaubriand.] Voilà ce qu'il a été donné aux poètes de voir et de faire voir aux autres. Le poète transmet l'impression sans peindre l'objet par des effets puisés dans les moyens techniques de l'art.[46]

The poet, whether he be working with words, pigment, or stone, is not an idealist seeking a generalized type; he works from a single model and brings out its individuality. Ballanche seems to be talking about personal style reached through a free use of technical means. This would be the opposite of those who recommended combining separate elements but reproducing them in a naturalistic way. Ballanche says,

[45] Ballanche, *Du sentiment*, p. 73.
[46] *Oeuvres* (1833 ed.), p. 313.

stay close to the individual model, find its salient characteristics but render them in a distinctive, impressionistic style.

Like Emeric-David and Quatremère de Quincy, he found that his own principles were practiced by the ancient Greeks; they too, he says, transmitted their impressions in their art, rather than trying imperfectly to copy the object itself. The ideal world where poetry (i.e., the arts) transports us is not the realm of the Platonic archetype but a happier place where man is free from the effects of his decline (*déchéance*), where purity of forms and expression have been less degraded by passions.

In *Oberman* and the *Rêveries* Senancour meditates on questions which have large implications for esthetics: the impenetrability of nature, the beauty and indifference of nature,[47] the mystery of man's relationships with nature, and the marvelous world of correspondences (*Oberman*, Letter 40). But he does not carry his meditations into the realm of the artist. His few remarks specifically on art are of interest though not very innovative: the passage on *le beau* in Lettre 21 of *Oberman* takes Diderot as point of departure, and this passage from the *Rêveries* (1809) shows us the ideal beauty of art as above that of any mortal or any human type:

> ... l'idée du beau absolu inspira les artistes de Chio, de Corinthe et d'Athènes; ils n'avaient à peindre, à sculpter que des hommes, mais ils surent leur donner quelque chose de céleste, en choisissant dans ce qui est possible, et en usant de l'imaginaire sans tomber dans le fabuleux. La nature met une grande distance entre l'habitant du Labrador et celui du Caucase: au lieu de rendre fidèlement les traits du Barbare ou de l'Ethiopien, le talent des Grecs fit l'homme plus beau que le Grec lui-même, sans cesser de faire des hommes.[48]

For Senancour art is nostalgic, it brings back to us what is absent, not as a copy of a sensible object but a representation of analogous traits.

> Alors il n'y a plus rien qui soit beau pour nous; car c'est surtout au loin que l'imagination voyait la beauté. L'imagination suppose toujours une nuance du beau idéal à tous les objets vagues et peu connus; elle aime surtout la mélodie des paroles chantées dans une langue qu'on

---

[47] *Rêveries sur la nature primitive de l'homme* (1809 ed.), ed. Merlant et Saintville (Paris: Droz, 1940), II, 94.
[48] In "Fragmens," pp. 150-51.

n'entend pas; elle découvre des intentions admirables et un sens prodigieux dans les passages des anciens auteurs, parce que leurs expressions nous sont moins familières. Un portrait lui paraît plus beau que
le modèle, lors même que l'artiste n'a point voulu *flatter*, parce que le
portrait n'est point une copie positive, mais un résultat d'effets
analogues, et que cette ressemblance n'était pas celle des abstractions,
lui présente l'image toujours arbitraire d'une réalité absente, qu'elle orne
à son gré comme une réalité idéale.[49]

A certain amount of the unknown remains, "heureux songes du beau
possible."[50] Creative imagination grasps relationships, which constitute
beauty, and establishes a synthesis. Ideal beauty is invariable and by
definition unattainable but we may sense it by perception of
relationships.[51] In the work of art these relationships are brought into order, which necessitates choice (*Oberman*, Letter 21).

Mme de Staël and the group around her not only rejected
naturalistic representation but brought into question the doctrine of
imitation itself. At first Mme de Staël herself is more traditional in
her ideas than some of the others. Her counsels in *Essai sur les fictions*
show her to be a moderate realist, allowing some dramatic effects as
long as they do not denature reality, cautioning against excessive use
of detail, a common Classical criticism, but strongly advocating depiction of everyday life as against fanciful fiction.[52] In *De l'Allemagne* she
will later express her preference for tragedy over the *drame*, on the
grounds that the latter is too close to everyday reality:

> On croit trouver plus d'intérêt dans le drame, parce qu'il nous représente
> ce que nous voyons tous les jours: mais une imitation trop rapprochée
> du vrai n'est pas ce que l'on recherche dans les arts. Le drame est à
> la tragédie ce que les figures de cire sont aux statues; il y a trop de
> vérité et pas assez d'idéal; c'est trop si c'est de l'art, et jamais assez pour
> que ce soit de la nature.(II.16; II.272)

The shift in emphasis. is not extreme: we are here dealing with the
theater, rather than prose fiction, and in any case reality is being contrasted with the ideal rather than with "fictions merveilleuses."

---

[49] *Rêveries* (1809), p. 134 (in Notes).
[50] *Ibid.*, p. 16.
[51] See Béatrice Le Gall, *L'Imaginaire chez Senancour* (Paris: Corti, 1966), II, 570-72.
[52] See A. Pizzorusso's paper in *Madame de Staël et l'Europe*, Colloque 1966 (Paris:
Klincksieck, 1970), pp. 281 sq.

In *Corinne* three pages devoted to the arts bear the mark of some of the new ideas circulating about her. It is true Mme de Staël does not always represent ideas as her own or those of her heroine, and she does not take sides when Corinne and Oswald disagree in their discussions. Corinne has read Winckelmann (she prefers serenity in the visual arts and finds that statues verging on the bisexual have the most sublime beauty) and Lessing (she does not like arts to be combined, as Oswald does). Mme de Staël returns to the idea made current by Chateaubriand, that Christianity has turned man inward: whereas paganism deified the human figure, Christianity has made our feelings divine. In the ancient world there was a closer union between physical and moral qualities than in modern man.[53] The human figure, which was also the figure of the gods, seemed symbolic. The shift that comes with an intellectual religion will inevitably change the artist's stance in relation to the human body in particular and the outer world in general. One consequence is that in Christian times the emphasis in visual arts has passed to painting. In painting as well as in sculpture, idealization is necessary to retain beauty when treating suffering and anguish.[54] With the exception of Philoctetes (the classic example, cited by Lessing), Oswald would exclude representation of physical suffering from painting. His remark, "L'art qui ne consisterait que dans cette imitation... est plus horrible ou moins beau que la nature même, dès l'instant qu'il aspire seulement à lui ressembler"[55] does seem, however, to have wider application to any artistic representation of visible reality, which should be distinct from the model.

In *De l'Allemagne* Mme de Staël emphasizes even more the inner sources of the work of art. She reports these conceptions as being those of German writers, but there can be little doubt that she herself subscribes to most of them, and her book is spreading the gospel. The chapter on Winckelmann and Lessing makes this clear: "Tout est symbolique dans les arts, et la nature sous mille apparences diverses dans ces statues, dans ces tableaux, dans ces poésies, où l'immortalité doit indiquer le mouvement, où l'extérieur doit révéler le fond de l'âme, où l'existence d'un instant doit être éternisée" (II.6; II.71). "Winckelmann a développé les vrais principes admis maintenant dans les arts sur l'idéal, sur cette nature perfectionnée dont le type est dans

---

[53] *Oeuvres complètes* (Paris: Treuttel et Würtz, 1820), VIII, 300, 307.
[54] *Ibid.*, IX, 377.
[55] *Ibid.*, VIII, 317.

notre imagination, et non au dehors de nous. L'application de ce principe à la littérature est particulièrement féconde" (II.6; II.74). The function of imagery based on nature is self-expression, as we shall see in chapter 4.

After Winckelmann, Kant:

> Kant soutient qu'il y a dans la poésie et dans les arts dignes comme elle de peindre les sentiments, deux genres de beauté, l'un qui peut se rapporter au temps et à cette vie, l'autre à l'éternel et à l'infini...
>
> Dans cette application du sentiment de l'infini aux beaux-arts doit naître l'idéal, c'est-à-dire le beau, considéré non pas comme la réunion et l'imitation de ce qu'il y a de mieux dans la nature, mais l'image réalisée de ce que notre âme se représente. (II.6; IV.136)

Whereas most French theoreticians looked upon ideal beauty as one principle of the imitation of nature, the Germans separate them, says Mme de Staël. Again, the sources are inside us. The artist gives form to his feelings in a work which evokes the same feelings in the spectator or the reader:

> Les Allemands ne considèrent point, ainsi qu'on le fait d'ordinaire, l'imitation de la nature comme le principal objet de l'art; c'est la beauté idéale qui leur paraît le principe de tous les chefs-d'oeuvre, et leur théorie poétique est à cet égard tout à fait d'accord avec leur philosophie. L'impression qu'on reçoit par les beaux-arts n'a pas le moindre rapport avec le plaisir que fait éprouver une imitation quelconque; l'homme a dans son âme des sentiments innés que les objets réels ne satisferont jamais, et c'est à ces sentiments que l'imagination des peintres et des poètes sait donner une forme et une vie. (III.9; IV.225)

Music, which imitates nothing, is the greatest and most moving of the arts.

Mme de Staël is not the first of her circle to deny that imitation is the principle of the arts. François Ancillon, though writing in French, reflects his German training (he was a disciple of Jacobi) in his *Mélanges de littérature et de philosophie*. Like the Germans of whom Mme de Staël speaks, he has a philosophical turn of mind and approaches the arts from that direction. His writings show clearly that he is not an artist. At home in a rational system in which the universe is but a reflection of the absolute, Ancillon sees the arts as a way of giving a finite form to the feeling for the infinite. The idea exists before forms. The plastic arts present specific forms with precise contours: the being that comes from the artist's ideal world takes on individual traits and through some secret of the artist awakens the feeling for the infinite in the spectator.[56]

There are two kinds of communication between the world of sensible forms and the intellectual world, says Ancillon: the philosopher ascends from sensible forms to intellectual ideas, but the artist proceeds in the opposite direction: "... on saisit les idées générales, puis on choisit ou l'on imagine des traits individuels qui puissent les tirer du champ des abstractions pour les réaliser aux yeux des sens."[57]

Poetry is the art which allows the greatest creative freedom; the poet may let his imagination run free, he may shake the dust of reality from his wings to soar above all that exists, in a universe of his own making.[58] But Ancillon does concede that in a sense poetry as well as the plastic arts does imitate nature, since it gives a high degree of individuality to the objects it creates. The difference is that nature works for its own conservation, whereas art aims to express an idea under individual traits.[59] The artist chooses the most perfect beings in nature as visible signs or emblems.

> Alors on pourroit peut-être dire que l'art imite la belle nature. Cependant il l'imite à son insu, et il puise ses formes dans l'imagination seule, enrichie par la contemplation et par l'étude de la nature. Dans ce sens encore, l'art est et doit être idéal.[60]

The emblems are not imitated directly from nature but pass through the imagination.

Also before Mme de Staël, Bonstetten, one of the Coppet group, had denied that the imitation of nature was the principle of the arts. Bonstetten is one of the most intelligent and interesting of the early nineteenth century writers who deal with these questions. Without entering here into the details of his theories, we may attempt to define how he saw the role of representation of the real world. The real objects given outward form by the artist serve, said he, to communicate to others the harmony which the artist feels and which awakens in him the *sentiment du beau*. Though there is, no doubt, in nature something which excites this feeling, beauty is not in the object.

[56] *Mélanges de littérature et de philosophie* (Paris: H. Nicolle et F. Schoell, 1809), I, 20.
[57] *Ibid.*, I, 155-56.
[58] *Ibid.*, I, 144-46.
[59] *Ibid.*, I, 175.
[60] *Ibid.*, I, 176-77.

> La beauté consiste dans des rapports tout spirituels, rapports nés de la combinaison de certaines sensations entr'elles et avec l'âme. Ce rapport n'est pas de nous aux choses, mais de nous à nous-mêmes, c'est-à-dire, des sensations aux sensations, et des sensations à l'âme.[61]

Artistic creation exteriorizes the feeling of harmony experienced by the artist, but it does not copy anything.

> L'imitation n'est... ni le but ni le principe des beaux-arts, mais bien un des *moyens* des beaux-arts. Il est important d'établir ce principe: l'opinion, que l'imitation est une des sources du beau, est dangereuse; nous lui devons déjà un grand nombre d'ouvrages sans goût. L'imitation parfaite peut bien donner le plaisir de la *surprise*, mais le sentiment de la surprise n'est pas le sentiment du beau, et n'a rien de commun avec l'harmonie.[62]

There is no imitation for its own sake: it is only a means of expression, and that is what we shall examine in chapter 4.

[61] *Recherches sur la nature et les lois de l'imagination*, 2 vols. (Geneva: Paschoud, 1807), I, 51 n.
[62] *Ibid.*, I, 55.

3. Expression

The term "expression," like "nature," is one of those vague words with multiple meanings which are used in various contexts and as often as not in an imprecise and ambiguous way. But it is a key word in esthetics, and the concepts it signifies are central to our subject, so we must contend with these multiple and often overlapping meanings. For purposes of analysis we shall separate some meanings that in the critical passages overlap and combine.

The first has to do with physical representation of the inner states of a model, usually human, what the artist calls his subject, or, in more philosophical terms, the object. In subsequent chapters we shall deal with art as self-expression, and then, in a more philosophical and theological acceptation, expression as a sensible form, in nature or in art, which clothes a higher reality. We shall not treat at any length expression in the sense of form of the work of art, though artistic technique and the problem of language are a logical continuation of our investigations. At the beginning of the nineteenth century, the common view was that conception and execution could be separated, and the former preceded the latter. At any rate, the inspiration of art preoccupied the critics of the early nineteenth century more than questions of form. Nor shall we deal with the arts as an expression of society, though this principle becomes one of the commonplaces of the time.

Expressiveness is one aspect of imitation and a necessary quality of art, for without some indication of the inner states of the model, the representation of appearances will produce a cold and lifeless work.

It also has a close link with the responsiveness of the spectator, reader, or listener, and one of the aims of the artist is to move the audience or to make it understand and admire. Commentary about expressiveness applies principally to the visual arts and the musical theater. An occasional remark includes the drama, on the grounds that it is, like painting, a direct representation of appearances, which must be expressive. Among other literary genres which are to some extent pictorial, descriptive poetry is reproached with lacking expression and leaving the reader cold, and the lush and poetic descriptions of recent masters of prose (Bernardin de Saint-Pierre, Chateaubriand) have not found a niche in this critical category.

For the eighteenth century, expression in the plastic arts was of prime importance. "Il n'y a que l'expression qui plaise," said Laugier.[1] The abbé Du Bos recommended that a painter concern himself first of all with expression, in order to "donner à chaque passion son caractère convenable."[2] Diderot also often wrote on the problem of expression, chiefly in his art criticism, but also in his *Lettre sur les sourds et muets*.[3] The depiction of emotions through facial expression had been systematized by Lebrun, whose *Méthode pour apprendre à dessiner les passions* (1696) showed a type configuration for every emotion. His method was based on the study of art rather than expression in living models or the study of anatomy.[4] Lavater's works on physiognomy, which set forth "le talent de connaître l'intérieur de l'homme par l'extérieur"[5] added their influence to the tradition already well established. He thought that his theories could be very useful to artists.[6]

Such a theory is predicated on the belief that there is a close and necessary link between emotions (*les mouvements de l'âme*) and outward signs, and the artist was supposed to make a study of emotions as

---

[1] *Jugement d'un amateur* (1973), p. 66, quoted in Alfred Lombard, *L'Abbé Du Bos* (Paris: Hachette, 1913), p. 328.

[2] *Réflexions*, I, 221-23, 311.

[3] See Michael T. Cartwright, *Diderot et le problème de l'expression*, Diderot Studies XIII (Geneva: Droz, 1969).

[4] See Gombrich, *Art and Illusion*, p. 348.

[5] Lavater was first published in France in 1803. *L'Art de connaître les hommes par la physionomie* dates from 1806. Balzac owned a copy of the 1820 edition of this work. See Jean Pommier, *La Mystique de Baudelaire* (Paris: Belle Lettres, 1932), pp. 42-46.

[6] J.B. Delestre followed in Lebrun's footsteps by publishing in 1833 his *Etudes des passions appliquées aux beaux-arts* (Paris: Joubert), which sets up a detailed classification of the passions and the manner in which the artist may delineate them.

well as the technique for representing them. Expression was concentrated in the human face, and to a lesser extent in bodily posture and gesture. The body was more important in ancient nude sculpture, the face and gesture more exclusively expressive in painting. Most critics did not recognize expressiveness outside human beings, though some also accepted it in animals. For Diderot inanimate objects were expressive; later, Chateaubriand and Ballanche saw a moral character in the landscape (see above, p. 31).

Among art forms, sculpture was traditionally said to be the least expressive, and the early nineteenth century will concur: according to Emeric-David, increasing degrees of expressiveness are found in sculpture, then painting, then theater, then narration (*le récit*). A statue is immobile and unchanging.[7] Guizot, too, disliked violent expression in a statue, for it had a tendency to harden, to become solid and more durable than on canvas.[8] He refers the reader to Diderot's *Salon de 1765* for similar views. Expressiveness lies in movement, and it is generally agreed that painting is better suited than sculpture for suggesting movement. Grace, too, is in movement and may be considered one kind of expressiveness.

The interest in classical archeology of the late eighteenth century lays emphasis on the least expressive genre and discourages the more extreme forms of dramatic expression. David after 1800 will seek to attenuate the dramatic qualities in his painting and follow Winckelmann. Quatremère de Quincy had read and absorbed Winckelmann and Lessing, especially the former, Mme de Staël knew them well, Guizot quotes Lessing at length and regrets that he is insufficiently known.[9] Lessing thought that the artist should "subject [expression] to the first law of art, the law of beauty."[10] Expression of extreme pain should be softened and veiled in the visual arts, as Laocoön's scream is softened to a sigh. Nor should the transitory, the peak of emotion be depicted in the visual arts, which freeze the moment for the contemplation of the spectator and in such case leave nothing to his imagination. Poetry, on the other hand, is not subject to the same conditions, and Virgil's Laocoön may scream. Drama is theoretically similar to the visual arts, since we actually see and hear a man

---

[7] *Recherches*, pp. 389-90.
[8] *Salon de 1810*, p. 116.
[9] *Ibid.*, p. 24.
[10] *Laocoön*, translated by E.A. McCormick (Indianapolis: Bobbs-Merrill, 1962), p. 17.

representing Philoctetes scream, but in practice the dramatic genius
of Sophocles can make us accept violent expression.[11]

Winckelmann pointed out that among the principal attributes of
the lofty beauty of ancient Greek art were lack of individuality and
of emotional expression which would mar the unity of the lines.

> Expression... changes the features of the face, and the posture, and
> consequently alters those forms which constitute beauty. The greater
> the change, the more unfavorable it is to beauty. On this account,
> stillness was one of the principles observed here, because it was regard-
> ed, according to Plato, as a state intermediate between sadness and
> gayety; and for the same reason, stillness is the state most appropriate
> to beauty, just as it is to the sea.[12]

Expression is not absent, it is simply not allowed to become so strong
that it would interfere with beauty of line. The comparative calmness
of Laocoön is expressive of a great and composed soul: such are suitable
objects for sculpture. The correct balance between passion and serenity
in order to make beauty prevail is found in the statue Apollo Belvedere
where, as Winckelmann points out, the nose shows indignation and
the chin shows contempt, but the glance is serene and the brow
unruffled. Winckelmann recognizes that beauty without expression
would be characterless, whereas expression without beauty is unpleas-
ant. As Bosanquet puts it, "expression is at once an element essential to beauty and tending to destroy it."[13]

Early nineteenth-century critics echoed many of these ideas.
Alphonse Leroy *fils* in a letter to the *Décade Philosophique* summarizes
Winckelmann's theories about facial expression, centered around the
eyes and mouth. The mouth depicts all emotions with a grimace, and
its only agreeable movement is a smile.

> Les yeux seuls peuvent peindre toutes les passions avec noblesse; aussi
> les anciens ont-ils pour leurs Dieux concentré toute l'expression dans
> les yeux, tandis qu'ils l'ont fait légèrement partager à la bouche pour
> les mortels. C'est au peu de mouvement de la bouche que les statues
> antiques doivent *cette sérénité* qui *forme pour elles un caractère distinctif*, comme
> l'observait Winckelmann.[14]

[11] *Ibid.*, pp. 19-25.

[12] *History of Ancient Art*, trans. G. Henry Lodge (New York: Frederick Ungar, 1968),
II, 245-46.

[13] *History of Aesthetics* (London: Macmillan, 1932), p. 24.

[14] 35 (An XI-1802), 110-11.

This noble and majestic expression of passions results in *la beauté idéale d'expression*.

When Corinne shows Oswald through the sculpture gallery of the Vatican museum, they (and their creator) admire the heroic calm of the ancient statues, which is even more noble than the suffering of modern men.[15] This calm, according to Mme de Staël, reflects the moral state of the ancients, who were almost never "mal à l'aise." Except for the two classic exceptions Laocoön (Lessing found his expression calm, but most others did not) and Niobe, no violent expressions are shown, and hardly a few traces of melancholy. If an ancient sculptor wished to indicate base or ferocious emotions, he had recourse to elements of animals, thus creating satyrs and centaurs; if, on the other hand, he wished to create the most sublime beauty, he combined the charms of the two sexes, thus joining gentleness to strength.[16]

The delicate balance between beauty and expression should be carried over into painting, though the emphasis may be different from that in sculpture. Guizot maintains this in his discussion of Girodet and Gros. He does not accept the argument that truth calls for the depiction of the horrible and the ugly in painting. Why hasn't Gros tried to keep beauty in his history paintings? "Je crains qu'il n'ait été souvent trompé par une idée trop répandue aujourd'hui dans l'Ecole, et contraire aux progrès de l'art; c'est que l'énergie de l'expression est le point le plus important."[17] Guizot does recognize Gros's talent for naturalistic representation, and he does not like figures in paintings to resemble statues, but when expressiveness results in ugliness, the line must be drawn. Such complaints are found throughout the period, and when the ugly in art does gain partial acceptance, it will be to some extent because it is expressive.

David, in whose paintings figures do sometimes look like statues, criticized Girodet's *Le Déluge* for excessive expressiveness and, when painting Leonidas at Thermopylae, was especially anxious to get away from dramatic effects, as he told Delécluze:

> Je veux essayer de mettre de côté ces mouvements, ces expressions de théâtre, auxquels les modernes ont donné le titre de *peinture d'expression*. A l'imitation des artistes de l'antiquité, qui ne manquaient jamais de

[15] Mme de Staël, *Oeuvres complètes*, VIII, 302.
[16] See also Quatremère de Quincy in *Archives Littéraires*, 7 (1805), 292.
[17] *Salon de 1810*, p. 24.

saisir l'instant avant ou après la grande crise du sujet, je ferai Léonidas et ses soldats calmes et se promettant l'immortalité avant le combat... Mais j'aurai bien de la peine... à faire adopter de semblables idées dans notre temps. On aime les coups de théâtre, et quand on ne peint pas les passions violentes, quand on ne pousse pas *l'expression* en peinture jusqu'à la *grimace*, on risque de n'être ni compris ni goûté.[18]

David was working not only against public opinion but against the Academy, which approved "energetic" expression. Though he and his school had for a time accustomed spectators to sculptural qualities in painting, the latter will soon reverse the situation by looking for pictorial qualities of movement and expression in sculpture.[19]

Ingres was much preoccupied with the exactness of facial expression, as befits a master portraitist. He characteristically places emphasis on draughtsmanship:

L'expression en peinture exige une très grande science du dessin, car l'expression ne peut être bonne si elle n'a été formulée avec une justesse absolue. Ne la saisir qu'à peu près, c'est la manquer; c'est ne représenter que des gens faux qui s'étudieraient à contrefaire des sentiments qu'ils n'éprouvent pas. On ne peut parvenir à cette extrême précision que par le plus sûr talent dans le dessin. Aussi les peintres d'expression parmi les modernes ont-ils été les plus grands dessinateurs. Voyez Raphaël![20]

He also made general observations concerning the expressive qualities of bodily lines and proportions and positions of the head and the chest. Here exactness is not quite so important as for the face: "Pour exprimer le caractère une certaine exagération est permise, surtout là où il s'agit de dégager et de faire saillir un élément du beau."[21] Expression is at the service of beauty, not, as for Winckelmann, in a precarious balance with it. As far as painting was concerned, the question of the desirable kind and degree ("énergie") of expression was an old one. Guizot points out that Vasari had regarded exaggerated expression as a sign of decadence.[22] Emeric-David deplores the fact that after Michelangelo most artists abandoned nature to seek a

---

[18] *Louis David*, pp. 226-27.
[19] See, for example, a comment in the *Globe* of 10 Sept. 1825, praising a statue of Prometheus for its expressiveness.
[20] Delaborde, p. 127.
[21] *Ibid.*, p. 130.
[22] *Salon de 1810*, p. 39.

chimerical beauty, trying to show the effects of passion without learning how the human body reacts, so that they fall into exaggeration of movement, at the expense of resemblance.[23] His adversary Quatremère de Quincy from the opposite vantage point attacks the expressiveness of the realists: "Je ne sais quoi d'expressif dans la physionomie par ces petitesses de l'imitation dont tout le monde peut être jugé..."[24]

As one would expect, partisans of naturalistic representation have a different conception from the idealists of what constitutes appropriate expression and whether or not expression is in conflict with beauty. The naturalists in general wish to stay closer to the true and the expressive, and nature herself furnishes this directly. When the natural model is full of life and movement and the face is animated, then imitation is expression. Art should first of all be beautiful, but without expression it is only carved stone or painted canvas.[25] The naturalists sought an illusion of life, but above all they wished to communicate something about the model, be it a portrait or a historical scene. "Le but véritable des arts du dessin," says Benoît of the naturalists, "est la traduction en langage visuel d'une 'pensée philosophique' ou d'un trait ingénieux de l'esprit, le 'tableau des passions humaines,' 'l'expression énergique' des affections de l'âme!"[26] Nobility comes not so much from the forms as from the feelings that animate them. And when the forms are individualized, the expression is all the more vivid.

As for the idealists, they followed Winckelmann in keeping facial expression to a minimum, avoiding "grimaces." An excessive vivacity of expression would speak too exclusively to the eyes, and such a "materialistic" appeal is unworthy of the noble and austere aspirations of art. Moreover, the idealist position tends toward a different kind of expression, that which is the embodiment of an intellectual essence. To this we shall return in chapter 5.

But some degree of expressiveness is accepted by almost everyone. Though some thought that it should be kept to a minimum, it was a necessary quality of the work of art, and its importance in relation to beauty will increase. It is curious to see expression listed as an element of painting, along with composition, color, line, and

---

23 *Recherches*, p. 450.
24 *Archives Littéraires*, 7 (1805), 7.
25 Benoît, *L'Art français*, p. 68.
26 *Ibid.*, pp. 72-73.

chiaroscuro.[27] Early in the century Ancillon pointed out that genius treats subjects so as to conciliate beauty and expression, which hides and reveals to the soul a world of feelings and ideas.[28] Joseph Droz finds that a masterpiece of physical perfection still does not attain ideal perfection without a noble expression.[29] In 1822, A.-H. Kératry, who like Droz is a middle-of-the-road critic, emphasizes the importance of expression for beauty: "Quant à notre espèce, le BEAU dans les formes éprouve... un grand déchet sans le Beau d'expression."[30] By the 1820s the term "beau d'expression" had become current. Expression is "l'âme d'un tableau," says Kératry in a chapter devoted to expression in painting.[31] He admires the expressiveness of the faces in Poussin and Gros, Raphael and David. Expression may even overtake and outweigh beauty as the supreme value.

Stendhal's writings on art often deal with expression, to which he gave the extreme importance it had for the eighteenth century.

> L'expression est tout l'art.
> Un tableau sans expression n'est qu'une image pour amuser les yeux un instant. Les peintres doivent sans doute posséder le coloris, le dessin, la perspective, etc.; sans cela l'on n'est point peintre. Mais s'arrêter dans une de ces perfections subalternes, c'est prendre misérablement le moyen pour le but, c'est manquer sa carrière.[32]

Stendhal uses the word in the conventional sense of the manifestations of emotions ("les mouvements de l'âme") in the face and body. The expressiveness of the figure portrayed was to awaken the sympathy and admiration of the spectator. "Par l'expression, la peinture se lie à tout ce qu'il y a de plus grand dans le coeur des grands hommes. *Napoléon touchant les pestiférés à Jaffa.*"[33]

Some modern critics have expressed disappointment with Stendhal for his essentially moral and sentimental approach to the arts. The

---

[27] See, for example, J.-F. Sobry, *La Poétique des arts* (Paris: Delaunay, Brunot-Labbe, Colnet, 1810), p. 90.

[28] *Mélanges*, p. 22.

[29] *Etudes*, p. 119.

[30] *Du beau dans les arts d'imitation* (Paris: P. Audot, 1822), II, 48-49.

[31] *Ibid.*, II, 165.

[32] *Histoire de la peinture en Italie*, I, 128. Hereafter abbreviated *Histoire*. See also II, 370, and a copy of a letter to F. Faure in *Oeuvres intimes* (Pléiade), p. 1014.

[33] *Ibid.*, I, 129.

moral approach was, as we have seen, characteristic of the time; art, though it did not necessarily aim to edify, should have some moral or cognitive effect. Stendhal's sentence, "La peinture n'est que de la morale construite,"[34] was repeated by Baudelaire, who accepted it as applicable to all the arts if taken in a broad sense (*Salon de 1846*). Stendhal was a student and lover of all the arts and he responded emotionally to them; in his view, emotion was the prime essential in the artist, in the subject matter, and in the spectator.

In spite of his categorical statements about the primacy of expressiveness in art, he does not extend it to sculpture. In his discussion of the *Beau Idéal Antique* in the *Histoire de la peinture en Italie*, he concurs with Winckelmann (whom he generally did not like) that the expression of passion is detrimental to beauty. Sculpture strives only for beauty and admits of little expression, says he. In other passages he speaks of the expressiveness proper to sculpture. In this respect Stendhal makes the distinction between character, that is, moral habits, or, according to the Stendhalian definition, one's habitual manner of seeking happiness, and passions, which alter habits and their physical expression. In the case of ancient Greek sculpture the subjects were gods, not men, and the sculptors brought out their character. The Jupiter Mansuetus, for example, expresses goodness, wisdom, and strength; his thick neck indicates strength and his protruberant forehead wisdom. The general impression is of inalterable serenity. Sculpture cannot exploit the most expressive feature, the eyes, but can express character which can be seen from all sides, not just the face.[35]

Among the plastic arts, painting best expresses passions as well as character. Historically, Stendhal places the beginning of expressiveness in Masaccio and its highest point of excellence in Raphael.[36] Painting, which in modern times tends to predominate over sculpture, more often portrays men, not gods. The passions of modern times are no longer those of antiquity. The nineteenth century is thirsty for strong emotion, and a new painting must satisfy this thirst. Stendhal calls

[34] *Ibid.*, II, 226 n.

[35] *Ibid.*, II, 10-84.

[36] Cf. Mengs: "Raphaël... conçut les premières idées de l'expression dans la peinture lorsqu'il vit les ouvrages de Masaccio," "car il y avait plus d'expression dans Massaccio que dans tous les autres de son temps," *Réflexions sur quelques peintres de differentes écoles*, pp. 334-35, quoted by Arbelet in notes to *Histoire de la peinture en Italie*, I, 335.

constantly for the depiction of passions in painting but on occasion prefers the portrayal of character. He asks the question: how far should the artist go in altering beauty or expression of character in order to represent passions? There is no answer: only the artist himself can decide this, brush in hand.

If "expression" for Stendhal meant the demonstration of passions, "idéal" also sometimes meant expressiveness, a reversal from the idealists' understanding of the term. After a description of Michelangelo's cartoon for *The Battle of Pisa*, in which he admires the expressive quality of the figures and the faces, the action of the muscles, the movement of the mouths, Stendhal says, "L'art d'idéaliser se montrait pour la première fois..." (in the Christian era, that is). This idealizing is quite different from the usual Neoclassic principle. "Le vulgaire [meaning Mengs] a coutume de dire que Michel-Ange manque d'idéal," says Stendhal, "et c'est lui qui, parmi les modernes, a inventé l'idéal." The difference between the ancient and modern conceptions of the ideal is crucial: "L'antique altère la nature en diminuant la saillie des muscles, Michel-Ange en l'augmentant."[37] The old idea is to smooth down and generalize; the new idea is to bring out salient features and individualize. And not only Michelangelo: Masaccio and Raphael individualized the expression of their subjects, says Stendhal.[38] The principle of simplification is the same, the manner different. This conception of the ideal is one of the most forward-looking in Stendhal's esthetics, which is a mixture of old and new ideas.

Stendhal is the first important critic to champion Michelangelo; in the following years the Romantics will take up the cause in their polemics with the *classiques*, who remain faithful to Raphael. Stendhal himself personally preferred Raphael.

Modern ideal beauty, according to Stendhal's description, is more expressive than the ancient, and he credited Canova, whom he greatly admired, with having invented a new kind of *beau idéal* closer to our taste for wit and sentiment than to the ancient Greek mores.[39] Modern ideal beauty does not, however, reflect the strong passions which the nineteenth century will supposedly demand. Among the desirable qualities (grace, gaiety, sensibility) only one feature, the most ex-

[37] *Histoire*, II, 324, 275, 85, 199, 201, 223.
[38] *Histoire*, I, 27. Cf. marginal remark in Stendhal's copy of *Lucien Leuwen*: "*idéaliser comme Raphaël idéalise dans un portrait pour le rendre plus ressemblant*" (II, 73).
[39] *Mélanges d'art*, III, 73.

pressive, is mentioned: "l'oeil étincelant." The ideal of modern beauty whose character is summed up by Stendhal as elegance, is clearly subjective, though he maintains that the public is aware of it.

Stendhal does not accept the idea that art can portray beauty of character shining through an ugly face, in contrast to Lavater, whom he quotes in a note. Lavater, according to this passage, would find a certain beauty in "toute bonne qualité qui est exprimée par les sens," (meaning, presumably, in material form), though the form itself would not be beautiful as in Raphael or Guido Reni. Not so, says Stendhal; in reality this may be valid, and it is true that a "grande âme" does betray itself in movement, but such a portrayal is inadmissible in sculpture. He cites the usual example: "S'il est vrai qu'avec les traits que nous lui connaissons Socrate ait porté une physionomie parfaitement ignoble, cette âme sublime fut à jamais hors de la portée des arts du dessin;..." As is well known, Stendhal was repelled by the ugly and the vulgar, which he called "base"; his "espagnolisme" was offended by the vulgarity of the subjects of Flemish realistic painting. However, though seized by the horror of parts of Michelangelo's *Last Judgment*, he does not react to this terrible and majestic visionary work as he does before the (for him) ignobly vulgar in the more realistic works: one of the faces, says he, "a toute la bassesse que peut admettre l'horreur du sujet"; the ideal of the demons was almost as difficult to achieve as the ideal of Apollo.

Though recognizing the importance of symbol and allegory in art, Stendhal does not discuss them at length nor seem to find them very expressive. He takes from Quatremère de Quincy some information about ancient bas-reliefs which constituted inscriptions of hieroglyphics, pointing out that when the figure is a sign it is no longer close to reality but must aim for clarity as a symbol. At the same time, if it is too far from reality, it loses its effectiveness and is no more than futile conventional language.

Stendhal knows enough about painting to discuss its technical aspects, though, as he says, these are only means to expressive ends. In addition to faces and figures, color can be expressive, and even brushwork; he is one of the rare critics of the time who perceives the importance of pictorial expression. But the emphasis is on the human subject, true to Stendhal's psychological approach. "... la peinture n'[a] que les corps pour rendre les âmes,..."[40] and Stendhal's complaint

[40] *Histoire*, II, 117, 135, 123, 268, 19, 26, 238.

is that David's school can paint only bodies and not souls.[41] Their figures have been frozen statue-like into dramatic gestures in imitation of Talma, which only leave the spectator cold. Even the greatest painters (and dramatists) are subject to limitations, for they cannot show passions themselves, but only their effects. "Ce que notre âme avide demande aux arts, c'est la peinture des passions, et non pas la peinture des actions que font faire les passions." Where else will he find it but in the novel, with its possibility of inner monologue? But Stendhal has little to say about the novel at this time (he has not yet become a novelist), though he cites the example of Werther when speaking of passions not visible externally.[42] Only a few comments point out literature's superior capacity for psychological depiction. The visual arts do not imitate man's moral character as closely as poetry, he says,[43] and among poetic genres dramatic poetry is more expressive than the epic.[44] The visual arts act on the imagination through the senses, whereas poetry acts on the senses through the imagination.[45] But Stendhal does not seem to believe in the expressive power of language except in relation to music.

For Stendhal music is the most sublime of all the arts, the one which touches the listener most directly, it is a language; a musical composition, says Stendhal, is speech made with sounds rather than with words.[46] The pleasure it gives is primarily physical, as against the more intellectual appeal of the visual arts. "Les expressions de cette langue vont droit au coeur, sans traverser, pour ainsi dire, l'esprit; elles produisent directement *peine* ou *plaisir*..." Better than speech it communicates nuances of feeling. "Il est tout simple que nos langues vulgaires, qui ne sont qu'une suite de signes convenus pour exprimer des choses généralement connues, n'aient point de signe pour exprimer de tels mouvements que vingt personnes peut-être, sur mille, ont éprouvés. Les âmes sensibles ne pouvaient donc se communiquer leurs impressions et les peindre."[47] The kind of music which would allow them to express feelings was invented in Italy in the early eighteenth century. However, it has the disadvantage of being unintelligible to

---

[41] *Salon de 1824* in *Mélanges d'art*, III, 27.
[42] *Histoire*, II, 32-33, 180.
[43] *Vies de Haydn, de Mozart et de Métastase*, p. 210.
[44] *Histoire*, II, 32.
[45] *Ibid.*, II, 122-23. Cf. P. Lahalle, *Essai sur la musique* (Paris: Rousselon, 1825), p. 83.
[46] *Haydn*, p. 93.
[47] *Ibid.*, pp. 349-51.

the other 980 listeners, who have never experienced these fleeting nuances of feeling. In line with Stendhal's relativistic esthetics, the expressive powers of music will also vary from country to country because of the differences in climate and the temperament of the people. In contrast to music, which comes the closest to direct communication and asks for the collaboration of the listener, a given piece of sculpture, which expresses only moderate and generalized emotion, can be appreciated by many peoples.[48] Music is not then for Stendhal a universal language but rather a superior language for a sensitive elite of homogeneous cultural formation. Its expressivity depends to a large degree on the ear of the listener.

The music to which Stendhal so ardently responds is vocal music, and his writings on music are principally devoted to the opera. Though he does pay homage to Haydn as a great genius of instrumental music, his preference is always on the side of the voice. Musical instruments please us, says he, only to the extent that they resemble and recall the human voice;[49] a voice always conveys some passion, whereas when we hear an instrumentalist we are impressed only by the "difficulté vaincue." Instrumental music is made chiefly to accompany the voice and be subordinate to it; it fulfills the same function as the landscape in a historical painting or ornaments in architecture.[50] The orchestra is supportive of the voice and can achieve some effects that the voice cannot: it can move faster, and it can represent such things as storms and wild beasts. The orchestral element of the opera (which Stendhal calls "harmonie") excels at depicting rapid and fleeting nuances which should capture our imagination only partially; it should not hold our attention too long, or its suggestive power is lost.[51]

Though music surpasses language as a vehicle of expression, it combines with it and uses it to reach the highest expressiveness. This it does in opera. Since music is vague by nature, a poet is needed to guide our imagination and bring clarity to our comprehension of the character's feelings.[52] At the same time, such clarification should not be detailed or over-subtle, and the emphasis remains on the melody. It turns out in practice that most opera librettos are absurd and badly written, so that it is enough that we have a word or two to tell us

[48] *Ibid.*, p. 210.
[49] *Vie de Rossini*, II, 131.
[50] *Haydn*, p. 18.
[51] *Rossini*, I, 314.
[52] *Haydn*, p. 351.

the situation and emotion of the character: "... [la parole] indique à l'imagination des auditeurs le genre d'images qu'ils doivent se figurer... les paroles ne sont dans la musique que pour y remplir des fonctions très secondaires, et pour n'y servir en quelque sorte que comme *étiquettes du sentiment.*"[53]

Stendhal occasionally chides himself with basing his criticism on an emotional response which lets him get carried away: "Comme en idéologie il faut savoir à chaque instant retenir notre intelligence qui veut courir, de même, dans la *théorie des arts*, il faut retenir l'âme, qui sans cesse veut jouir et non examiner."[54] It is the *idéologue* in Stendhal that would like to systematize expression in music as Lebrun had done for painting, but according to scientific methods. "La musique attend son Lavoisier." This genius would conduct experiments in psychology ("le coeur humain") and physiology (the ear itself), after which he would deduce the rules of music. For various emotions (anger, jealousy, happy love, etc.) he would give us the twenty melodies (*cantilènes*) which best expressed the feeling, with appropriate accompaniment. Then a real theory of music would be scientifically established, displacing the present theories based on nothing.[55]

Villoteau, though unlike Stendhal in most respects, had expressed a similar desire in his *Recherches sur l'analogie de la musique avec les arts qui ont pour l'objet l'imitation du langage*. Such a collection of the "divers accents naturels de l'expression, rendus musicalement" would constitute a real dictionary of music.[56] According to Villoteau, the choice of sounds is determined by nature, since they are to stay close to the natural inflections of the voice; a musician who departs from the natural inflections expresses poorly or not at all the feeling he wishes to communicate.[57] The most expressive sounds are those which are in phase with the rhythm of our bodies:

[53] *Rossini*, II, 132-33.

[54] *Ibid.*, I, 168.

[55] *Ibid.*, I, 165-67: "La plupart des règles, qui oppriment dans ce moment le génie des musiciens, ressemblent à la philosophie de Platon ou de Kant; ce sont des billevesées mathématiques inventées avec plus ou moins d'esprit ou d'imagination, mais dont chacune a grand besoin d'être soumise au creuset de l'expérience."

[56] G.A. Villoteau, *Recherches sur l'analogie de la musique avec les arts qui ont pour objet l'imitation du langage*, 2 vols. (Paris: Imprimerie Impériale, 1807), II, 159-60 n. Grétry, whom Villoteau respected, devoted the second volume of his *Mémoires* to an analysis of passions with its application to musical composition. Villoteau does not mention this.

[57] Villoteau, II, 98.

[Les sons] se rapprochent de l'ordre qui existe habituellement en nous, et l'harmonie de tous les mouvements qui nous animent tant extérieurement qu'intérieurement, de cette harmonie qui se manifeste évidemment dans les battements de notre coeur, dans les pulsations des artères, en un mot dans l'action de toutes les parties matérielles de notre être...[58]

Villoteau finds an invariable order in sounds which is absent in colors: "... ils ont toujours un rapport constamment le même avec l'étendue des corps, la rapidité du mouvement et la densité de l'air qui les produit. Ils ont toujours, dans la voix, un rapport constamment le même avec les sentiments et les passions dont ils sont l'expression."[59] Such a compilation of sounds would be an infallible guide to perfect expressiveness and invaluable to all musicians, who are supposed to know how to express all emotions, whether they have ever felt them or not.[60]

The abbé Morellet cites examples of expressive devices but makes no effort to be complete. After the obvious analogies between muffled sounds and an aching heart, between rhythmic and emotional agitation, the commonly known suggestiveness of major and minor modes, he points out the use of certain intervals: the sweet and gentle effect of ascending minor thirds and sixths, fourths and diminished fifths as against the firmer and more decided effect of ascending fifths and major thirds and sixths.[61]

Many writers of the early nineteenth century echoed Stendhal's choice of music as the best communication of feeling, the most direct, the most penetrating. According to Chênedollé, "La musique attaque plus vivement les fibres que la poésie."[62] Mme de Staël's Corinne finds that music acts immediately upon the soul.[63] Bonstetten like Stendhal stresses its nonrational operation: "La musique est de tous les arts celui qui parle à l'âme de plus près. C'est que la musique n'a pas besoin d'aller toujours aux idées pour toucher la sensibilité; elle peut, au contraire, y arriver directement par le mouvement et l'harmonie."[64]

[58] *Ibid.*, II, 114.

[59] *Ibid.*, II, 157 n.

[60] *Ibid.*, II, 68-69.

[61] "De l'expression en musique," *Archives Littéraires*, 6 (1805), 164-65.

[62] *Journal*, quoted in F. Baldensperger, *Romantisme et sensibilité musicale* (Paris: Presses Françaises, 1925), p. 80.

[63] *Oeuvres complètes*, VIII, 169.

[64] *Recherches sur la nature et les lois de l'imagination*, p. 36.

He is approaching the idea common today, that music is expressive in itself without being the expression of something.

Again, Villoteau has definite ideas to present on the subject: the laws of expressiveness in singing, says he, are more dependent on the laws of natural expression than are those of words. There are two different languages, that of unarticulated sounds, which is natural and always true (unarticulated sounds and gestures constitute natural expression), and the conventional one of words, but we have only one way of feeling, and singing is the true imitation of its expression. (Actually, music and poetry should always be joined together, as we shall see below.) If the ear is the principal organ by which we naturally transmit ideas, feelings, and knowledge, it is for definite physical reasons:

> ... l'organe de l'ouïe a cet avantage sur tous les autres, qu'étant placé très près du cerveau, et conséquemment près de la source et du foyer de nos sensations, de nos idées, ainsi que du siège de la mémoire, les impressions qu'il reçoit par l'action de l'air extérieur, qui est le véhicule du son, et qui s'identifie en quelque façon avec l'action de l'air qui nous anime, se communiquent aussi bien plus vivement à notre imagination et à tout le système de notre sensibilité, se gravent plus profondément dans notre mémoire, et s'y conservent beaucoup plus longtemps que les impressions que nous recevons par les autres organes.[65]

Since expressiveness is based on physical laws, it is independent of human convention and the same for all peoples.[66]

According to Fabre d'Olivet, the communication of feeling through music involves more than air vibrations striking the ear drum. First of all, in order to move others, the composer must himself be moved; his emotion is a fluid that will pass by magnetism to others: "Sachez qu'il existe une correspondance entre les âmes, un fluide secret et sympathique, une électricité inconnue qui les met en rapport les unes avec les autres. De tous les moyens de mettre ce fluide en mouvement, la musique offre le plus puissant."[67] If the emotion is strong enough and the composer is trained in the principles of his art, the means of communication — the music, the melody — will come to him without his searching for them.

---

[65] Villoteau, II, 391-92.
[66] *Ibid.*, II, 98, 490.
[67] *La Musique*, p. 87. See Léon Cellier, *Fabre d'Olivet*, p. 224.

In the early nineteenth century musicians and writers of the most diverse tendencies carried on a running debate concerning the virtues of instrumental as against vocal music, of symphony as against opera. Here again, Stendhal is typical of his time in his preference for vocal music and his love for opera. No one is more contemptuous of orchestral music than Villoteau:

> Est-il quelqu'un assez dépourvu de sensibilité et de jugement, pour préférer une symphonie agréable, mais dont l'expression vague et presque nulle ne peindrait rien, à ces morceaux admirables de chant de nos meilleurs opéras, et dont l'expression énergique et vraie remue si fortement le coeur et remplit l'âme d'un trouble si délicieux?[68]

Fabre d'Olivet too is categorical in rejecting instrumental music: it is a kind of soul deprived of a body; lacking the means of making its beauties felt, that is, words or gesture, it falls into vagueness.[69] For the abbé Morellet, it is like a language without vowels. French music lovers are slow to acquire a taste for orchestral music, partly for lack of a chance to hear it.[70] Parallel to this deprivation is another, the lack of good writing on music; music criticism hardly exists before 1820. The opera had been the most popular musical form in the eighteenth century, and this dominance continued in the early part of the nineteenth. As the Romantic generations came onto the scene, opera, with its color and its pathetic situations, continued to please them. For many years the nineteenth century seemed to agree with Grétry and others that declamation was the principle of operatic music. Castil-Blaze in 1820 declares: "Si on reconnaît que la déclamation est une imitation de la nature, pourquoi refuserait-on cette qualité à l'expression musicale, qui ne fait que renforcer les tons de la voix parlante et les assujettir à un rythme déterminé?"[71] But declamatory music was losing its hold on the new generation. In *Le Globe* Ludovic Vitet mockingly portrays a musician of the old school giving advice to a young composer:

> Vous voulez être dramatique; il n'y a qu'un chemin pour vous conduire à votre but, c'est la mélodie, et non pas toute espèce de mélodie,

---

[68] Villoteau, II, 78.

[69] *La Musique*, p. 92.

[70] A Beethoven symphony was first performed in Paris in 1826. (See *L'Artiste*, 29 [1837], 322.)

[71] *De l'opéra en France*, p. 138.

mais seulement la mélodie déclamée ou *syllabique*; car pour ces chants qui ne sont qu'agréables sans rien dire à l'esprit, il faut en faire un sobre usage. Chantez, sans vous mettre en peine de la basse, sans même vous inquiéter du plaisir de l'oreille. Pourvu que vous traduisiez exactement les inflexions du langage, pourvu que vous nous fassiez de la déclamation notée, nous serons contents, nous vous proclamerons dramatique par excellence.[72]

The word "vague" can designate vocal music not based on declamation, church music rather than theater music. "La musique d'une expression vague," says Grétry, "a un charme plus magique peut-être que la musique déclamée; et c'est pour les paroles saintes qu'il faut l'adopter... Vouloir faire sortir la musique d'église du vague mystérieux qui lui est propre, est, je crois, une erreur."[73] Cabanis, in speaking of the possibilities of the various arts, also finds that the vague impressions of music make it more suitable to the temple than to the theater.[74]

Mme de Staël in *De l'Allemagne* gives an example of the expressivity which opera can achieve by the combined forces of words, song, and orchestra. She praises Gluck for having so wonderfully adapted the song to the words and rivaled the poet in the contrast between the serenity of Orestes's song in *Iphigénie en Tauride* (words and melody) and the agitation of the orchestra, which thereby shows that Orestes is lying. Mozart has brought this technique to a point of perfection in the contrast between the gay and the somber in *Don Giovanni*. She sees a parallel with the use of words in Poussin's *Bergers d'Arcadie*:

Il y a de la pensée dans cette manière de considérer les arts, comme dans les combinaisons ingénieuses de Gluck; mais les arts sont au-dessus de la pensée: leur langage ce sont les couleurs ou les formes, ou les sons. Si l'on pouvait se figurer les impressions dont notre âme serait susceptible, avant qu'elle connût la parole, on concevrait mieux l'effet de la peinture et de la musique. (II.32; III.377)

Rather than follow a text closely, she likes to see a composer use it as a springboard for a purely musical expression. There are two ways of looking at expressive music, says she: "... les uns veulent trouver en elle la traduction des paroles, les autres, et ce sont les Italiens,

---

[72] 15 Jan. 1825.
[73] *Mémoires*, I, 75-76.
[74] *Oeuvres complètes*, V, 349-50, "Lettre... sur les poèmes d'Homère."

se contentent d'un rapport général entre les situations de la pièce et l'intention des airs, et cherchent les plaisirs de l'art uniquement en lui-même" (II.32; III.380). Stendhal says something similar about badly written librettos (see above, p. 54); Mme de Staël is more inclusive; for her the text is a pretext.

Some others preferred that the music take precedence over the words, which become indistinct. According to Lahalle, poetry has a tendency to demand our full attention and prevents music from taking possession of our sensibility; as a consequence, when the two are combined, one should be subordinated or even sacrificed to the other.[75] Senancour's Oberman too finds that words stand in the way of the beauty of the melody, and he prefers songs whose words he does not understand (*Oberman*, Letter LXI). This is the preferred situation for Preromantic reverie. "Quand on aime véritablement la musique," says Mme de Staël, "il est rare qu'on écoute les paroles des beaux airs. On préfère de se livrer au vague indéfini de la rêverie qu'excitent les sons."[76]

Song without words approaches the vague and indeterminate expression of instrumental music. Most listeners, who preferred to know what feeling was being expressed, found instrumental music too abstract and were likely to react by asking, "Sonate, que me veux-tu?" (a sentence attributed to Fontenelle). "La musique nous émeut," says Joseph Droz, "par ce qu'elle a d'expressif et par ce qu'elle a d'incertain et de vague."[77] Music uses sounds whose expressive value results from their more or less vague relationships with our moods. But later in the same work Droz finds less charm in vagueness of expression. Yes, music should captivate the ear, says he:

> Mais la musique veut aussi nous inspirer des sentiments, des idées; elle nous captive surtout lorsqu'elle embellit nos théâtres; et c'est en devenant expressive qu'elle approche de la perfection.
>
> L'infériorité de la musique instrumentale, comparée à la musique dramatique, résulte de ce que la première ne s'adresse pas aussi directement que la seconde à notre âme. Des symphonies flattent le sens de l'ouïe, et ce n'est pas assez pour nous intéresser longtemps.[78]

[75] *Essai*, pp. 83-84.
[76] *De la littérature*, I, 55.
[77] *Etudes*, pp. 71-72.
[78] *Ibid.*, p. 148.

Symphonic music has too few ideas, he continues (he is not aware of the existence of musical ideas). Castil-Blaze too prefers something more easy to grasp to what he calls the Protean character of symphonic music.

L'expression de la musique n'est parfaite que quand la poésie vient lui prêter son secours et retenir sur une idée fixe l'imagination prête à s'égarer dans le vague des sons; alors tout tend au but principal qui est de plaire et de séduire. La musique donne aux vers une harmonie délicieuse, un coloris enchanteur, elle aiguise les traits que le poète a dirigés sur le coeur, et ces deux arts s'unissent pour former un langage divin.[79]

The dreamers with their taste for the vague are joined in their love of wordless or abstract music by some others of a different temperament. A.-J. Morel, a mathematician, thinks that the pleasure of music is physiological. (F. B. Hoffman, who reviews his book, agrees with Euler that it is metaphysical.) According to Morel, "les gens de lettres ne reconnaissent point de beautés musicales sans le secours des beautés poétiques."[80] He disdains most opera-goers: "La multitude veut tout comprendre, ne veut pas perdre une parole, et se trouve au supplice quand le chanteur ne prononce pas nettement; tandis qu'un véritable amateur ne pense aucunement au sens des paroles."[81] The partisans of instrumental music were slowly gaining ground. As Delécluze tells us in the *Lycée Français* in 1820, the revolution brought about by Handel, Gluck, Haydn, and Mozart is making itself felt. Before them, vocal music was the principal object, now it is the orchestra. "Le violon est le rival heureux de la voix humaine."[82] Within a few years Fétis and others will take up the cause of instrumental music.

While the realities of musical life and musical composition were leading gradually to a greater acceptance of wordless music, yet another strain of thought tended to hold music and poetry together. The nostalgia for the primitive, which urged a return to the wonders of ancient music, would ultimately have considerable impact on poetry,

---

[79] *De l'opéra en France*, p. 114. Castil Blaze was the *chroniqueur musical* of the *Journal des Débats* starting 1820.
[80] *Principe acoustique*, quoted by Hoffman, *Oeuvres* (Paris: Lefebvre, 1829), X, 61.
[81] *Principe*, p. 393.
[82] "Musique sacrée, Concert spirituel," 4, 78-79.

if but little on music. Villoteau, who made a long and detailed study of ancient music, was a partisan of this point of view. Since words and singing were direct developments of natural expression, i.e., unarticulated vocal sounds, it is logical and right that they should stay together. (Dance developed from gesture, the other kind of natural expression.) The principles and rules of music and poetry were originally the same and can be again. Separating the two arts is a "dismemberment" and a sign of corruption.[83] Villoteau traces the history of musical corruption, which started when instrumentalists, who were modest accompanists, playing simple pieces and staying close to the vocal line, began to develop their instruments, adding strings to the lyre and making other improvements. They became jealous of the singers and wished to attract attention to themselves. (The corruption is moral as well as musical.)[84] The use of ornamentation is a further step downward, pushing music away from its true object, which is the imitation of natural expression, "d'où il est résulté que cet art a dû nécessairement se perdre dans le vague, en changeant de direction, et ne rencontrant aucun obstacle qui pût le contenir dans ses limites naturelles, ainsi que le langage est contenu par la forme matérielle des mots et par sa construction grammaticale."[85] He agrees with Rousseau that the development of harmony, that is, instrumental music, has been disastrous to the art. "En quittant l'accent oral et s'attachant aux seules institutions harmoniques," said Jean-Jacques in his *Essai sur l'origine des langues*, "la musique devient plus bruyante à l'oreille, et moins douce au coeur. Elle a cessé de parler, bientôt elle ne chantera plus; et alors, avec tous ses accords et toute son harmonie, elle ne fera plus aucun effet sur nous."[86]

Villoteau places great emphasis on the oral tradition, both in the development of the arts and for transmission of knowledge and general civilizing influence. The merits of sung poetry are not only artistic and spiritual; it has had other and higher functions and can again: mnemonic and instructive (for the retention of knowledge), social and moral (the carrying out in life of the noble feelings expressed).

Ainsi la raison, d'accord avec la nature, exige donc que la poésie et la musique soient étroitement unies entre elles. L'une est le corps, l'autre

---

[83] Villoteau, II, 144.
[84] *Ibid.*, I, 291.
[85] *Ibid.*, II, 141-42.
[86] Quoted by Villoteau, II, 91-92.

est l'âme; c'est de leur correspondance réciproque et du concours de leurs moyens que résultent toute l'efficacité et toute l'utilité de leurs effets. Sans la musique, la poésie se décolore et perd une grande partie de son énergie; et sans la poésie, la musique ne rend que de vains sons, elle n'est plus qu'un langage vide de sens. La musique doit être à la poésie ce que l'inflexion naturelle de la voix est à la parole; et la poésie doit être à la musique ce que les mots sont à l'accent inarticulé du sentiment. Toutes les deux réunies, elles ne sont autre chose... que le langage même réduit en art; et c'est aussi pour cette raison que chez les anciens, où ces deux arts s'éloignaient le moins possible de l'objet naturel de leur imitation, l'expression en était aussi plus rapprochée de la vérité, et produisait des impressions d'autant plus fortes et plus sensibles.[87]

According to Fabre d'Olivet also, music and poetry complete each other. The essence of music is the melody, which consists not in a succession of sounds, but in the thought which presides over this succession.

Il n'existe pas plus de mélodie sans pensée, qu'il n'existe de tableau ou de poème. Les sons, les couleurs et les mots, sont les moyens que la musique, la peinture et la poésie mettent en oeuvre pour en revêtir diversement la pensée et donner une forme extérieure à ce qui n'existait d'abord que par l'intelligence... La poésie animée d'une pensée générale la particularise pour la faire saisir; la musique, au contraire, frappée d'une pensée particulière, la généralise pour en augmenter la douceur ou la force... Ainsi la poésie et la musique se prêtent un secours mutuel et s'embellissent réciproquement; car la poésie détermine ce que la musique a de trop vague, et la musique étend ce que la poésie a de trop restreint. En sorte que l'on peut les imaginer comme deux ministres de la poésie, dont le premier, transportant les idées du ciel à la terre, particularise ce qui est universel et dont le second, les élevant de la terre au ciel universalise ce que la poésie a de particulier...[88]

Music is even dependent on poetry for its physical existence: "La musique, tout intellectuelle dans son essence, ne peut recevoir de formes physiques qu'au moyen de la poésie. Sans le secours de la poésie qui en fixe les idées, elle resterait toujours vague et indéterminée."[89] That is why these two sciences were never separated in antiquity. They

---

[87] Villoteau, II, 325-26.
[88] *La Musique*, p. 52.
[89] *Ibid.*, pp. 91-92.

were even joined by the dance, and no perfect music can exist without the union of the three: "la parole qui détermine l'idée, le chant qui lui communique le sentiment et le mouvement rythmique qui en caractérise l'expression."

4. Self-Expression

According to the mimetic theory, the primary impulse as well as the subject matter for the work of art comes from the artist's perception of the world outside himself; though his imagination may considerably alter the natural model, his attention is fixed upon it. The external passes through the artist to again take external form. At the same time, many in the late eighteenth century believed that the impulse for artistic creation lies in the emotions of the artist, whether they are the primary subject matter, as in lyric poetry, or the primary cause of the will to create in any art, or simply a requisite property of the artist's character. In practice, these two opposite factors, the emotional and the mimetic, more often than not combine, especially in the visual arts. The idea that in order to move, the artist must first himself be moved, dates back at least to Cicero and Horace, but there the emphasis is on the desired effect rather than the artist's desire to express his own emotions.[1] The phrase from Horace, "Si vis me flere" (if you would have me weep) sums up this idea. Or, as Boileau said, "Pour me tirer des pleurs, il faut que vous pleuriez."

In France the emphasis on the internal sources of art dates from the middle of the eighteenth century, and in particular from Condillac's *Essai sur l'origine des connaissances humaines* (1746). As Folkierski points out, it is when the theorists begin to speculate on the origins of art that self-expression comes to assume primary importance.[2]

---

[1] See M.H. Abrams, *The Mirror and the Lamp* (New York: Oxford University Press, 1953), p. 71.

[2] *Entre le classicisme et le romantisme* (Cracovie: Académie des Sciences et des Lettres; Paris: Champion, 1925), p. 120.

65

Condillac speculates that speech and the arts are derived from the first language of the earliest times: natural (inarticulate) cries and the *langage d'action*. The latter, which in the beginning consisted of violent movement, evolved into gesture and symbolic acts (Jeremiah breaking an earthen pot before the Hebrew people) and gave man his first art, dance. One kind of dance, the *danse des gestes*, served to communicate thought; the other, the *danse des pas*, was an outlet for certain moods or emotions ("situations de l'âme"), particularly joy, and Condillac found that dance in the eighteenth century, though it was more varied in kind and sometimes more elaborate, still had the character of emotional expression. Music and dramatic art also sprang from the need for self-expression, uniting pantomime and articulated language (*langage d'action* and *langage parlé*). The earliest poetry, patterning itself after the violent physicality of gesture, consisted of an accumulation of figures and metaphors. Just as pantomime sought to give a picture in terms of physical movement, so the earliest writing too was a simple picture. Thus from the need to set down a thought the visual arts were born.

Rousseau picks up Condillac's theories but places even more emphasis on the role of the emotions. In his *Essai sur l'origine des langues* he differentiates between gesture, which sprang from need, and speech, which sprang from the passions (Ch. 2). Taking his cue from the oriental languages, Rousseau deduces that the first languages were poetic, and this is logical, for we begin not by reasoning but by feeling (Ch. 3). From unarticulated vocal sounds, the starting point, primitive men presumably found it natural to sing before speaking, and the first words were onomatopoeic. Thus poetry, singing, and speaking have a common origin, and poetry precedes prose (Ch. 12).

Villoteau follows these two sources fairly closely: words, singing, and dancing are an outgrowth of the unarticulated speech and gesture (mimic) which constitute natural expression. The arts had their origin in the need to communicate feelings or ideas by language or gesture. Words, music, and pantomime are both imitative and naturally expressive. Villoteau imagines how the ancients must have worked out a musical system based on these emotional cries: "Il est... probable que les anciens musiciens, qui étaient philosophes aussi, sont parvenus, par une longue suite d'observations, à déterminer et à classer les principales modifications de la voix qui caractérisent l'expression des diverses émotions de l'âme..."[3]

[3] Villoteau, I, 35, 33, 122.

This original joining of the three arts, and even more often, of poetry and music, as the basic vehicles of expression by primitive man, seems to be generally accepted in the early nineteenth century. Sometimes the three arts are all included in the name "poetry," as Charles Loyson explains:

La poésie fut dans la première origine un art ou plutôt une faculté dans laquelle se confondaient trois choses que le temps a distinguées depuis, et dont il a fait des arts différents; la musique, la danse et la parole toutes trois ayant leur origine et leur source naturelle dans le coeur humain; la musique rendait les sons et les bruits de la nature, la danse peignait les images, la parole exprimait les sentiments et les passions.[4]

Loyson makes of "the word," that is, poetry, the one of the three that originally gave direct expression to feelings, whereas the other two are imitative.[5] An anonymous writer in the *Archives Littéraires* also gives the pre-eminent place in the trio to poetry as expression of feeling, while dance was pantomime and music an exaggerated declamation. The first feelings expressed by poetry, he thinks, must have been gaiety, love, and regret for lost loved ones. It had the power to banish sadness and recall happy memories; thus Orpheus recalled his past happiness by the power of poetry, whose illusions were lost as soon as he stopped singing.[6]

On the other hand, the music of ancient times included even more than the three arts, it was the foundation of education, as Ballanche reminds us, it was "une doctrine tout entière; c'était l'ensemble même des lois sociales."[7] The emotional sources of the art are not often discussed outside the context of primitive or folk music, though it is understood that they extend into modern times. The critics are more likely to emphasize the effect of music on the listener and its expressivity, which belongs ambiguously to both composer and listener.

Some writers believe that modern man has not entirely lost the affectivity of his primitive ancestors, thus Preromanticism rediscovers the lyric impulse in its own time. Diderot and others in the second half of the eighteenth century point out the creative power of emotion and

---

[4] Review of *Traduction complète des Odes de Pindare, Archives Philosophiques*, II (1817), 456-57.
[5] Cf. J.-J. Ampère, *De l'histoire de la poésie* (Marseille: Feissat aîné et Demonchy, 1830), p. 23.
[6] "Considérations sur l'origine et les progrès de la poésie," 9 (1806), 24-26.
[7] *Essai sur les institutions sociales* (1833 ed.), p. 203.

spiritual exaltation which is in accord with the aspirations of the "âme sensible" characteristic of the time. Even Voltaire said, "La poésie est la musique de l'âme, et surtout des âmes grandes et sensibles."[8] Diderot, who in his early works would let sensibility overflow, later became wary of it and recommended controlled emotion, recollected emotion.[9] Emotion and enthusiasm were closely associated and sometimes confused.[10] Sabatier in his ode "L'Enthousiasme" gives way to his "transports brûlants."[11] André Chénier believed in emotion as the fountainhead of poetry: "L'art ne fait que des vers; le coeur seul est poète."[12] Without it poetry is cold: "L'homme insensible et froid en vain s'attache à peindre / Les sentiments du coeur que l'esprit ne peut feindre." Emotion becomes the sacred fire: "Aimer, sentir, c'est là cette ivresse vantée / Qu'aux cèlestes foyers déroba Prométhée."[13] Thus the fire stolen from the gods now belongs to man; but Chénier also knew that enthusiasm of the primitive poet who felt himself possessed by a god.[14]

In the early nineteenth century Mme de Staël and Stendhal most clearly proclaimed the necessity of emotion for the artist. "La première condition pour écrire, c'est une manière de sentir vive et forte," says the former (II.1; II.12). Not that it suffices by itself: every sensitive person has a bit of the poet in him, but only a few have the creative gift. "Le poète ne fait pour ainsi dire que dégager le sentiment prisonnier au fond de l'âme," says Mme de Staël (II.10; II.114). Her friend Bonstetten concurs on the importance of feeling: "Ce n'est pas le besoin d'imiter qui a produit les beaux-arts, mais le besoin de sentir."[15]

For Stendhal, too, the capacity for deep feeling is absolutely essential. All great artists are passionate men or men of extreme sensibility, he says on several occasions.[16] One of his complaints about the *Beau Idéal Antique* is that painters who have recourse to it do not put

---

[8] Article "Poètes," *Dictionnaire philosophique, Oeuvres complètes* (Paris: Garnier, 1879), XX, 232.

[9] See Margaret Gilman, *The Idea of Poetry in France from Houdar de la Motte to Baudelaire* (Cambridge: Harvard University Press, 1958), pp. 50-57.

[10] By Marmontel, for example, in his *Poétique* (1763), I, 73; see Gilman, p. 95.

[11] Quoted by Gilman, p. 96.

[12] "Epilogue," *Oeuvres complètes* (Paris: Bibliothèque de la Pléiade, Gallimard, 1958), p. 614.

[13] "Epître III," *ibid.*, p. 143.

[14] "L'Invention," v. 257 sq., *ibid.*, p. 131.

[15] Bonstetten, *Recherches*, p. 56.

[16] *Histoire*, I, 259; II, 79; *Rossini*, I, 56; *Mélanges*, III, 26.

their own soul into their painting but rely solely on technique ("la mécanique") and emphasize line rather than color, which requires some feeling in the artist.[17]

All feelings may serve as a source of inspiration: "... amour, patrie, croyance, tout doit être divinisé dans l'ode, c'est l'apothéose du sentiment" says Mme de Staël (II.10; II.118). Among emotions, a privileged place already belongs to sorrow and suffering. According to Lacépède, music, because of its origin as an expression of grief, retains its sorrowful character and even when gay, has an undertone of sadness.[18] Stendhal relates artistic creation to unhappiness in love (see below, p. 74) and in general to a melancholy temperament.[19]

The most famous literary texts of the early years of the century suggest that the artist's work receives impetus not so much from emotional response to personal experience or from physical temperament as from existential anguish, that "sentiment douloureux de l'incomplet de notre destinée" which according to Mme de Staël is at the source of all of mankind's greatest acts.[20] In much of the writing from now on the artistic impulse is difficult to distinguish from that which lies at the base of any kind of creative activity; a poet may be any noble and elevated soul, a scientist, a philosopher, a soldier. Thus an esthetic dimension is added to all kinds of creative activity, as well as to a simple disposition of the mind. (A generation later he can even be a gifted criminal like Vautrin, who presents himself as a poet.) The need to fill a spiritual emptiness which is predominant in Chateaubriand is associated with the artistic impulse, and we understand that the "vague des passions" is a kind of poetic disposition. Its fictional embodiment, René, himself an *artiste manqué*, sees Italian architecture as a projection of this poetic impulse, a purely subjective art: "L'architecte bâtit, pour ainsi dire, les idées du poète et les fait toucher aux sens."

If the "vague des passions" is a product of a Christian society, Christianity can also have more enriching effects, since it contributes to a tragic view of life and a deepening of emotion and of all aspects of spiritual life. This idea pervades *Le Génie du christianisme* though

---

[17] *Histoire*, II, 156.
[18] Bernard, Comte de Lacépède, *La Poétique de la musique* (Paris: L'Imprimerie de Monsieur, 1785), pp. 6-7.
[19] *Histoire*, II, 78.
[20] *De la littérature*, I, 183.

it is not often explicitly dealt with. Chateaubriand treats at length the effects of Christianity on the spirit, the passions, and the characters in works by Christian artists, though his specific comments on artistic creation lie, as we have seen (p. 31), within the framework of the mimetic doctrine. But Christianity itself is a passion: "Non contente d'augmenter le jeu des passions dans le drame et dans l'épopée, la religion chrétienne est elle-même une sorte de passion qui a ses transports, ses ardeurs, ses soupirs, ses joies, ses larmes, ses amours du monde et du désert" (II.iii.8). This Christian passion opens up nature to us in a new way, leading us to commune with God as he is manifested in the universe; there is usually more emphasis on the tears than on the joys: "Or, le christianisme, considéré lui-même comme passion, fournit des trésors immenses au poète... Comme toutes les grandes affections, [la passion religieuse] a quelque chose de sérieux et de triste; elle nous traîne à l'ombre des cloîtres et sur les montagnes" (II.iii.8). The inspiration the poet is searching for, he finds in the mountains and the forests:

> Oh! que le poète chrétien est plus favorisé dans la solitude où Dieu se promène avec lui! Libres de ce troupeau de dieux ridicules qui les bornaient de toutes parts, les bois se sont remplis d'une Divinité immense. Le don de prophétie et de sagesse, le mystère et la religion, semblent résider éternellement dans leurs profondeurs sacrées. (II.iv.1)

It is in the chapters on music that Chateaubriand speaks most directly of the expression of feeling in the artist or performer. Sorrowful music is a "soupir de l'âme." The composer should limit himself to a single emotion:

> *Diverses* raisons peuvent faire couler les larmes; mais les larmes ont toujours une *semblable* amertume; d'ailleurs il est rare qu'on pleure à la fois pour une foule de maux; et quand les blessures sont multipliées, il y en a toujours une plus cuisante que les autres, qui finit par absorber les moindres peines. Telle est la raison du charme de nos vieilles romances françaises. Ce chant *pareil*, qui revient à chaque couplet sur des paroles variées, imite parfaitement la nature: l'homme qui souffre promène ainsi ses pensées sur différentes images, tandis que le fond de ses chagrins reste le même. (III.i.2)

The performance of religious song brings men to the height of spiritual exaltation:

> Enfin c'est l'enthousiasme même qui inspira le *Te Deum*. Lorsque, arrêtée sur les plaines de Lens ou de Fontenoy, au milieu des foudres

et du sang, des fanfares et des trompettes, une armée française, sillon-
née des feux de la guerre, fléchissait le genou et entonnait l'hymne au
Dieu des batailles; ou bien, lorsqu'au milieu des lampes, des masses
d'or, des flambeaux, des parfums, aux soupirs de l'orgue, au balance-
ment des cloches, au frémissement des serpents et des basses, cette
hymne faisait résonner les vitraux, les souterrains et les dômes d'une
basilique, alors il n'y avait point d'homme qui ne se sentît transporté,
point d'homme qui n'éprouvât quelque mouvement de ce délire que
faisait éclater Pindare aux bois d'Olympie, ou David au torrent de
Cédron. (III.i.2)

In Chateaubriand we see the same combination of emotion and
enthusiasm which is already evident in the eighteenth century. Even
if the ancient Greeks did not know melancholy, as Mme de Staël believed, they did know poetic madness, which is akin to religious exaltation. In most of the theories of primitive beginnings, prehistoric
man gives outward expression to feeling rising from within, while Pin-
dar and David, as well as the singers of the Christian hymn feel
themselves possessed by a force stronger than themselves.

Some writers retain a distinction between the two. Bonstetten points
out that the painter or poet feels and expresses, as opposed to moral
man, who only feels: "[l'artiste] *transforme le sentiment en sensation* en faisant *voir* ce que l'on doit sentir."[21] However, truly religious inspiration seems to be superior to the simply emotional: "... c'est à la religion
que nous devons tout ce qu'il y a de grand et de sublime dans les
beaux-arts; il fallait une inspiration surnaturelle, émanée des sentiments religieux, pour inspirer de grandes idées plus dignes des dieux
que des hommes."[22]

But in the early years of the century, when religion is a passion
and passionate love is sacred, the line between the human and the
divine is often erased. Religion is internalized and pervades our emotional as well as our spiritual life. "[Les anciens], avec une religion
naturelle, mettaient toute leur poésie dans les sens," says Sismondi;
"[les modernes], dont la religion est toute spirituelle, placent toute
la poésie dans les émotions de l'âme."[23]

---

[21] Charles-Victor de Bonstetten, *Etudes de l'homme*, 2 vols. (Geneva: Paschoud, 1821),
I, 121-22.

[22] Bonstetten, *Recherches*, II, 143.

[23] J.C.-L. Simonde de Sismondi, *La Littérature du midi de l'Europe*, 4 vols. (Paris:
Treuttel et Würtz, 1813), II, 156; quoted by E. Eggli in E. Eggli and P. Martino,
Le Débat romantique en France 1813-1830 (Paris: Les Belles Lettres, 1933), I, 326.

In *Corinne* the enthusiasm the heroine feels while improvising is a noble and generous exaltation which raises her to moral heights where she surpasses herself and thus feels possessed by a superior force: "Je crois alors éprouver un enthousiasme surnaturel; et je sens bien que ce qui parle en moi vaut mieux que moi-même:..."[24] In *De l'Allemagne* Mme de Staël gives enthusiasm a more explicit religious character; it is *Dieu en nous*, and it includes "l'amour du beau, l'élévation de l'âme, la jouissance du dévouement" (IV.10; V.187-88). Though the famous chapter "De l'enthousiasme" places enthusiasm in a moral and religious context, the love of beauty also ties it to art; it rejoins the classic meaning of the term. It is a disposition of an artistic people, here the Germans: "l'enthousiasme est tout pour les nations littéraires..." (IV.10; V.196)

Poetry, like its wellspring enthusiasm, links all that is noble and beautiful: "le génie poétique est une disposition intérieure de la même nature que celle qui rend capable d'un génèreux sacrifice: c'est rêver l'héroïsme que composer une belle ode" (II.10; II.114). It is a kind of expansion of the soul. Though Mme de Staël sees in Christianity the richest source of poetic inspiration, like Chateaubriand she appreciates more primitive and popular sources: "Il est bon de retourner quelquefois à l'origine de toute poésie, c'est-à-dire l'impression de la nature sur l'homme avant qu'il eût analysé l'univers et lui-même" (II.30; III.314-15). This implies a kind of mythic awe.

A few comments suggest that hidden feelings and impulses well up from the unconscious of the artist: for A. W. Schlegel, poetry is "la vive expression de ce qu'il y a de plus intime dans notre être."[25] Joubert is more explicit about unconscious self-revelation, though he does not link it to the emotions: "L'homme se peint lui-même dans ses ouvrages et ne parvient à les trouver beaux qu'en leur donnant ses propres proportions correspondantes aux siennes, non toujours à celles qu'il voit en lui-même, mais à celles qui y sont cachées et qu'il ne rend visibles que dans ces imitations qu'il en fait à son propre insu."[26] To the word "imitation" we should give a more extended meaning: man imitates himself.

Some inner impulse, emotional or otherwise, is necessary, not just to poetry and music, but also to painting, the imitative art par excellence. Though most of Stendhal's remarks deal with the artist in

[24] VIII, 94.
[25] *Cours de littérature dramatique* (Paris and Geneva: Paschoud, 1813), I, 83, quoted by Eggli and Martino, p. 84.
[26] *Carnets*, I, 305 (11 Nov. 1801).

general, some others refer to painters in particular (no doubt because he is writing about painters). Only the artist with emotional depth will be able to break away from his master and develop his own way of seeing; "... dans les beaux-arts, ainsi appelés parce qu'ils procurent le plaisir par le moyen du beau, il faut une âme, même pour imiter les objets les plus froids." A lack of emotional reaction to the natural world will lead only to mediocre art.[27] Quatremère de Quincy too recognized that creative power lies in feeling: "Le sentiment," says he, "est la puissance vitale de l'art."[28]

On the other hand, it is claimed that an artist's strong feeling is unfailingly communicated to the spectator. Delécluze recognizes that it is David's personal knowledge of and emotional involvement with the Revolution that gives such force to his paintings of that period, especially the *Marat*.[29]

The primitivists, as we have seen, thought the lyric impulse strongest in the earliest times. "Dans les arts d'imitation," says Fr. Koeppen, a German, writing in the *Archives Littéraires*, "c'est par lui-même que l'homme commence, et par la nature qu'il finit."[30]Poetry begins with feelings and only later describes objects; painting begins with gods and heroes and ends with landscape. But this gradual externalization does not prevent painting from being a personal expression, since each painter mixes the color of his own talent with that of objects.[31]

Bonstetten goes even farther: he challenges the prevailing opinion that imitation is the basic principle of the visual arts more than any other. On the contrary, says he, they are, along with music, the arts best suited to the expression of feelings:

> Le véritable langage de l'harmonie, ce sont les beaux-arts: les beaux-arts *expriment* ce que nous *sentons*, bien mieux que le langage parlé, ne peut exprimer ce que nous *pensons*. C'est que les beaux-arts n'ont que des signes naturels, tandis que le langage parlé, ayant perdu tout ce qui était naturel dans l'origine du langage, ne présente plus que des signes de convention, qui ne sont propres qu'à l'abstraction.[32]

The fine arts have retained the directness of expression which language has lost since the Edenic days when the word was the thing.

[27] *Histoire*, I, 169, 259.
[28] *Considérations morales*, pp. 47, 64.
[29] *Jacques-Louis David*, pp. 405-06.
[30] "Lettre sur le paysage," III (1804), 301.
[31] *Ibid.*, III, 307.
[32] Bonstetten, *Recherches*, p. 54. We shall have more to say about harmony in chapter 5.

Neoclassic critics were able to see some expressiveness in ancient sculpture, but it is unusual to read that it was also a means of personal expression. (As far as we know, the ancient Greeks did not look upon it that way.) According to Kératry, for example, the conditions of sculpture held down personal expression, but literature was more free and the ancients could express their sorrow in elegies.[33] However, Mme de Staël does not exclude it:

> Quelquefois un sculpteur ancien ne faisait qu'une statue dans sa vie; elle était toute son histoire. Il la perfectionnait chaque jour: s'il aimait, s'il était aimé, s'il recevait par la nature ou par les beaux-arts une impression nouvelle, il embellissait les traits de son héros par ses souvenirs et par ses affections. Il savait ainsi traduire aux regards tous les sentiments de son âme.[34]

The work of art becomes a record of all impressions from inside and out.

If the personal emotion of the artist is at the source of his creation, it cannot serve this function while fresh and overpowering. Only attenuated emotion, "recollected in tranquility," will be fruitful. In the case of Stendhal the emotion is, of course, love. He tells us how the memory of unhappy love sets in motion certain mental processes which send the painter down the path to creation:

> La distraction la plus facile pour l'homme que les passions tendres ont rendu malheureux n'est-elle pas celle qui se compose presque en entier du souvenir même de ces passions? L'autre partie, c'est l'art de toucher les coeurs, art dont il a si bien éprouvé la puissance.
>
> Travailler, pour un artiste, dans ces circonstances, ce n'est presque que se souvenir avec ordre des idées chères et cruelles qui l'attristent sans cesse. L'amour propre qui vient se mettre de la partie est l'habitude de l'âme la plus ancienne. Elle n'impose pas de gêne nouvelle, et dans la mémoire des choses passées fait trouver un nouveau plaisir. Peu à peu les sensations de l'art viennent se mêler à celles que donne la nature. Dès lors le peintre est sur la bonne route.[35]

For Mme de Staël also, excessively strong feeling is not fruitful. In this passage, which prefigures Musset, Corinne, in the grasp of powerful emotion, is unable to turn her suffering into artistic channels:

[33] *Annales Littéraires* (1814), quoted by R. Canat, *L'Hellénisme des romantiques*, I, 155.
[34] *Corinne*, VII, 301.
[35] *Histoire*, I, 172.

Se sentant alors incapable de détourner sa pensée de sa propre situation, elle peignait ce qu'elle souffrait; mais ce n'était plus ces idées
générales, ces sentiments universels qui répondent au coeur de tous
les hommes: c'était le cri de la douleur, cri monotone à la longue, comme celui des oiseaux de la nuit; il y a trop d'ardeur dans les expressions, trop d'impétuosité, trop peu de nuances: c'était le malheur, mais
ce n'était plus le talent. Sans doute il faut, pour bien écrire, une émotion vraie; mais il ne faut pas qu'elle soit déchirante. Le bonheur est
nécessaire à tout; et la poésie la plus mélancolique doit être inspirée
par une sorte de verve qui suppose et de la force et des jouissances intellectuelles. La véritable douleur n'a point de fécondité naturelle: ce
qu'elle produit n'est qu'une agitation sombre qui ramène sans cesse aux
mêmes pensées.[36]

The creative process involves much more than a spontaneous out-
poring. Joubert too recommends that the poet wait until the immediate
storm of feeling has passed.[37] He does not agree with Mme de Staël
about the role of intelligence in the composition of poetry:

L'esprit n'a point de part à la véritable poésie; elle est un don du ciel
qui l'a mise en nous; elle sort de l'âme seule; elle vient dans la rêverie;
mais, quoi qu'on fasse, la réflexion ne la trouve jamais. L'esprit, cependant, la prépare, en offrant à l'âme les objets que la réflexion déterre,
en quelque sorte. L'émotion et le savoir, voilà sa cause, et voilà sa
matière.[38]

To prepare himself for composing, the poet tunes himself like an instrument, says Joubert.[39]

In addition to personal emotion and religious enthusiasm, *sentiment*
and *sensibilité* play their role. For Ballanche, *sentiment* includes the affective and the intuitive, but also other faculties: "... dans les beaux-
arts et dans les belles-lettres j'appelle sentiment ce tact heureux, plus
sûr que le goût; tantôt cette inspiration créatrice qui élève sans qu'on
s'en aperçoive, tantôt cet abandon d'un coeur qui se déborde, et qui
laisse aller ses pensées sans songer à les produire ni à les retenir."[40]
It is a kind of esthetic faculty, giving rise to artistic creation:

---

[36] *Oeuvres complètes*, IX, 378. See comment on the first part of this passage by Madelyn
Gutwirth in *Le Préromantisme: hypothèque ou hypothèse*, Colloque 29-30 June 1972, ed.
P. Viallaneix (Paris: Klincksieck, 1975), pp. 243-44.
[37] *Carnets*, I, 45.
[38] *Pensées et lettres*, I, 167. Cf. *Carnets*, I, 419.
[39] *Carnets*, II, 622; 26 Feb. 1816.
[40] *Du sentiment*, p. 15.

La faculté de sentir ce que la nature a de beau, avant de l'imiter; cette faculté qui précéde l'observation, qui est la force motrice du génie, et qui devient habitude d'être ému par le beau, est précisément *cette puissance du sentiment* que nous avons défini plus haut. Le sentiment, parvenu à un certain degré d'énergie et d'exaltation, devient enthousiasme.[41]

For Bonstetten, *sentiment* gives the idea of pleasure or displeasure; he gives much more attention to sensibility, and especially to imagination, which is *"le mouvement des idées, produit par l'action de la sensibilité."* Music is the art that speaks most directly to the soul (see above, p. 56). Poetry, on the other hand, must be embodied in images, which belong to the imagination: "... comme l'artiste ne sent que par les images, qu'il faut pour ainsi dire un corps à son sentiment, il cherche à exprimer par les images ce qu'il a vivement senti."[42] These images, drawn from sensible reality, are one of the means of art.

It is interesting to see how Mme de Staël's ideas on the subject evolve. In her *Essai sur les fictions* she separates deep feeling from imagery:

> ... il est rare... qu'un sentiment ou une idée soient dans toute leur force, quand on peut les exprimer par une image... Les images, les tableaux, sont le charme de la poésie et de tout ce qui lui ressemble; mais ce qui appartient à la réflexion acquiert une plus grande puissance, une intensité plus concentrée, lorsque l'expression de la pensée ne tire sa force que d'elle-même.[43]

These images are *plaquées*, after the manner of the eighteenth century. We see the same dichotomy in *De la littérature*: images belong to the imitation of nature and feelings to "l'éloquence des passions": "En exprimant ce qu'on éprouve, on peut avoir un style poétique, recourir à des images pour fortifier des impressions; mais la poésie proprement dite, c'est l'art de peindre par la parole tout ce qui frappe nos regards" (I.48). When she writes *De l'Allemagne* ten years later, her idea of the image and of poetry has been transformed: the image drawn from nature is now the essential means by which poetry translates emotions in primitive societies or in more civilized ones: "... les nations peu civilisées commencent toujours par la poésie, et

---

[41] *Ibid.*, p. 32. *Sentiment* is also at the center of the esthetic faculty in the spectator of the arts (p. 33).

[42] Bonstetten, *Recherches*, pp. 7, 55.

[43] *Oeuvres complètes*, II, 182-93.

dès qu'une passion forte agite l'âme, les hommes les plus vulgaires se servent, à leur insu, d'images et de métaphores; ils appellent à leur secours la nature extérieure pour exprimer ce qui se passe en eux d'inexprimable" (II.10; II.114-15). Modern man has lost the primitive spontaneity, but Christianity has replaced it with a new depth which also seeks poetic expression in imagery:

> Les modernes ne peuvent se passer d'une certaine profondeur d'idées dont une religion spiritualiste leur a donné l'habitude; et si cependant cette profondeur n'était point revêtue d'images, ce ne serait pas de la poésie: il faut donc que la nature grandisse aux yeux de l'homme pour qu'il puisse s'en servir comme de l'emblème de ses pensées. Les bosquets, les fleurs et les ruisseaux suffisaient aux poètes du paganisme; la solitude des forêts, l'Océan sans bornes, le ciel étoilé peuvent à peine exprimer l'éternel et l'infini dont l'âme des chrétiens est remplie. (II.10; II.119)

Poetry depicts the idea of time with the passing of the seasons, the externalizing par excellence of the internal, and mental reflection becomes a reflection of the universe:

> Schiller ne présente jamais les réflexions les plus profondes que revêtues de nobles images: il parle à l'homme comme la nature elle-même; car la nature est tout à la fois penseur et poète. Pour peindre l'idée du temps, elle fait couler devant nos yeux les flots d'un fleuve inépuisable; et pour que sa jeunesse éternelle nous fasse songer à notre existence passagère, elle se revêt de fleurs qui doivent périr, elle fait tomber en automne les feuilles des arbres que le printemps a vues dans tout leur éclat: la poésie doit être le miroir terrestre de la divinité, et réfléchir par les couleurs, les sons et les rythmes, toutes les beautés de l'univers. (II.13; II.177-78)

On the whole, those who attempt during these years to define the creative process (Ballanche, Bonstetten, Joubert, Girodet, Mme de Staël) lay as much, or more, emphasis on other elements than deep emotion, in particular the quality of imagination and the process of meditation. Two examples will suffice at this stage to show how several elements interact and the artist moves back and forth between the inner and outer worlds. In both cases we are dealing with the fine arts.

First, Bonstetten on "l'invention dans les beaux-arts": "Le phénomène physiologique de l'invention dans les beaux-arts n'est que la sensibilité concentrée dans l'unité des rapports harmoniques. L'artiste, qui compose, commence par sentir vivement: ce sentiment rare et sublime n'est pas volontaire, puisqu'on l'appelle *inspiration*."[44] The artist chooses the order and disposition of parts; the "sentiment moteur" of harmony acts on subordinate feelings; a circle of first conceptions grows around a center. After the first conception, the mind goes back to make corrections. After sensibility, intelligence plays an increasing role in the inventive process.

> L'imagination, arrivée au point de développement où elle compose des ouvrages, prend la marche de l'intelligence, aussitôt qu'elle voit devant elle un objet réel auquel elle peut se fixer: voilà pourquoi, en parlant des beaux-arts, on emploie si souvent le langage de l'intelligence. Voyez travailler l'artiste: ce qu'il a d'abord senti, il le *pense* aussitôt qu'il le *voit devant lui*; il sent et réfléchit tour à tour; son ouvrage a-t-il pris du corps, est-il sorti de son âme sous une forme matérielle, il est devenu un objet non seulement de sensibilité, mais encore de connaissance. Dès lors la pensée reprend le caractère de l'intelligence, son aplomb, sa fixité, sa durée. Bien plus, la sensibilité, d'abord muette, trouve tout à coup un langage, et le plus sublime des langages, celui des beaux-arts, qui est l'expression naturelle et unique de l'imagination développée.
>
> C'est ainsi que l'imagination invente, et que l'intelligence achève et finit les ouvrages des beaux-arts.[45]

If it is unusual to find an interesting work at this period on the workings of the imagination in the arts, it is even rarer to find a passage where a professional painter, and a famous one, bears testimony to the process of creation within himself. Such a passage Girodet has left us. Whereas Mme de Staël shows us the poet reaching outward in search of images, Girodet in the throes of creation retires within himself.

> S'il arrive... que les facultés de l'intelligence et la sensibilité dont émane le génie, soient dans leur plus haut degré possible, les idées et les images sur lesquelles elles éprouvent alors le besoin de s'exercer, sont à la fois plus abondantes, plus vives et plus judicieusement ordonnées; elles sont présentes, comme la réalité même, au génie qui en est frappé. L'excitation, que réveille en lui la surabondance des puissances créatrices qu'il ne peut laisser oisives et dont il ne peut contenir la fougue, l'agite en tous sens, le concentre et l'absorbe enfin tout entier dans de profondes méditations. Un monde intellectuel remplace, dans sa pensée,

---

[44] Bonstetten, *Recherches*, pp. 71-72.
[45] *Ibid.*, p. 76.

le monde matériel qui s'éclipse à ses yeux. C'est en lui-même qu'il poursuit, sans cesse, ces types de beauté idéale dont la nature lui avait, il est vrai, révélé les premières traces, mais dont son imagination et son jugement peuvent seuls lui faire trouver la perfection. Il en saisit, il en combine, il en étend les rapports, il invente réellement: c'est l'instant de la création, et il se passionne pour ce qu'il crée. Comme la vague qui se gonfle, comme la flamme qui s'allume, sa passion exaspérée s'accroît rapidement et par les succès et par les obstacles; la lumière jaillit de ces grands chocs, et le chef d'oeuvre du génie est enfanté.[46]

The artist must keep these forces, which have been called divine inspiration, under the control of "l'harmonie modératrice," lest he be like a ship without a rudder, or, to use the classical image, Phaethon dragged off by runaway horses.

When art is thought of as the expression of deep feeling, religious aspiration or some undefinable impetus, when it originates in personal and inner sources, then theorists will speak less and less of it as a direct imitation of nature and will turn their attention to the complex relationships between inner and outer worlds. Emotional warmth will stimulate the artist to attain a new ideal beauty: Mme de Staël relates ideal beauty not to imitation but to the expression of innate feelings (III.9; IV.225; see above, p. 39), and feeling is indispensable to Stendhal's *Beau Idéal moderne*. In the following years critics and poets alike will stress the importance of sincere and spontaneous feeling, but along with it, all that marks the quiddity of the artist: character, temperament, an idiosyncratic view of the world.

[46] *Oeuvres posthumes* (Paris: Renouard, 1829), II, 117-18.

5. Mystics and Illuminists

The essence of lyricism is the expression of the artist's inner state, but, as we have seen, he must draw upon the outer world for his means of expression, whether it be visual images, sounds, or verbal metaphor. An artist who ascribes a moral character to the universe is often projecting his own feelings onto it or looking for natural elements that will, so to speak, vibrate sympathetically with his own emotions and serve to communicate them to others. Thus Chateaubriand, who even before his return to Christianity speaks of the moral character of nature (in "Lettre sur le dessin") and afterward excels in the *paysage état d'âme*. Even when he is taking a religious view of nature, as in *Le Génie du christianisme*, his approach is more lyric than visionary, for here the chief effect of religious belief is to awaken in us a quickened emotional response to nature. God is manifested in the wonders of nature, but Chateaubriand prefers that He remain mysterious and does not attempt to penetrate behind phenomena.

But at the same time the desire for the infinite which Christianity creates in us, whether through its emotional effects, chiefly melancholy, or more directly through divine inspiration (enthusiasm), becomes an esthetic impulse. The desire for the infinite, says Ancillon, turns us toward *le vague*, not in the sense of emptiness, as in Chateaubriand, but rather the indeterminate. Since we cannot know or conceive of the infinite, says he, we change it into the indefinite. "C'est en nous perdant dans l'immensité du vague et en aimant à nous y perdre, que nous charmons le besoin d'infini, et que nous en nourrissons le sentiment." We find traces of the feeling and the need for the infinite in the contemplation of nature, the pleasures of art, religion, or even sciences. All the arts awaken *le sentiment de l'infini*, and this gives them all a religious character, though some bring us closer to the infinite than others. The plastic arts have definite forms, precise contours, exact proportions, which at first seem quite foreign to the infinite; there is no vagueness in the execution of the arts. This does not refute the great principle of post-Kantian esthetics as stated by Ancillon: "Mais le grand secret de l'artiste est de donner à l'âme le sentiment de l'infini, en lui présentant des formes finies."[1]

Music and poetry have even stronger effects, says Ancillon. Music is like a limitless ocean. So is poetry, to some extent, though poetic expression is more precise and determinate than musical expression. It is great poets that most often make us taste the pleasures of the infinite, rather than great artists, partly because poetry will always be more vague and indefinite than the visual arts, no matter how individual its features may be, and also because it depicts a succession of traits, whereas the visual arts seize only a moment. Poetry may be either beautiful or sublime; the beautiful pleases us but is circumscribed and limited, whereas the sublime contains an element of dread: "tel autre [morceau] nous atterre, nous accable et nous fait jouir de notre accablement même, parce qu'il est sublime." Proportion, measure, and limits are inseparable from beauty, but the sublime is unhindered by limits. "L'infini est ce qu'il y a de plus sublime, et le sublime est ce qui nous donne l'idée de l'infini."[2]

The artist of genius may satisfy his thirst for divine revelation by a spiritual elevation which in his poetry takes the form of a cosmic journey. Chénier gives us an outstanding example of this in his "L'Amérique," where the disembodied soul of the poet rises toward the divine light:

> Que je m'élève au ciel comme une flamme ardente.
> Déjà ce corps pesant se détache de moi.
> Adieu, tombeau de chair, je ne suis plus à toi.
> Terre, fuis sous mes pas. L'éther où le ciel nage
> M'aspire. Je parcours l'océan sans rivage.
> Plus de nuit. Je n'ai plus d'un globe opaque et dur

---

[1] *Mélanges* pp. 9, 16, 21.

[2] *Ibid.*, pp. 25-26, 28. Ancillon in a subsequent passage defines sublime poetry as that in which poetic energy dominates, whereas poetic truth dominates in the beautiful (p. 163).

Entre le jour et moi l'impénétrable mur.
Plus de nuit, et mon oeil se perd et se mêle
Dans les torrents profonds de lumière éternelle
......
Abîmes de clarté, où libre de ses fers,
L'homme siège au conseil qui créa l'univers;
Où l'âme remontant à sa grande origine
Sent qu'elle est une part de l'essence divine.[3]

In another fragment Chénier has the poet speak of his visions and of his verses which reveal them:

Le poète divin, tout esprit, tout pensée,
Ne sent point dans un corps son âme embarrassée.
Il va percer le ciel aux murailles d'azur,
De la terre, des mers, le labyrinthe obscur.
Ses vers ont revêtu, prompts et légers Protées,
Les formes tour à tour à ses yeux présentées.[4]

In his poetic vision the verses themselves take on the form of torrents, lava, a windstorm, then warm, calm weather. While in the first passage the poet rises above earthly phenomena, in the second he enters into their labyrinth and his work takes on their forms. The poet presents himself as dematerialized.

In the early years of the nineteenth century it was principally the Germans and the Germanophiles, on the one hand, along with the illuminists on the other, who opened up poetry to mystic aspirations. Ancillon considered himself as much German as French. Charles de Villers, who before Mme de Staël did the most to introduce German literature and thought to the French, expounded his conception of poetry, which derives from the German Romantics:

Le talent poétique est dans l'homme un précieux reflet de la toute-puissance de son Créateur: c'est le besoin de créer aussi nous-mêmes, et que notre nature limitée tient de sa nature divine: c'est le besoin d'échapper au monde vulgaire qui nous entoure, qui gêne et oppresse ce que nous avons de meilleur en nous; de nous élever vers le beau et le sublime éternels; de trouver en nous, et au-dessus de nous, un monde idéal aussi épuré, aussi noble, aussi rayonnant de lumière et d'amour qu'il convient à l'âme humaine glorifiée par l'idée du Beau.

[3] *Oeuvres complètes*, p. 428.
[4] *Ibid.*, pp. 437-38.

Voilà pourquoi l'esprit poétique a été mis par les anciens au même rang que l'esprit prophétique et placé parmi les Dieux sous les figures symboliques d'*Apollon* et des *Muses*; pourquoi les vers ont été nommés par eux "le langage des Dieux."

Mais ce qui dans l'Etre tout-puissant est une immense réalité, n'est plus dans l'homme qu'un jeu idéal, qu'un essor de son intelligence. Dieu dispose à la fois souverainement de la matière et de la forme: sa poésie est donc création et son épopée est l'univers. Le talent poétique de l'homme n'est qu'une simple forme, mais une forme de feu, un creuset embrasé qui résout en figures vaporeuses et aériennes les choses et les figures terrestres qu'on lui confie.[5]

According to A. W. Schlegel, it is *le sentiment* which brings the poet close to the secret of the universe; he knows it intuitively.

L'art et la poésie antiques peuvent être considérés, pour ainsi dire, comme des lois rythmiques, comme la révélation harmonieuse et régulière de la législation sage et bien ordonnée d'un monde idéal. La poésie romantique, au contraire, est l'expression d'une force mystérieuse, tendant toujours vers une création nouvelle, et faisant sortir comme un monde merveilleux du sein du chaos.

L'inspiration des Anciens était simple, claire et semblable à la nature, dans ses oeuvres les plus parfaites. Le génie romantique, dans son désordre même, est cependant plus prés du secret de l'univers, car l'intelligence ne peut jamais saisir qu'une partie de la vérité, tandis que le sentiment embrassant tout, pénètre seul le mystère de la nature.[6]

Schlegel like Ancillon emphasizes the contemplation of the infinite by modern man and "le néant de tout ce qui a des bornes." As in Chateaubriand, the thirst for the infinite brings about an indefinable melancholy. "C'est ainsi que la poésie des anciens était celle de la jouissance, et que la nôtre est celle du désir; l'une s'établissait dans le présent, l'autre se balance entre les souvenirs du passé, et les pressentiments de l'avenir."[7] The rise toward the infinite, which is the glory of the modern poet, is also his dilemma. Greek poetry, says Schlegel, gave a soul to sensations and a body to thoughts; they sought a determinate perfection and achieved their end. The moderns, having launched into the limitless, always remain unsatisfied.

---

[5] *De la manière essentiellement différente dont les poètes français et les allemands traitent l'amour*, commonly called *L'Erotique comparée* (Polyanthea, Munster, 1806),sec. 9 quoted in Eggli and Martino, I, 23.

[6] *Cours de littérature dramatique*, II, 329; quoted in Eggli and Martino, I, 84.

[7] *Ibid.*, quoted in Eggli and Martino, I, 329.

Ancillon, for all he wrote about the infinite and the sublime, warns the poet against getting lost in abstractions. In great poetry an infinite world of ideas is hidden under precise forms. "Cette idée, dont les formes ne sont jamais que le signe et l'enveloppe, constitue l'idéal de l'art, ou, en d'autres termes, le sublime et l'énergie d'un ouvrage poétique."[8]

Mme de Staël, as we have seen, urges the poet to push his vision to the farthest reaches of the universe in order to express the eternal and the infinite (see above, p. 77); it is a question of choosing the most vast and awesome natural elements as emblems of his thought. Likewise, in the following passage the supraterrestrial spheres may furnish the symbols for the poet's emotions: "... il faut, pour concevoir la vraie grandeur de la poésie lyrique, errer par la rêverie dans les régions éthérées, oublier le bruit de la terre en écoutant l'harmonie céleste, et considérer l'univers entier comme un symbol des émotions de l'âme" (II.10; II.118). This kind of ecstatic experience lifts the poet temporarily out of terrestrial existence, after which he returns to the plane of emotional expression.

There is a correspondence between our souls and nature, which also has a soul:

> L'âme de la nature se fait connaître à nous de toutes parts et sous mille formes diverses. La campagne fertile, comme les déserts abandonnés, la mer, comme les étoiles, sont soumises aux mêmes lois, et l'homme renferme en lui-même des sensations, des puissances occultes qui correspondent avec le jour, avec la nuit, avec l'orage: c'est cette alliance secrète de notre âme avec les merveilles de l'univers qui donne à la poésie sa véritable grandeur. Le poète sait rétablir l'unité du monde physique avec le monde moral; son imagination forme un lien entre l'un et l'autre. (II.13; II.171)

If these correspondences exist, then analogies are more than metaphors, and the imagination is indeed the essential poetic faculty. This passage has a Baudelairean ring.

One other passage in *De l'Allemagne* indicates even more clearly the possibility of the real existence of correspondences between physical and moral worlds; it is placed in the context of German scientific investigation:

> ... pourquoi... l'intelligence suprême, qui a formé la nature et l'âme, n'aurait-elle pas fait de l'une l'emblème de l'autre? Ce n'est point un

[8] *Mélanges* I, 165.

vain jeu de l'imagination que ces métaphores continuelles, qui servent à comparer nos sentiments avec les phénomènes extérieurs, la tristesse, avec le ciel couvert de nuages, le calme, avec les rayons argentés de la lune, la colère, avec les flots agités par les vents; c'est la même pensée du créateur qui se traduit dans les deux langages différents, et l'un peut servir d'interprète à l'autre. (III.10; IV.246)[9]

During her visit to Germany Mme de Staël had been struck by the unity of thought among writers, philosophers, and scientists and the constant exchange of views among them. Her German sojourn also awakened her interest in theosophy, and afterward, encouraged by A. W. Schlegel, she read and discussed many illuminist writers at Coppet. (Bonstetten in a letter mentions Boehme and Saint-Martin in particular.)[10] Chapter 7 of the fourth part of *De l'Allemagne* is devoted to them, and many other passages show traces of their influence, including those we have just quoted. She distinguishes between theosophists, such as Boehme and Saint-Martin, and mystics: "les premiers veulent pénétrer le secret de la création; les seconds s'en tiennent à leur propre coeur" (IV.5; V.87). Following the lead of Friedrich Schlegel, she speculates that language came into existence not by a long gradual development from the savage's cry, but by revelation, and she admits the possibility of an occult explanation of the universe (III.7; IV.193 and III.10; IV.265).

According to the common belief of the time, an abundant use of metaphor was characteristic of primitive man. As we have seen, primitive language considered from a naturalistic point of view, was an insufficient means of expression unless fortified by an accumulation of metaphors. But the illuminists had a different view, or rather vision, of primitive man and his language, and many others shared their ideas. Rather than being the result of a slow development starting from inarticulate cries, language was given to man by God: "Quoique le langage soit l'application des sons aux objets qui ont quelque rapport avec eux, il n'en est pas moins d'une origine divine. Ce ne sont point les hommes qui ont formé ces sons et ces rapports; c'est

---

[9] Cf. *De la littérature*, II, 362: "… la providence a mis une telle relation entre les objets physiques et l'être moral de l'homme, qu'on ne peut rien ajouter à l'étude des uns qui ne serve en même temps à la connaissance de l'autre."

[10] Quoted in Auguste Viatte, *Les Sources occultes du romantisme*, 2 vols. (Paris: Champion, 1928), II, 103.

Dieu qui fit de l'homme un être parlant."[11] In the Edenic language the word gave the essence of the thing. After the Fall, this identity was lost, and after the Tower of Babel, the single universal language was broken up into myriad tongues. But since language originally came from God, it still contained a germ for regeneration.[12]

In Saint-Martin, the most important of the French illuminists, the basic division is not between the finite and the infinite but between the sensible and the suprasensible. "La matière n'est qu'une représentation et une image de ce qui n'est pas elle."[13] Man and nature are mirrors of the divine,[14] and nature is also a mirror for man. In Edenic times the sensible world was a perfect mirror and revelation of the divine world, but since the Fall, nature is altered and degraded. "Ne sais-tu pas que la nature avait été accordée à l'homme pour lui servir de miroir, et que, le frappant à grands coups, ils l'ont brisé?"[15] To him who looks the mirror will send back a broken and deformed reflection.

In other passages, however, the reflection assures man of his greatness, for in spite of his fall, he is still made in the image of God and directly linked to Him. All elements and actions of the universe are for man "comme autant de miroirs, sur lesquels il élance, continuellement, toutes les effluves de son âme, et qui les lui renvoyant avec des couleurs et des formes, lui donnent par-là le témoignage visible de sa grandeur et de sa destination dans l'univers."[16] Or, rather than a mirror, the visible world (*la nature actuelle*) is like a screen or sifter through which its hidden properties show; or it is "un fruit dont tous les objets visibles ne sont que l'écorce, et dont la chose admirable est le germe ou la substance par excellence, mais ne peut être connue qu'autant qu'on enlève toute l'écorce qui l'enveloppe" (I.90). Sensible objects are only signs of the invisible, but nature is precious to us, says Saint-Martin, because it is an embodiment in which the sign is always in an exact relationship to the invisible properties it should

---

[11] Court de Gébelin, *Histoire naturelle de la parole*, quoted by Anne-Marie Amiot in *Le Préromantisme*, p. 387. Court de Gébelin, though not strictly an illuminist, adopted some of their ideas.

[12] See remarks by L. Cellier (*ibid.*, p. 375).

[13] *Le Ministère de l'homme esprit*, p. 82, quoted in Viatte, *Les Sources occultes*, I, 276.

[14] *De l'esprit des choses* (Paris: Laran, Debrai, Fayolle, An 8), I, 35.

[15] *L'Homme de désir* (Lyon: 1790), p. 234.

[16] *De l'esprit des choses*, I, 37.

manifest (I.256). They are sufficiently clear so that practiced eyes can read in present nature the tableau of nature as it was (*la nature antérieure*). Such beauty as natural objects may have does not belong to them but is projected onto them in divine rays, as plants are illumined by the sun.

For the philosopher Saint-Martin, nature is dominated by man, who stands at the center of existing things, type and model of everything. His face is the archetype of beauty among all forms, the most expressive part of his being, the part that is the best conserved since the Fall (I.54-55). Just as God is mirrored in spiritual beings, which is His only way of knowing himself, so we need to see ourselves in the images born from our thoughts; thus we know our own treasures. Hence our need to cultivate the sciences and the arts and our need for the regard and esteem of others; these are mirrors which increase the intensity of our own (I.50-51). Man is also impelled to artistic creation by his need to introduce order and regularity around him; in primitive times he beautified his habitation (I.45). Man's role, a considerable one indeed, is to extend the reign of truth by manipulating and thus purifying matter. He cultivates nature's treasures and adds to their perfection by passing them through himself, producing inventions and arts. "Ne purifie-t-il pas, par ses manipulations, toutes les substances de ce bas monde? ne fait-il pas sortir, par son industrie, des sons harmonieux de ses doigts?... n'enfante-t-il pas par la peinture l'image de toutes les productions?" (I.48). If man can produce such marvels in the lower order, what would his power not be, says Saint-Martin, if they were integrated into true reality?

The arts are here presented among other productions and accomplishments of men; they are also limited to man's efforts toward regeneration and toward perfection. Like a lens, he has the property of concentrating in his thought the rays projected from the heavenly world, and this perfection is shown in all his person. The first consequence deduced by Saint-Martin is a separation between true beauty and concrete (lower) reality. He gives a new meaning to *la belle nature*.

... le principe de la beauté n'appartient point à la nature altérée où nous habitons à présent;... notre forme actuelle n'est plus qu'un faible reste de celle qui nous appartenait par notre origine;... la définition du beau qui nous le peint comme l'imitation de la belle nature, ne se peut réaliser qu'en nous élevant jusqu'au monde supérieur, dont celui-ci n'est qu'une effluve, et comme un extralignement, et... les artistes nous prouvent cette vérité en allant chercher dans ce qu'ils appellent

> le beau idéal, tous les principes de la régularité et de la perfection qui
> ne se trouvent plus dans le beau visible,... ils ont grand tort de donner
> à ce beau idéal un sens imaginaire, qui prouve seulement que ce beau
> idéal n'est plus à leur portée, mais non point qu'il n'existe pas. (I.54)

Ideal beauty is not an abstraction; it exists, but on the suprasensible
level.

Man's face must become the most living and complete expression
of his thought. We can recover our true beauty only by renewing the
pure and revivifying springs which originally flowed in us. As Saint-
Martin sees it, man's artistic creation, like creation by God, moves
from the suprasensible to the sensible, and can be considered a true
creation, since it is an embodiment of his thought. At the same time,
by manipulating and purifying matter, he tends to dematerialize it;
the human artist is trying to increase the heavenly substance, which
is immaterial both in himself and in the work he produces. Artistic
activity is a form of the personal striving for regeneration; physical
beautification, operated on matter, and moral beautification, wrought
inwardly, go hand in hand.

> Il n'est plus douteux que l'accroissement et l'extension de cette chose
> admirable, au milieu du sensible altéré et corrompu d'ici-bas, ne soit
> cet embellissement que nous avons reconnu comme étant la tâche de
> l'homme primitif,...
> Il n'est pas douteux que cet embellissement ne tienne à celui que
> l'homme a maintenant à opérer sur lui-même, et qui consiste à rendre
> à sa propre forme les propriétés de cette substance admirable, ou de
> ce sensible immatériel qui constituait originairement sa beauté, de façon
> que sa première forme et le sensible immatériel devaient avoir une par-
> faite analogie, et n'être que la même substance... (I.90-91)

One might say that man's greatest work of art is himself, insofar as
he can bring himself close to his primitive state and the original
substance.[17] We can see Saint-Martin's tendency to dematerialize matter in his preference for the dematerialized in his own imagery: fire,
reflections, and the vapor in the line quoted by Viatte: "Mes jours
sont la vapeur des jours de l'Eternel."[18] Such metaphors are

---

[17] See comment by Annie Becq in "L'Imagination selon Saint-Martin," *Le Préromantisme*, pp. 421-22.
[18] *Oeuvres posthumes*, 2 vols. (Tours: Letourmy, 1807), I, 342, quoted in Viatte, *Les
Sources occultes*, I, 193.

characteristic of religious texts; we have already seen them in Charles de Villers.[19]

The visual arts receive less attention from the illuminists than poetry or music, and this is not surprising, since they are concerned first of all with concrete appearances and are the least subject to dematerialization. Usually the visual arts are not, in their present form, dependent on the word, but Saint-Martin (like Condillac!) believes that painting derives from the written word or sign, as poetry and music are derived from the spoken word. The true language, that is, the universal primitive language, has an infinite multitude of characters, as many as there are beings in nature: the word and the thing are the same. Those men who studied these signs, in order to remember them, needed to copy them: this was the first painting. Painting would have done better to stop here, says Saint-Martin, with exact copies of these models, which showed the very nature of things.[20] But man in his imprudence lost confidence in these true guides.

> Il n'a plus cherché ses modèles dans les objets utiles et salutaires, et dont il eût pu continuellement recevoir les secours, mais dans des formes passagères et trompeuses, qui ne lui offrant que des traits incertains et des couleurs changeantes, l'exposent tous les jours à varier sur ses propres principes et à mépriser ses ouvrages.[21]

The objects that man represents today are only the appearance of those he should study, with the result that painting as it now exists is only the appearance of appearances. (This sounds Platonic; the difference is that for Plato ideal beauty is abstract while for Saint-Martin it is not.) "Peuvent-ils prendre leurs sujets ailleurs [than in material beings], puisque la peinture n'étant que la science des yeux, elle ne peut s'occuper que du sensible, et par conséquent ne se trouver que dans le sensible?"[22] Saint-Martin does not accept the argument that a painter

---

[19] The tendency to dematerialize is also evident in the Platonic idealism of Joubert: "Que fait le poète? A l'aide de certains rayons, il purge et vide les formes de matière et nous fait voir l'univers tel qu'il est dans la pensée de Dieu même." (*Oeuvres*, ed. Paul de Raynal, 5th ed. [Paris, 1869]), quoted in Paul Bénichou, *Le Sacre de l'écrivain 1750-1830* (Paris: Corti, 1973), pp. 153-54, and in Ward, *Joseph Joubert*, p. 66. See the chapter on Joubert in Georges Poulet, *Mesure de l'instant* (Paris: Plon, 1968).

[20] *Des erreurs et de la vérité*, Vol. I of *Oeuvres majeures*, ed. R. Amadou (1775; rpt. Hildesheim and New York: Georg Olms Verlag, 1975), p. 499.

[21] *Ibid.*, p. 500.

[22] *Ibid.*, p. 501.

can choose subjects in his imagination, for though he may represent a fanciful or bizarre being, all the parts of this being came from nature. Man invents nothing. (So also said Batteux.) He also advises the painter not to depict a supernatural or marvelous subject (as Raphael painted the Transfiguration) unless he has himself had a vision of it, and even then, painting cannot really render such subjects and tends to make us confuse them with mythology.[23] But the painter does transpose appearances, idealizing and dematerializing as we have seen above.

Painting as it exists is justified because it is descended from a higher art and is one proof of the single universal language. Moreover, it seeks to give a good resemblance of all sensible nature in its representations. In *L'Homme de désir* Saint-Martin places painting, as "l'oeuvre sensible de la vérité" on the same plane with poetry and music: "La poésie, la musique et la peinture, sont trois soeurs, qui devraient être inséparables... La poésie devrait annoncer les vérités, la musique leur ouvrir l'issue, et la peinture les réaliser..."[24]

Music occupies a much larger space than painting in illuminist writings, since it is the image of that universal harmony from which all arts stemmed and by which works of art were to be judged.[25] In the Orphic tradition it is united with poetry and esoteric gifts. Music like language was often said to be of divine origin. Ballanche and Fabre d'Olivet thought so, and so did Villoteau (though he was not an illuminist):

> La musique... ne fut point *inventée* par les hommes, dans le sens que nous donnons ordinairement au mot *inventer*; elle ne fut que découverte par eux. Cet art vient réellement de Dieu; c'est lui qui l'a inspiré aux hommes; c'est lui qui en a établi les principes et les règles dans les accents de nos besoins; c'est lui qui en a noté tous les sons dans notre coeur: c'est là qu'il a déposé tous les secrets de la science musicale, de cet art de peindre le sentiment par la voix, et d'en imiter les accents par des sons.[26]

Ancient music contained the essential principles of language; it had, moreover, the highest moral, religious, and social effects. For these

---

[23] *L'Homme de désir*, pp. 262-63. Cf. *Des erreurs*, p. 503.
[24] *Ibid.*, p. 263.
[25] See Villoteau, I, lviii.
[26] Villoteau, II, 127-28.

reasons, says Villoteau, only God could have inspired its first principles in man. For Saint-Martin, it had its source in the original universal language and was the true measure of things.[27] Music, as the ancients defined it, says Fabre d'Olivet, was "la connaissance de l'ordre de toutes choses, la science des rapports harmonieux de l'univers; elle repose sur des principes immuables auxquels rien ne peut porter atteinte." Music exercises its true power not through its sound or its forms, but by the principles which govern them, says Fabre d'Olivet. Ancient music did not achieve its effects by melody or harmony: "Cette mélodie, cette harmonie, n'étaient que l'enveloppe physique d'un principe intellectuel connu, dont la présence éveillait dans l'âme une pensée analogue, et produisait par son moyen, non seulement le plaisir des sens dépendant de la forme, mais l'affection morale dépendante du principe."[28] While for modern man, music is theoretical or practical, the ancients considered it as speculative, intellectual, or celestial. The principles of ancient music were hidden to all but initiates.

> ...la musique intellectuelle et céleste était l'application des principes données par la musique spéculative, non plus à la théorie, ou la pratique de l'art pur et simple, mais à cette partie sublime de la science qui avait pour objet la contemplation de la nature et la connaissance des lois immuables de l'univers. Parvenue alors à son plus haut degré de perfection, elle formait une sorte de lien analogique entre le sensible et l'intelligible, et présentait ainsi un moyen facile de communication entre les deux mondes. C'était une langue intellectuelle qui s'appliquait aux abstractions métaphysiques et en faisait connaître les lois harmoniques, de la manière que l'algèbre, partie scientifique des mathématiques, s'applique, parmi nous, aux abstractions physiques et sert à calculer les rapports.[29]

Pythagoras recommended to his pupils that they reject the judgment of their ears, which were susceptible to error; immutable musical principles should be the "analogical and proportional harmony of numbers."[30] Music, like science, says Fabre d'Olivet, brings together the outer or visible effects with the inner or hidden.

As he does for other domains, Saint-Martin divides music into the sensible (*musique artificielle, musique naturelle-temporelle*) and suprasensi-

---

[27] *Des erreurs*, p. 523.
[28] *La Musique*, pp. 1, 16-17.
[29] *Ibid.*, p. 19.
[30] *Ibid.*, p. 22.

ble. Dissonance, which is part of sensible music, is an image and reminder of "le crime primitif," but also makes us strive for assonance, the perfect chord, divine unity. Music is the only *fil d'Ariane* that all men have been given to lead them in the labyrinth, our best link with regions lost to us.[31] It was possible in primitive times for music to move through the air from the audible to the channels of the higher realm.[32] Combined with words, it can purify the air, now corrupt, and the singer can rise to the divine region or make it come down into his own being. Even if temporal music should cease to exist, divine music, "le musique *principe*" will never cease. It exists outside of time and auditory sensation.

Theatrical productions have their origin in admiration for the heavenly spectacle and should lead us back to a contemplation of it. As for the dance, it too is an image of the freedom men should enjoy; its movements are impulses (*élans*) toward a region less inert than earth.[33]

Every art is in a sense a language and every artist a poet, but it is above all poetry in the strict sense of the art of the word which claims access to the suprasensory world. Saint-Martin calls poetry "la plus sublime des productions des facultés de l'homme, celle qui le rapproche le plus de son Principe, et qui par les transports qu'elle lui fait sentir, lui prouve le mieux la dignité de son origine."[34] Though the primitive language, the true mother tongue, has been degraded since the Fall, it has been given back to man in part, since he pursued it.[35] It is the poet in particular who has undertaken the quest for the primitive language, which gives him an intuition of the supernatural. This is the role of the "homme de parole."[36] In the first days of the world, when God's light had not yet darkened, says Saint-Martin, poets had magical powers:

> ...ils semblaient dans leurs vers traduire la nature,
> De l'univers entier dessiner la structure,

[31] *De l'esprit*, I, 170-75.
[32] *L'Homme*, p. 177.
[33] *De l'esprit*, I, 174-86.
[34] *Des erreurs*, p. 492.
[35] *De l'esprit*, II, 212-13.
[36] See Anne-Marie Amiot, "'L'Homme de parole' martiniste," *Le Préromantisme*, pp. 380-92.

> Servir partout d'organe à la vertu des cieux;
> Tout leur être était plein de l'image des Dieux.[37]

Since then poetry has fallen into decadence, with its descriptions of passions or imitations of things. Lyric poetry has become subjective, and love one of its greatest resources. While we all understand these feelings, they do not teach us anything, and poets would do better to show us how to rule our passions; however, in order to do this, they would have to know the order of higher laws.[38] Descriptive poetry, in the eighteenth century manner, is rejected. The only kind of description Saint-Martin finds acceptable in lyric poetry is that in which faithful depictions of natural objects strike us by their moral relationships, where mountains, rivers, and all natural phenomena celebrate the glory of God. But especially, it should depict what we cannot see. Epic poetry reveals the hidden springs of great events and has power over men, though it is false; there is some reflection of truth in its illusions. Prophetic poetry is the only truly powerful poetry. Since it has its roots in Asia, it has the most daring images and the most picturesque allegories.[39] In speaking of this genre, Saint-Martin again affirms that natural phenomena have no place in poetry unless the poet shows them penetrated by "un rayon divin qui fait de tous les êtres une espèce de sanctuaire sacré pour nous,..." Nature becomes a temple. "Aussi, la nature matérielle n'entre-t-elle dans la poésie prophétique, que comme comparaison avec les objets supérieurs, et on ne s'y occupe point de la Poésie descriptive."

This indicates a symbolic use in literature of material objects, which are signs of the invisible world. But true poetry must rise above even symbolic objects onto the heavenly plane.

> Enfin le véritable objet de la Poésie, ce sont les tableaux des faits suprêmes qui, par l'analogie de leur principe avec la substance qui nous anime, peuvent développer chez nous le feu divin qui y est contenu et concentré, et mettre notre poésie dans le cas d'en faire réfléchir les rayons sur les moindres objets qui nous environnent.[40]

Metaphor is central to poetry, in Saint-Martin's view, for simile and metaphor tend to elevate us to a higher plane. However, they should

---

[37] *Phanor*, in *Oeuvres posthumes*, II, 293.
[38] *Oeuvres posthumes*, II, 274.
[39] *L'Homme*, pp. 277, 376-77.
[40] *Oeuvres posthumes*, II, 275-76.

be used sparingly, lest the image encircle and shrink the model, rather than letting the model enter into the image to develop it.[41] Saint-Martin's own style is highly metaphorical, even taking into account that certain objects such as mirrors and rays are perhaps to be taken literally.

Court de Gébelin states more clearly the metaphorical or allegorical character of poetry in a universe whose objects are emblematic; here he speaks of primitive poetry:

> Le propre de la poésie étant de donner du corps aux pensées les plus sublimes, et aux connaissances les plus intellectuelles, elle ne put y parvenir qu'en personnifiant tout, qu'en animant tout, qu'en prêtant à l'Univers son enthousiasme, qu'en s'élevant toujours au-dessus de ce qu'elle voit...[42]

Saint-Martin essentially agrees that the composition of poetry, like the creation of any work of art, involves passing back from the suprasensory to the sensory, but he is loath to dwell on this *corporisation*, so that the poet seems already on his way back into the empyrean. Perhaps this is because the artist is seeking not so much transcendental beauty, which may have an earthly reflection, as divine truth. As Sigmond Czerny points out, truth, under the aspect of the sublime, replaces beauty as the highest aspiration in Saint-Martin's system and pushes it into second place.[43]

Texts dealing with literature and the arts are scattered through Saint-Martin's work; they are fragmentary and occupy only a minor place. In general, the illuminists' writings are not greatly concerned with the arts, and up to 1815 they had little impact on esthetics. Though their ideas were in the air, they were read mostly by an elite minority. Among those writers who followed the eighteenth-century occultists, Ballanche (though he disavowed Saint-Martin's influence) and Fabre d'Olivet, as we have seen, showed the greatest interest in the arts. Some others, such as Senancour and Nodier, knew the illuminists but left no significant texts dealing with our aspect of the subject. (Oberman's letters on music and Romantic harmony, reminiscence

---

[41] *De l'esprit*, II, 241.

[42] *Du génie allégorique*, art. VII, sec. 6, p. 150, quoted in Brian Juden, *Traditions orphiques et tendances mystiques dans le romantisme français (1800-1850)* (Paris: Klincksieck, 1971), p. 93.

[43] *L'Esthétique de Louis Claude de Saint-Martin* (Leopol, Warsaw: Ed. de la "Ksiaznica Polska T.N.S.W.," 1920), p. 99.

and Swedenborgian correspondences do not deal specifically with artistic creation.) It was undoubtedly Mme de Staël through *De l'Allemagne* who spread the word most effectively and wielded the greatest influence on the upcoming generation.

For the arts in general, one important consequence of illuminist esthetics is immediately evident: if the sensory universe has no autonomous existence but is only a sign of a spiritual universe, then art, rather than being mimetic and expressive, becomes symbolic. The illuminist influence joins with that of other groups we have already studied to attack the doctrine of art as imitation. We can accept the idea that the arts are an imitation of nature, says Fabre d'Olivet, only if we correctly understand what that means:

> La nature, qui est l'objet de l'imitation des arts, n'est point, comme l'imagine le vulgaire des artistes, la nature physique dont les phénomènes frappent les sens, mais celle dont les merveilles se manifestent à leur intelligence. Prendre pour unique modèle les formes particulières de la première, c'est s'astreindre à n'être qu'un copiste servile, un froid imitateur. Ce n'est qu'en cherchant à rendre sensibles les beautés intellectuelles de la seconde, qu'on peut prétendre à devenir créateur, qu'on peut s'élever jusqu'au sublime dans quelque genre que ce soit.[44]

[44] *La Musique*, p. 84.

6. The Balance Shifts

Up to this point we have been concentrating on the first fifteen or twenty years of the nineteenth century, with some attention to eighteenth-century antecedents; we are now going to turn our attention to the years following. A division at the beginning of the Restoration might be justified because of the change in the political regime, or at 1820, the date marked by the publication of the *Méditations poétiques* of Lamartine and so often chosen as the beginning of the Romantic era in literature. At any period diverse tendencies make clear-cut divisions difficult, but in the midst of the diverse, even contradictory tendencies of the Empire, changes in the general climate have gradually taken place and would accelerate in the following years. If, as is sometimes said, the Romantic period is the time when the dominant esthetic moved from imitation to expression, it is during the early years of the Restoration that the shift in emphasis becomes evident.

It is particularly evident in literature that these years were a prelude to the intense activity of the 1820s, when a new generation of gifted writers arrived on the scene. They are marked by a few important events: the publication in France of *De l'Allemagne* in 1814, followed within a few years by the death of Mme de Staël; the publication of Chénier's poetry by Latouche in 1819; the entry into France of Scott and the historical romance early in the period and of Byron somewhat later (the Pichot translation dates from 1819).

The pattern is somewhat less clear in painting. One could point to David's exile in 1816; Géricault's *Le Radeau de la Méduse*, first exhibited in the Salon of 1819; the official encouragement given to landscape painting, which was already flourishing and would soon know a real flowering, by the Academy, which for the first time offered a prize for *paysage historique* in 1817. Etienne Delécluze speaks of the sudden changes in the art world following David's departure but thinks that these changes would have taken place even if he had stayed in France.[1] The young "restaurateurs de l'art," says Delécluze, did not share David's respect for antiquity, exactness of drawing, and imitation of forms. "L'idée de la recherche du beau visible comme l'avaient fait les anciens fut réputée fausse et ridicule dans son application chez les modernes, et il fut reconnu que les ouvrages de la statuaire antique, uniquement faits pour plaire aux yeux, laissent l'âme froide et inactive." This seems to indicate a movement toward expressiveness at the expense of formal beauty. But Delécluze emphasizes the diversity and independence of young painters who study and paint nature as they please. Hence a great confusion of systems, of which the predominant one is "l'admission, la recherche même du *laid*, ce qui a fait admettre dans l'art l'imitation du naturel, quel qu'il soit et sous quelque forme qu'il se présente."[2] Delécluze will constantly complain of the ugliness of post-Davidian painting and regret the abandonment of the *beau visible* and the nude. He emphasizes the importance of foreign influences in France after the fall of the Empire.

Present-day art historians do not see such sudden changes taking place in painting. Pierre Rosenberg does not believe in the sectarian reign of David which Delécluze sees breaking up after 1815,[3] and in general French painting before 1815 is so diverse in subject matter, mood, and technique that it is difficult to define a trend. Delécluze's attitude toward David is no doubt colored by the fact that he is a former pupil of the master. But his observation about the confusion of systems is borne out by a study of the artistic production of those years. Robert Rosenblum points out (among others) the following characteristics of the painting of this period: the *grand genre* of history painting in no way dominates the field, as theoreticians would prefer, but shares it with large numbers of portraits, still lifes and genre paintings in the Dutch manner; the erotic, the bizarre, and the oneiric penetrate

---

[1] Stendhal, who frequented Delécluze's salon, speaks of the "tyranny" of David (*Mélanges*, III, 26).

[2] *Louis David*, pp. 379, 380.

[3] See his comment in the catalogue to the exposition *French Painting 1774-1830*, Detroit Institute of Arts, Metropolitan Museum of Art, New York; in France: *De David à Delacroix*, Grand Palais, Paris, 1974-1975, p. 14.

into mythological subjects; the Gothic and the *genre troubadour* share the stage with sharp focus realism.[4]

In these years, esthetic theory and criticism reach a middle period where little new is written in France. It is occupied by the debate over *De l'Allemagne*,[5] and in spite of the reaction against statue-like figures in painting, a continuation of the Winckelmann tradition of the *beau idéal* in the unflagging activity of Quatremère de Quincy. But though the esthetic of the *beau idéal* is the most generally accepted, it seems to be evolving into something else. The end of its predominance is at hand, and Stendhal, whose first publications on music and painting date from these years, helps to hasten its eclipse with his attacks on the traditional doctrine and his distinctions between the *beau idéal antique* and the *beau idéal moderne*. The well-known terms are still used, by Stendhal and by others, but the word "idéal" in particular takes on new meanings, as we shall see in the next chapter. Stendhal's influence was not immediate but would be felt in the next decade: in 1828 Delécluze says of *Histoire de la peinture en Italie*, "C'est le Koran des peintres dits romantiques."[6]

At this time there appeared on the horizon another new figure, one who may truly be considered transitional, Victor Cousin, the professor of philosophy whose eclecticism looks both backward and forward and makes of him a pivotal figure in esthetic theory. He is the only one figuring in this study who formulated his esthetic fully in philosophical terms and incorporated it into a general system. (Théodore Jouffroy had less breadth as a philosopher, but he developed his esthetic doctrine in greater detail than Cousin.) In the summary of Cousin's doctrine which follows, the reader will recognize some ideas already set forth in previous chapters.

Victor Cousin is an interesting phenomenon: while not a major philosopher, he was a very influential figure in the intellectual life of the Restoration. He arrived at just the right time to play a decisive role in the shift from sensualism to spiritualism as the dominant philosophy in France. He was in touch with eminent thinkers in France and Germany, a regular dinner companion of Ampère and Maine

---

[4] *Ibid.*, pp. 166-71.
[5] See I.A. Henning, *"L'Allemagne" de Madame de Staël et la polémique romantique* (Paris: Champion, 1929).
[6] *Précis d'un traité de peinture* (Paris: Bureau de l'Encyclopédie portative), p. 225.

de Biran, and, after 1818, a friend of Hegel. His lectures at the Sorbonne and the Collège de France drew large and enthusiastic audiences. Among the students a group of disciples soon formed around the young and eloquent professor; he was hardly older than themselves but became a *maître à penser* for the generation just reaching maturity.[7]

Cousin formulated for himself an esthetic which was chiefly a mingling of Platonism (through Plotinus and Shaftesbury), Neoclassicism (through Winckelmann and Quatremère de Quincy), and recent German philosophy, in particular Hegel, in that order of importance. Much has been made of the German influence on Cousin, especially because his 1818 course, the basic statement of his philosophy, immediately followed his first trip to Germany, but Frederick Will has shown that it is less important than the two others.[8] I shall not deal with the question of Cousin's sources here, except as certain esthetic concepts relate to the Neoclassicism discussed in the previous chapters.

The lecture notes for the 1818 course, drawn up by A. Garnier and approved by Cousin, were first published in 1836 under the title *Du vrai, du beau et du bien*. Cousin subsequently revised the book extensively and issued three other editions, between 1840 and 1853, but the first edition is the one which gives us the most accurate account of the lectures as the listeners heard them and others heard about them. We may supplement the section on *le beau* with an article on "Le Beau réel et le Beau idéal" (1818) and some manuscript notes.

As the Platonic triad of the title indicates, Cousin's esthetics is part of a metaphysical system. We do not grasp the infinite in itself but in the forms of the true, the beautiful, and the good (59).[9] The beautiful is the true in visible forms, the good is the true transported into human action (111). In loving truth, beauty, and goodness we constantly try to rise above them to the love of infinite being (77).

Art is in harmony with religion: "la religion est un regard vers l'infini du sein du fini, et l'art une reproduction de l'infini par le fini" (78). Such was its mission in Greece and Italy, but in modern times in

---

[7] For Stendhal's observations on Cousin, see A. Hoog, "Un Intercesseur du romantisme: Victor Cousin vu par Stendhal," in *Revue des Sciences Humaines*, fasc. 62-63 (1951), 184-200.

[8] See his study of Cousin's esthetics in *Flumen Historicum: Victor Cousin's Aesthetic and Its Sources* (Chapel Hill: University of North Carolina Press, 1965). This work has been helpful to me in composing this chapter.

[9] *Du vrai, du beau et du bien*, 59 (subsequent page references to this work will appear in the text).

France and England, art has lowered itself by representing only the finite. In Germany it has got lost in space in an attempt to represent the infinite by forms in themselves infinite, obviously an impossibility, since the infinite can manifest itself only in determinate forms. (Likewise, if religion rejects all determinate forms, it falls into the ecstatic.)

Real beauty, that existing in men and nature, whether it be physical, moral, or intellectual, is recognized by a combination of a feeling of disinterested love, which is individual, and a rational judgment, which is universal. If judgment is lost in the feeling, we have not the beautiful but the agreeable; if universality dominates, we arrive at a kind of intellectual mysticism.[10] When in harmony, these two faculties constitute taste.

Outer beauty contains a mixture of two elements, the general and the individual; the human face, for example, has both individually distinguishing features and the general lineaments of the species. In Cousin's epistemology we always start with a complex fact containing on one hand the individual, the variable, the non-essential, which is phenomenon; and on the other, the general, the unchanging, the essential, the absolute, which is substance. The opposing elements are always presented together, and we perceive them simultaneously. In the first spontaneous perception, we do not distinguish them but have a complex and primitive intuition of real beauty.[11]

Ideal beauty, though the negation of real beauty, is within it, a part of the amalgam of which real beauty is composed. It is the absolute which has been disengaged, or abstracted from the individual part which enveloped it; it is the real minus the individual. There are two kinds of abstraction: one is comparative abstraction, which forms a general idea from a multitude of examples; the other is practiced from a single example, by neglecting the individual part and disengaging the general (cf. 206-14). This second abstraction is immediate, since we need not have recourse to comparison of objects. This is the abstraction which Cousin proposes. Indeed, the comparative abstraction does not produce ideal beauty but what he calls a *beauté réelle collective* (188). He also rejects "l'hypothèse désespérée du beau idéal inné." The ideal

---

[10] "Du beau réel et du beau idéal," *Archives Philosophiques*, 3 (1818), 7. Cousin sometimes had occasion to protest when others saw in him this same intellectual mysticism.

[11] *Ibid.*, 3:8-13.

is neither previous to experience nor does it lag behind it while making comparisons. Ideal beauty is immediately discoverable from a single example, just as the ideal triangle is immediately constructed by a geometrician from the first triangle he meets in nature. "La nature nous le cache à la fois et nous le révèle; elle ne réfléchit la beauté éternelle que sous des formes qui s'évanouissent sans cesse; mais enfin elle la réfléchit, et pour le voir, il suffit d'ouvrir les yeux."[12]

So ideal beauty is there before us, within real beauty, but it is an abstraction, a pure intellectual conception. If real beauty contains the ideal, one might believe that faithful imitation would suffice, but since ideal beauty is veiled in nature, the artist must not only show the real but bring out its meaning, simplify and clarify. His genius determines the proportion between living reality and ideal beauty (208).

The artist starts with the concrete world and physical sensation, but physical beauty is only a reflection of moral and intellectual beauty. The visible beauty of a statue such as the Apollo Belvedere is only the manifestation of an inner beauty, an incorporeal beauty which shines through its envelope; the word which sums up this visible beauty is "expression" (255).[13] The same thing is true of human beings, says Cousin; physical beauty is beautiful only on condition that it place itself at the service of moral beauty. A common or even an ugly face may be illuminated by the soul it reflects; it takes on a character of morality, hence of beauty. We recognize Quatremère de Quincy's argument, and the example cited, Socrates, is always the same. But, says Cousin, "Ce ne sont pas les contours de la matière, en tant que pure étendue et pure forme, qui sont empreints de sublimité, c'est la matière vivante, animée, c'est-à-dire, la matière expressive, la matière manifestant l'âme, déchirant elle-même ses voiles" (256-57).

The point Cousin is making here is the dominant strength of moral beauty, necessary for physical beauty and even triumphing over physical ugliness. The reader may be disconcerted to see Cousin failing to differentiate between man and a work of art, and he will look in vain for a statement of whether moral beauty can show through physical ugliness in a statue or a painting. He does not enter into these questions but limits himself to the enunciation of his main principles. He will speak of the artist later in his discussion of genius.

---

[12] *Ibid.*, 3:15-16.
[13] In the 1846 edition, the word "expression" is replaced by "beauté morale."

Cousin's use of the word "sublimité" points up the lack of agreement between visible contours and moral beauty. The difference between the beautiful and the sublime, says he, lies in the proper proportion and harmony of reason, which grasps the unity of a person, a place, an object, or an act, and intuition, which perceives the variety in them.

> Lorsque... on saisit l'unité, et que l'intuition ne peut comprendre toutes les variétés renfermées dans l'objet, la beauté que nous découvrons, et qui nous fait éprouver un déplaisir dans notre organisation sensible en même temps qu'une joie intellectuelle, a été nommée sublime. Mais quand les parties de l'objet ne sont ni assez variées ni assez nombreuses pour n'être pas embrassées par l'intuition, et qu'en même temps l'ensemble est facile à saisir, que nous sentons un accord harmonique entre la variété et l'unité, entre les sens et la raison, nous nous arrêtons délicieusement sur ce spectacle, et c'est le beau proprement dit. (245)[14]

The sublime is then a special kind of beauty, though the causes and effects of the two are different. It is the kind of beauty in which "la matière expressive" can transform the ugliness of physical forms.

Cousin seems to hesitate as to whether visible beauty exists. Here he tells us that it has the existence of a reflection (elsewhere, as we have seen, it is an envelope or a veil):

> L'intérieur seul est beau: il n'y a pas de beau que ce qui n'est pas visible; cependant, si le beau n'était pas, sinon montré aux yeux, du moins indiqué, et pour ainsi dire esquissé par la forme visible, il n'existerait pas pour l'homme; il se manifeste par des traits sensibles, mais dont toute la beauté n'est que le reflet du beau incorporel. Ce n'est que par l'expression que la nature est belle. (257-58)

When we understand expression as the outer manifestation of an inner beauty, the conflict disappears and we see a new unity between the visible and the invisible. Victor Cousin stays close to the Hegelian concept that art is the sensible expression of the idea.

The expressiveness of nature is not limited to men and higher animals, as Quatremère de Quincy would have it, but extends to all levels of natural phenomena, because everything that exists is the expression of an intelligence. "La métaphysique nous apprend que tout ce qui existe est vivant, que l'âme de la nature rayonne à travers les

---

[14] When only intuition is satisfied and reason can grasp no unity, then we have the agreeable.

enveloppes les plus grossières. L'observation physique nous amène à des conclusions semblables: ces corps, dits inorganisés, sont soumis à des lois; là où il y a des lois il y a de l'intelligence" (258-59). The artist has much in common with the scientist, who seeks to discover these laws, and Cousin makes their work smack of alchemy:

> Aux yeux du physicien et du chimiste, la physique et la chimie ne sont belles que parce qu'elles pénètrent dans les secrets de l'intelligence suprême. Tout est symbolique dans la nature: la forme n'est jamais une forme toute seule, c'est la forme de quelque chose, c'est la manifestation de l'interne. La beauté est donc l'expression, l'art sera donc la recherche de l'expression. (260)[15]

Cousin has given a new, metaphysical dimension to the word "expression." This "manifestation of the internal," which he also calls a symbol, communicates not only the character and moral states of sentient beings but is also, says he, a revelation of that incorporeal beauty which is truth itself and the infinite.

The artist's task is to find the *beau idéal* in natural forms, then give it real expression: "Dégagez le beau de ses formes naturelles, vous trouverez le beau idéal; si vous cherchez à réaliser ce beau idéal, vous faites de l'art; si vous croyez que les formes, si pures qu'elles soient, altèrent la beauté, vous vous élevez à l'idée absolue, vous touchez presque à Dieu lui-même" (262). The highest cultivation of taste is that of a feeling for beauty, which means a constant effort to break the material envelope to arrive at moral beauty. The artist has the power to see this obscure beauty, but he is not a mystic: he tries to render in sensible form what was hidden in the concrete. Or, as Cousin says, "L'art c'est la nature détruite et recréée." (264).[16] The recreation brings out its essence and makes it more intelligible. The artist must conceive of nature as a symbol and consecrate his art to the search for a symbol purer and closer to the moral idea. Thus Cousin continues and extends the Neoclassic view of art as superior to nature.

To those who would object to this view, saying that if man surpasses nature, he is superior to God, Cousin replies: God in creating nature wished to show not his power but his will, and he wished to show it in symbols. He wished man to be superior to nature.

---

[15] Here again, the word "expression" is missing in the 1846 edition.
[16] Cf. Shaftesbury: "Man destroys nature in order to recreate it." See F. Will, *Flumen Historicum*, p. 44.

Le génie est ce qu'il y a de plus éminent dans l'humanité, et le génie détruit la nature, tout en l'adorant; et après l'avoir renversée, il la rétablit plus pure, et plus conforme à l'idée morale, gravée en elle de la main de Dieu; ainsi, les caractères du génie sont: destruction et création... L'artiste en détruisant et en reformant la matière, marche à la fin de l'art qui est le triomphe de la nature humaine sur la nature physique: élever le réel jusqu'à l'idéal, telle est la mission du génie. (267)

Man's superiority to the rest of God's creation is brought out in some manuscript notes for the Sorbonne course which are still extant:

L'homme est trop supérieur au monde pour le laisser tel qu'il est, il le change, le transforme, l'idéalise,... On préfère les ouvrages de la nature à ceux de l'art; parce que la première fut l'ouvrage de Dieu, comme si Dieu n'agissait pas d'une manière beaucoup plus profonde par le moyen de l'homme. Les ouvrages de la nature passent, se détériorent—ceux de l'art sont [illegible]; car l'art est l'expression de l'Esprit—et non imitation de la nature.[17]

"Man" here means the artist, who must know how to handle matter and to make it express the immaterial, otherwise he will not be superior to nature; not only vision but technical skill is necessary.

The sympathy that man has for nature is explained by the presence of God in both man and nature. If man is able to perceive an idea in its outer symbol, nature, it is because he already possesses it within himself: "c'est par notre côté moral seul que nous pouvons nous mettre en rapport avec le moral de la nature (273)." But man must also be endowed with the faculty which perceives the beautiful, says Cousin. Man is neither pure receptivity nor the opposite. Unfortunately, Cousin does not develop these thoughts nor try to deal fully with the subject of the interaction between the artist and the universe. Genius remains elusive.

Since moral expressiveness is the highest law of art, Cousin chooses it as the basis for his classification and ranking of the arts. If the criterion is pleasure, says he, the highest art is music; if clarity is the criterion, painting is the highest art (279). But since Cousin's criterion is expressiveness, he places poetry in the highest rank. It expresses beauty in a way both determinate and indeterminate, both finite and infinite. The poet's medium is words, which are both visible and invisible, material and immaterial. A simple word can awaken in us

---

[17] Feuillet 26, Bibliothèque Victor Cousin.

a multitude of feelings and ideas. "Le mot est donc le symbole le plus vaste et la plus clair; il est aussi déterminé que les lignes et les couleurs, mais il est mille fois plus compréhensif; c'est la manifestation la plus simple et la plus riche de l'absolu" (281). After poetry, he places in second place music, which he equates with melody: "Sous une forme déterminée, la mélodie est après la parole, l'expression qui altère le moins l'idée universelle et infini que nous appelons le beau... et par son vague même elle ouvre une vaste carrière aux jeux de l'imagination" (282). Then in descending order come painting, sculpture, architecture, and the construction of gardens. (Dance is not mentioned; perhaps it is to be included in music.)

This classification bears considerable resemblance to Hegel's, but Cousin does not attempt an exposition of the character and evolution of the different arts, as Hegel does. He adds only a few remarks to his brief presentation. In the idea (*fond*), all arts are identical, but they differ in their form. Of the five senses, only sight and hearing are involved in the arts. These two senses are less indispensable than the others to the conservation of the individual; they serve for the beautifying but not the sustaining of life. A subordination to useful ends kills architecture; poetry and music, painting and sculpture are freer. The musician and the painter can evoke the same emotions, but the forms do not overlap (268-88). And he cites the well-known example of Haydn, who, after having tried and failed to depict a stormy sea in music, realized that he must arouse the same emotion as that given by a stormy sea, but in musical terms. As for the old coupling of poetry and painting, the axiom *ut pictura poesis*, says he, should be regarded in a certain sense as false, since each art can do something the other cannot. The most varied and complete of the arts is poetry:

> Avec la parole, la poésie arrive à peindre et à sculpter; elle construit des édifices comme l'architecte; elle imite, jusqu'à un certain point, la mélodie de la musique. Elle est, pour ainsi dire, le centre où se réunissent tous les arts: c'est l'art par excellence; c'est la faculté de tout exprimer, avec un symbole universel. (290)

To interpret the symbolic universe Cousin sees, the most suitable medium is also symbolic. The rise of spiritualism as the dominant philosophy seems to correspond to the increasing acceptance of poetry as the major art form. Ancillon had many years earlier praised poetry as the freest of the arts. In the 1820s we shall find a number of critics ranking the arts in the same order as Cousin or declaring the superiority of poetry. His former pupil Adolphe Garnier, for example, is even more spiritualist than Cousin, when he makes the word almost identical with the thing or the concept, and in itself transparent:

> ... outre la grande puissance de ses moyens, la poésie a l'immense avantage d'employer des signes qui ont une liaison plus étroite avec l'intellectuel et d'y arriver ainsi bien plus nettement à l'idée qu'il veut rendre. Par exemple, quand elle prononce le mot de générosité, tout le monde saisit aussitôt la pensée, et personne ne fait attention à la forme matérielle du mot qui l'exprime. Dans les autres arts, au contraire, on est toujours arrêté plus ou moins par la configuration matérielle.[18]

In general, sculpture, the exemplar of Neoclassic art, is yielding to the Romantic trio, painting, music, and poetry, and the greatest of these, say many, is poetry.

---

[18] "Observations sur le beau," *Revue Encyclopédique*, 30 (1826), 617. See also Jos. Bard in the *Annales*, 26 (1827), 61 sq.; N. Massias in *Théorie du beau et du sublime* (1824), p. 85; Quatremère de Quincy in *L'Imitation* (1823), pp. 114-47 (Quatremère includes the ballet, which he places immediately after *les arts du dessin*).

7. *The Real and the Ideal (I)*

Under the Restoration the dichotomy real–ideal continues to preoccupy the critics, but the relations between the two theoretical opposites change and become more complex. Especially, the connotations attached to the word "ideal" become more diverse. In Neoclassical theory, real and ideal beauty were not widely separated and theoretical opinion was not polarized. Ideal beauty existed behind or within beauty in nature, and the artist derived it from real beauty or went through real beauty to perceive it, after which he gave it form in the work of art according to certain principles. Whatever the meaning given to "ideal," whether it be a choice and combination of real beauties, a generalization and search for type, an abstracted essence and clarification, a moral or spiritual quality, or a mental conception, real and ideal remained closely tied. In his writings on real and ideal beauty, Victor Cousin, though he gave a new dimension to the meaning of the terms, did not depart from Neoclassicism in this respect.

Traditional attitudes naturally continued, usually couched in the traditional vocabulary. According to Delécluze, idealization has its point of departure in the real; after long study, the artist fashions types, which are the artistic categories of the ideal.[1] Aignan places emphasis on a *nature choisie*, a mixture of real elements: "... l'illusion ne peut résulter que des rapports intimes de la représentation avec le modèle, modèle choisi, modèle savamment combiné..."[2] Or this comment in

---

[1] See Robert Baschet, *E.J. Delécluze témoin de son temps, 1781-1863* (Paris: Boivin, 1942), p. 249.
[2] *Courrier Français*, 9 Sept. 1821.

a critique of the 1824 Salon: "Le peintre, pour produire ces types, n'a fait qu'imiter avec un goût élevé les modèles qu'il avait sous les yeux; et le véritable idéal ne doit être en effet qu'une belle nature copiée avec goût."[3] The writers of *Le Globe* are closer to the spiritualism of Quatremère de Quincy and Victor Cousin: "... l'idéal... n'est ni le faux, ni le factice, ni même l'invraisemblable; il doit rappeler la réalité, dont il n'est pas l'exacte copie, mais la pure conception."[4] Since works of art can never render all that is beauty in life, says Charles Magnin, "il faut, par compensation, qu'ils ajoutent d'autres beautés prises dans le type éternel que nous portons en nous-mêmes."[5] The artist, by his conception of the type, supplies what is missing, obscure, or unreproducible in nature.

The concept of ideal beauty, taking Greek sculpture as point of departure, has spread into other arts, but in its original acceptation it no longer seems sufficient. Stendhal and Sismondi both maintain that that beauty praised by Winckelmann is no longer related to modern times. René Canat, in his *L'Hellénisme des romantiques* has shown how the original doctrine was attacked and lost ground during the 1820s. Victor Cousin's translation of Plato, published beginning in 1822, revealed to readers what the concept was at its source, before Aristotelian modifications, and served to reinforce Cousinian spiritualism.[6]

The sculptural models themselves changed aspect. As the literate and art-loving public came to know Greek art and literature better, their discovery of Aeschylus, of the Elgin marbles, and of Phidias (this latter 1825-1830) showed them a realism in the ancient Greeks of which they had been unaware. The lectures of Raoul-Rochette were particularly effective in instructing the public concerning new discoveries and new ideas of Greek art; he attacked Winckelmann at the same time that Villemain was attacking Barthélemy's *Anacharsis*. The Greeks no longer seemed so calm as formerly, nor the beauty of their statuary so serene. The slow breakdown of belief in the superiority of the formal ideal beauty of ancient Greek sculpture begins to have important implications for modern sculpture only near the end of the 1820s long after most practitioners and commentators of the other arts have adopted the ideal as a moral or spiritual quality or else have abandoned it.

[3] *Constitutionnel*, 23 Sept. 1824.
[4] Review of *Bug Jargal*, 2 March 1826.
[5] *Le Globe*, 26 July 1828.
[6] Didier, I (1959), 166.

Ingres used the term "beau idéal" ambiguously, making it sometimes the equivalent of *beau antique* or of *beau visible* (*beau de la nature*). What some would call "beau idéal" he would probably call "belle nature." "Phidias," says he, "parvint au sublime en corrigeant la nature avec elle-même, et, à l'occasion de Jupiter Olympien, il se servit de toutes les beautés naturelles réunies pour arriver à ce qu'on appelle mal à propos le beau idéal."[7] It must be this pejorative meaning of unnatural and conventional that he has in mind when he exclaims that "le beau idéal est une sottise."[8] The true beauty of ancient Greek art is, as he says, nature corrected by nature, or natural beauties brought together in one being.[9]

A curious passage by Baron Nicolas Massias links the ideal with contemporary science. Geoffroy Saint-Hilaire's discoveries in anatomy, says Massias, have confirmed what Plato's genius had revealed concerning the existence of primitive types on which sensible objects are modeled. The organization of different species is only the application of a single *idea*. The oldest forms are the simplest and have been modified, not destroyed, through the ages.

> D'où il résulte évidemment que la raison de chaque être n'est point en lui-même, puisque, avant d'exister, il était déjà lié à un modèle antérieur, et que lui-même il sert de base et comme d'échelon aux analogues qui doivent en dériver et lui être coordonnés; *il existe donc un type idéal pour les espèces.*[10]

Having opened up the interesting subject of what implications the theory of *unité de composition* might have for the age-old search for the archetype, Massias fails to follow his thought to its logical conclusion, which is that the continuing modification of forms destroys the concept of the immutable type. He simply returns to the conventional Aristotelian search for perfection of the species through multiple individual examples. "Plus l'artiste transporte dans ses ouvrages de ces beautés partielles éparses sur les individus, plus il est parfait, plus il se rapproche de l'idéal."[11]

The word "idéal" may refer to the conception of the subject of a work or to its form. Quatremère de Quincy says that it is in both

---

[7] Delaborde, *Ingres*, p. 139.
[8] See Canat, *L'Hellénisme*, II, 194.
[9] See Robert Baschet, "Ingres de Delacroix: une esquisse de leur doctrine artistique," *Revue des Sciences Humaines*, 34, no. 136 (1969), 625-43.
[10] *Théorie du beau et du sublime* (Paris: Didot, 1824), pp. 255-56.
[11] *Ibid.*, p. 256.

the notions which exist in our mind and in the works which inspire impressions other than those of physical sensations, which is to say, those that evoke a primarily emotional response.[12] Adolphe Garnier uses the traditional terms; his 1826 article, "Observations sur le beau," bears the Cousinian stamp, but he places even more emphasis than the master on the rational and intelligible. The ideal is "la matière soumise à l'idée," and art is "la production de l'idéal." The difference between "beau idéal" and "beau réel" is simply that between art and nature; they are in essence the same:

> ... l'idée que saisit notre raison dans les ouvrages de la nature, est enveloppée de matière; un trait ou deux, qui se rapportent à cette idée, ont suffi pour la faire découvrir; les autres s'en écartent, ou lui sont opposés. L'art, au contraire, partant de l'idée qu'il veut rendre, emploie seulement les traits matériels qui sont en rapport avec elle. Le rationnel, ou le beau, est donc le même dans les deux cas; la différence existe dans le mode d'exécution. Ce qui donne l'avantage à la forme de l'art, c'est qu'en elle l'idée est plus claire, puisque la matière lui est tout à fait soumise. La forme de la nature étant moins bien ramenée à l'unité de l'idée, est nécessairement inférieure.[13]

We recognize the Neoclassic idea that art brings out the meaning in nature; it is because men have interpreted nature, says Garnier, that they find it beautiful.

Kératry contrasts "ce que nous appelons *beau idéal* dans les formes" with "le *beau moral* dans l'expression."[14] He hardly believes in the *beau idéal* which, according to Winckelmann, the sculptors of antiquity placed in "l'épuration des formes corporelles" (II.84), but rather looked for the expressiveness of art which was to be achieved by the exact representation of emotions ("mouvements de l'âme"), no doubt through facial expression, and bodily forms. "Tel est leur moyen d'ascension vers le seul Beau idéal qu'avoue notre nature" (II.113). Kératry believes that nature ("le monde organique") is perfect, having come from God; it is an error for men who are struck with the moral imperfection of their own kind to disdain nature also as imperfect (II.163). For him the *beau idéal* is the idea of beauty toward which we ascend; returning to Plato, he has removed the *beau idéal* from artistic form. Kératry tells us that "[l'expression] est l'âme d'un tableau" (II.165), which is

---

[12] *L'Imitation*, pp. 186-87.

[13] *Revue Encyclopédique*, 30, 612-13.

[14] *Du beau dans les arts d'imitation* (Paris: P. Audot, 1822), II, 65.

in agreement with the way the majority opinion is moving, but he also calls David a "peintre d'expression," which is exactly what David himself and most others said he was not (II.174). Such confusion of vocabulary is of course not limited to Kératry.

In any case, the critics often hesitate between the "inner" and "outer" meanings of ideal beauty, as when a critic of the *Revue Française* contrasts two of David's pupils: Girodet, who wished to attain "le béau idéal comme forme," and Guérin, who strove for "le beau idéal comme expression."[15]

In *Histoire de la peinture en Italie* Stendhal had already called for a *beau idéal moderne* to replace the *beau idéal antique* (see above, p. 51). He kept the traditional vocabulary, though the most important quality of this new ideal beauty was expressiveness. In his writings of the 1820s he again uses the Neoclassic formula, in the sense of what is considered most beautiful. He accentuates even more than before its changeable character. Sometimes it is a long slow change, brought about by fundamental historical forces; here he contrasts this evolution to changes in fashion:

> L'essence de la mode est de changer sans cesse; la classe riche veut à toute force se distinguer de la classe bourgeoise, qui s'obstine à l'imiter, tandis que le *beau idéal* ne varie que tous les dix siècles avec les grands intérêts des peuples. L'invention de la poudre à canon, par exemple, a exclu du beau idéal moderne *l'expression de la force.*[16]

Canova has invented a new kind of *beau idéal* which is closer to our mores than to the ancient Greeks: the Greeks esteemed physical force above all else, while we esteem mind (*l'esprit*) and feeling.

Cyprien Desmarais, another writer sympathetic to the Romantics, also lays emphasis on the relativity of the *beau idéal*, or rather, "le sentiment du beau idéal" which, he says, is innate in all men, being "la conscience intime du type de l'éternelle beauté," but varies in character.

> Chez les nations heureuses par la douceur du climat, par les jouissances du luxe, et par la puissance politique, le sentiment du beau idéal est plus positif, plus correct, et j'oserais dire plus classique; chez celles, au contraire, qu'une nature âpre, qu'un sol aride, qu'un ciel nébuleux, qu'une civilisation grossière condamnent à plus de souffrances physiques, l'idéal s'élève davantage; c'est là qu'il est vague et profond com-

[15] *Ibid.*, I (1828), 191.
[16] *Mélanges*, III, 71.

me l'abîme, triste et solennel comme la nuit des pôles... L'idéal est comme le supplément de notre nature morale: nous y avons d'autant plus recours que les réalités nous manquent davantage.[17]

Here the *beau idéal* is determined by reality but does not correspond to it; it is in inverse relationship to real beauty. Religion also has a strong influence on the feeling of ideal beauty: mythological religions, by exaggerating the power of men and lowering that of gods, brought the two closer together and kept the ideal within bounds. But the classical *beau idéal*, which rested upon Greek theogony, can no longer bring inspiration to the European poetic genius. After the Revolution the French looked to the north and tried to borrow the ideal of northern countries but failed, hence the disorders of Romanticism in France. The Romantic ideal, says Desmarais, is sad and severe, unlike the gaiety natural to the French. More time is necessary for it to become assimilated. The ideal is in the inspiration of the arts, as opposed to the *beau positif*, the outer form of highly developed pagan art.[18]

The term "idéal" has a limited place in the esthetics of Théodore Jouffroy, a student of Cousin and one of the most important *Globe* critics. Cousin is the point of departure for his esthetics, but he does not follow Cousin's use of "real" and "ideal"; he chooses other terms to expound his theory of reality and what is behind it; of this we shall speak in chapter 10. In his course on esthetics he passes in review the different accepted meanings of the term. It means first of all the elimination of detail in order to bring out the main traits of the outer form of a species. Jouffroy does not accept the Platonic hypothesis of absolute types in our intelligence. He ridicules the belief that raising forms from the real to the ideal by elimination of detail suffices to make them beautiful. "Quand on change les formes réelles de l'âne et du porc en leurs formes idéales, on arrive à l'idéal de l'âne et du porc, et cet idéal est beau; au moins, on l'a cru."[19] This is not an entirely fair description of a traditional position: those who, like Quatremère de Quincy, admitted "la laideur idéale" into art, did not equate it with ideal beauty. Jouffroy continues: "Or, supprimer les détails des traits, ce n'est pas rendre beaux les traits qui ne le sont

---

[17] *Essai sur les classiques et les romantiques* (Udron: Vernarel et Tenon, 1824), pp. 88, 89.
[18] *Ibid.*, pp. 90-94.
[19] *Cours d'esthétique*, Preface Ph. Damiron (Paris: Hachette, 1843), p. 68.

pas." If this kind of idealization pleases us, it is because we like imitation and we like simplicity; through generalized imitations we may immediately see the physiognomy of a species. Though an ideal pig is not beautiful, Jouffroy does concede that it is less ugly than a real pig.

Jouffroy does not entirely dissociate the beautiful and the ideal. He distinguishes several kinds of beauty: *le beau d'expression, le beau d'imitation* and "la beauté de l'idéal," by which he means suppression of the irrelevant to make the natural object more coherent; the beauty which is the basis of all these and which exists in itself is "le beau spirituel."[20] To this we shall return later.

Vigny is not ill at ease with the term "idéal," as Jouffroy seems to be. His dictum, "L'ART ne doit jamais être considéré que dans ses rapports avec sa BEAUTÉ IDÉALE,"[21] has a distinctly Classic ring. "L'art est la vérité choisie," says an 1829 entry in his *Journal d'un poète*. "Si le premier mérite de l'art n'était que la peinture exacte de la vérité, le panorama serait supérieur à la *Descente de croix*" (II.901). Certainly no one could quarrel with this. In his "Réflexions sur la vérité dans l'art" (1827), attached as a preface to *Cinq-Mars*, he distinguishes between the visible and concrete "vrai," which others might call "réel," and "la vérité," which is the soul of the arts.

> Cette vérité... un choix du signe caractéristique dans toutes les beautés et toutes les grandeurs de VRAI visible; mais ce n'est pas lui-même, c'est mieux que lui; c'est un ensemble idéal de ses principales formes, une teinte lumineuse qui comprend ses plus vives couleurs, un baume enivrant de ses parfums les plus purs, un élixir de ses sucs les meilleurs, une harmonie parfaite de ses sons les plus mélodieux; enfin c'est une somme complète de toutes ses valeurs. (II.21)

This truth should be the object of the aspirations of authors of dramatic works (including the novel), which are "une représentation de la vie." To know the factual truth of each period is not enough; one must choose the proper elements and group them around a center of the artist's invention.

Vigny's passionate outburst against tepid reality shows to what extent his theory grows out of his personal experience and outlook:

---

[20] *Ibid.*, pp. 177 sq.
[21] "Réflexions sur la vérité dans l'art," *Oeuvres complètes* (Paris: : Bibliothèque de la Pléiade, Gallimard, 1948), II, 25.

A quoi bon les Arts, s'ils n'étaient que le redoublement et la contre-épreuve de l'existence? Eh! bon Dieu, nous ne voyons que trop autour de nous la triste et désenchanteresse réalité: la tiédeur insupportable des demi-caractères, des ébauches de vertus et de vices, des amours irrésolues, des haines mitigées, des amitiés tremblotantes, des doctrines variables, des fidélités qui ont leur hausse et leur baisse, des opinions qui s'évaporent; laissez-nous rêver que parfois ont paru des hommes plus forts et plus grands, qui furent des bons ou des méchants plus résolus; cela fait du bien. Si la pâleur de votre VRAI nous poursuit dans l'Art, nous fermerons ensemble le théâtre et le livre pour ne pas le rencontrer deux fois. (II.22)

Real people, things, and events do not satisfy us either esthetically or morally. They are not in themselves meaningful, and meaning is what we look for in art.

Le fait adopté est toujours mieux composé que le vrai, et n'est même adopté que parce qu'il est plus beau que lui; c'est que l'HUMANITÉ ENTIÈRE a besoin que ses destinées soient pour elle-même une suite de leçons; plus indifférents qu'on ne pense sur la RÉALITÉ DES FAITS, elle cherche à perfectionner l'événement pour lui donner une grande signification morale; sentant bien que la succession des scènes qu'elle joue sur la terre n'est pas une comédie, et que, puisqu'elle avance, elle marche à un but dont il faut chercher l'explication au delà de ce qui se voit. (II.23-24)

The classic conception of cognitive art fits this *poète-philosophe*.

It is the spiritual and religious concept of the ideal that has real richness and vitality. Baron Eckstein in a review of B. Constant's *De la religion* affirms the strong presence of the ideal in ancient Greece, but in the context of drama, which showed a struggle of cosmic forces. The ideal of the ancient dramatists consisted in "imprimer à toute chose une signification supérieure à celle de la sphère de la vie commune;… Leur conception de la nature était empreinte d'une grande idée de la vie divine, qui l'animait dans toutes ses parties; leur conception de l'idéal était celle de cette vie divine, visible en toutes choses…"[22] This suffusion of divine life in all things removed poetry from the limits of imitation and brought it under the conditions of art.

In his theory of beauty, Eckstein again represents the ideal as God penetrating matter: "L'idéal, sous sa forme de l'univers, est l'image, le reflet de la beauté suprême du monde en Dieu: mais une image

---

[22] *Le Catholique*, 1 (1826), 81-82.

animée de ce feu d'amour céleste qui circule, comme vie et Providence, dans les veines de la création."[23] The modern ideal differs from the ancient in having the dimension of the infinite which has given a new depth to the work of Christian artists. "Cet infini, et si je puis dire, cet *au-delà des choses*, visible dans l'art, tel que le christianisme l'a fait, a dû lui imposer un genre d'idéalité que les anciens n'ont pu deviner que très rarement, parce que leur religion n'en offrait aucun germe positif."[24] Art, he continues, will never succeed in expressing the ideal beauties of Christianity with the complete perfection we find in Phidias and Socrates, but in the expression of the infinite that Leonardo, Raphael, and Calderón struggle with, there is an element of mysterious beauty superior to the ancients' art.

Since we have entered a decade of polemics between *classiques* and *romantiques*, it is not surprising to find that some critics try to define the difference between them in terms of the real and the ideal. Nor is it surprising that they do not all agree, for in the early 1820s the appellations "classique" and "romantique" are even more imprecise than the term "idéal." The political difference (Romantic–royalist, Classic–liberal) is perhaps the clearest one perceived at this time. The polemic stance of much of the writing augments the confusion, since the perception of the critics varies according to their own position in the dispute.

Among the critics who placed the Romantics among the partisans of the ideal, those who were sympathetic to them emphasized their religious inspiration, their spiritualist orientation in philosophy, their introspective nature, their exaltation, their aspiration toward the infinite. "La littérature romantique sera plus aérienne et plus idéale que la littérature classique," says Cyprien Desmarais.[25] In the Preface to his *Odes et poésies diverses* (1822), Victor Hugo postulates an ideal world beneath the real: "Sous le monde réel, il existe un monde idéal, qui se montre resplendissant à l'oeil de ceux que des méditations graves ont accoutumés à voir dans les choses plus que les choses."[26] Eckstein

---

[23] "Du beau," *Le Catholique*, 4 (1826), 518.

[24] *Ibid.*, 4:532.

[25] *Essai*, p. 97. See below, Ch. 10, for continuation of this passage.

[26] *Oeuvres complètes*, ed. Jean Massin (Paris: Club Français du Livre, 1969), II/1, 5. Unless otherwise indicated, all subsequent references from Hugo will come from this edition.

has no doubt taken his clue from Hugo in the following observation: "La nature est l'oeuvre de la main de Dieu; c'est là qu'il a inscrit sa pensée en caractères symboliques; elle sert de voile à tout un monde idéal. C'est ce monde surtout que le poète doit chercher à deviner, au lieu de s'en tenir à l'apparence des phénomènes."[27]

A debate which took place two years later in the columns of the *Journal des Débats* between Hugo and the critic Hoffman (who signed his articles Z...) shows how complex the cross-currents were and how differently they were perceived by different people. The debate started with a review by Hoffman of Hugo's *Nouvelles Odes*, in which he theorized on some differences, supposed and real, between the Classics and the Romantics. According to the critic, the Romantics' ideal tends to be fantastic and arbitrary. It is true that "sous le monde réel existe un monde idéal," but "ce n'est qu'à travers le prisme du monde réel que nous pouvons concevoir les abstractions. Les classiques ont bien senti cette vérité que les romantiques ne veulent point reconnaître; les classiques se renferment dans le monde réel, les romantiques s'égarent dans le monde idéal: voilà la ligne de démarcation,..."[28] He presents the arguments of the Romantics thus: since the spiritual world is superior to the material, images and comparisons should be drawn from the former. "Cette conséquence, qui fait prévaloir les abstractions sur les réalités, a tellement égaré les romantiques, et ils en ont porté si loin les développements, qu'ils ont été jusqu'à mépriser toutes les formes naturelles; et ils ont fini par dire: *Il n'y a de beau que ce qui n'existe pas!*" How can a soul be expressed, asks Hoffman, except through a body? The ideal world can be perceived only through the real world; the Romantics take their models, forms, and colors, not from nature but from "le monde idéal et fantastique."

In a letter to the *Débats* Hugo answers and refutes Hoffman's arguments point by point. When it comes to the question of style, specifically imagery, for that is the crux of the matter, he finds that he and Hoffman are recommending basically the same thing.

Des *formes* et des *couleurs* appartiennent nécessairement à des objets physiques; indiquez-moi donc, Monsieur, quel moyen ces heureux romantiques emploient pour trouver des *formes* et des *couleurs* dans le monde idéal, c'est-à-dire des choses matérielles dans le monde immatériel. Comment ont-ils fait pour découvrir la *couleur* de la pensée, la *forme* de la

[27] Review of Victor Hugo, *Odes et ballades, Le Catholique,* 7 (1827), 247.
[28] 14 June 1824.

rêverie? Ne leur a-t-il pas fallu la toute-puissance du créateur pour tirer des *corps* d'un monde où il n'existe pas de corps?... Mais une chose m'embarrasse: ces *formes*, ces *couleurs*, ces *corps*, une fois trouvés aux pays des abstractions, appartiennent nécessairement, en leur qualité de *corps*, au monde physique; c'est donc au monde physique que les *romantiques* ont, en définitive, emprunté leurs *formes* et leurs *couleurs*; or, comme, suivant votre définition, on ne peut emprunter de formes et de couleurs au monde réel sans être *classique*, les *romantiques* sont donc des *classiques*!... Souffrez que je vous le dise, la littérature *romantique*, d'après votre distinction, serait une littérature impossible; aucune langue humaine ne pourrait l'exprimer.[29]

We know that up to this time Hugo had declined to call himself and his friends "Romantic," finding that the term was so ill-defined as to have no meaning. In this article, however, he places himself within the new group.

What is true of imagery is true of language itself. Hugo goes on:

Il n'est pas plus donné aux *romantiques* qu'aux classiques de concevoir le monde idéal, abstraction faite du monde réel. Vous avez parfaitement raison de dire que "toutes les affections morales, toutes les facultés intellectuelles, ne peuvent se représenter à l'esprit que par des images, par des expressions empruntées au physique; que les mots mêmes qui expriment des abstractions sont tirés de l'ordre matériel." Les images sont le fondement de tout langage humain; et il serait aussi impossible de parler sans images que de peindre sans couleurs. Nous ne pouvons concevoir que selon ce que nous avons vu; et nous ne saurions inventer des formes imaginaires qui ne fussent le résultat de quelque combinaison des formes réelles. Le travail simultanée de la pensée et de la parole est une traduction perpétuelle des réalités en abstractions et des abstractions en réalités. En un mot, sans les images du monde réel, non seulement une littérature, mais même une langue, ne saurait se former...[30]

Subsequent discussion, in this letter, plus one more by Hoffmann and three more by Hugo, centers on the use of such images as "avoir le mystère pour vêtement" and "le corps bleu du cauchemar"; Hugo overwhelms his adversary by citing numerous examples of similar associations of abstract ideas and terms and physical images drawn from Classic and Neoclassic authors.

Actually, the Romantics were more often characterized as adhering to reality. Quatremère de Quincy, the Neoclassic spiritualist, not

---

[29] *Oeuvres complètes*, II/1, 537.
[30] *Ibid.*, pp. 537-38.

unexpectedly sees the description of physical nature as the basic characteristic of the *genre romantique*. The Romantic poet seems to want to make an exact copy of material objects. "Il s'efforce de s'attacher à leur réalité, comme s'il pouvait s'en prendre à l'organe visuel."[31] He has borrowed the painter's eyes and his imitative procedures, says Quatremère. According to Baron Massias, the classically trained writer rises to the *beau idéal*, while "l'école romantique se contente de peindre les individus tels qu'ils tombent sous son pinceau."[32] Again, the comparison with painting. Nodier, on the other hand, is sympathetic to the young writers, and though his own favored domain is the imaginary, he praises their depiction of the real:

> Si les auteurs romantiques sont quelquefois admirables, c'est qu'ils cessent d'être faux et exagérés, pour se rapprocher de la vérité, c'est qu'ils sont naturels... Le génie consiste à voir et à peindre les choses comme elles sont, et le don le plus rare est d'être susceptible de recevoir et de rendre dans toute leur force les impressions les plus opposées...[33]

Audin also emphasizes the naturalistic side of Romanticism:

> Le poète classique, cherchant un beau qui ne peut tomber sous les sens, éternel, immuable, veut pour juge une substance immortelle, l'intelligence et non des organes périssables, tels que l'oeil ou l'oreille: aussi toutes ses merveilles sont spirituelles; il ne trace presque jamais que des douleurs morales; rarement vous le verrez étaler à vos regards des souffrances physiques... [He quotes a brief description of Ulysses returning home.] Mais que le poète romantique ait la même scène à peindre; comme le beau n'est pour lui que la représentation exacte de la nature, il s'attache à donner à cette représentation la ressemblance la plus parfaite avec son modèle.[34]

Classic poetry is an imitation of "la nature choisie et parée," while Romantic poetry imitates "la nature nue" with its irregularities and bizarre aspects.[35] But Romantic poetry encompasses both the real and the ideal; it may be made with a little mud, but the poet has breathed life into it. The poet moves at ease in the two worlds:

[31] *L'Imitation*, p. 82.

[32] *Principes de littérature* (Paris: F. Didot, 1826), p. 59.

[33] *Pensées de Shakespeare, suivies de quelques scènes de ses tragédies et de son testament* (Paris: Librarie nationale et étrangère, 1822), quoted in Raymond Setbon, *Libertés d'une écriture critique: Charles Nodier* (Geneva: Editions Slatkine, 1979), p. 249.

[34] J.M.V. Audin, "Du romantique," preceding *Florence* (Paris: Pigoreau et Ponthieu, 1822), pp. xxiii-xxv.

[35] *Ibid.*, p. cxiv.

On n'a point assez remarqué les harmonies de la réalité et de l'idéalité, des sens et de l'esprit, du naturel et du possible, que crée le romantisme: harmonies qui étendent l'espace où le poète déploie les merveilles de son art...

Premier anneau de cette chaîne d'inspirations imaginée par Platon, il tient attaché le lecteur, qu'il emporte incessamment du monde visible au monde invisible, des ténèbres à la source de la lumière, de la contemplation des choses divines, au spectacle des misères humaines.[36]

But the two worlds are combined especially in the union of thought with expression, specifically the imagery. Two years before Hoffman's critique, Audin takes the contrary position, basing his opinion on Schiller and Shakespeare, among others;

Ce que le génie des anciens a moins souvent hasardé, c'est ce mélange de la nature morale et de la nature physique; ces transitions du monde visible dans le monde spirituel; cette confusion de la réalité et de l'idéalité; ces comparaisons dont un terme est pris dans le sens propre et l'autre dans le sens figuré.[37]

Rather than claim the universality of this kind of imagery, as Hugo does slightly later, Audin claims it for the moderns. Most of his remarks are based on English and German literature, though he sees that the Romantic muse is now penetrating into all domains in France: politics, science, philosophy, the arts—especially the novel. The basic difference between real and ideal often lies, as we have seen, in the distinction between the inspiration or aspiration of the poet on one hand, and on the other the form his work takes. As the poet is himself a dualism, so also is his work.

M. de Sismondi prétend que les anciens plaçaient la poésie dans les sens, tandis que les poètes romantiques la placent dans les émotions de l'âme. Ceci semblerait détruire ce que nous avons cherché à établir, l'union du romantisme avec les sens; mais il faut prendre garde que l'écrivain ne considère ici que la poésie dans son origine. Né d'une religion qui la première vint révéler aux hommes un dieu sans corps, ni figure ni couleur, qu'il fallait adorer en esprit et en vérité, le romantisme en ce sens, est la poésie de l'intelligence; tandis que, fondée sur un culte tout matériel, offrant à l'adoration des hommes des dieux de chair et d'os, la poésie antique peut être regardée comme la poésie des sens. Enchaînée au présent, limitée dans sa durée, l'une était la poésie

[36] *Ibid.*, pp. lxix-l.
[37] *Ibid.*, p. lxxxv.

de la jouissance et du moment: l'autre est celle de l'espérance et de
l'avenir. Mais l'homme est à la fois composé de matière et d'intelligence.
En lui se trouvent deux êtres que le poète romantique appelle à la fois
à la contemplation de l'infini, de l'éternité, de tous les mystères de l'autre
vie: l'être doué de l'immortalité, et l'être périssable et matériel. Et voilà
pourquoi le romantisme, spirituel dans l'objet de ses chants, est matériel
dans l'expression dont il les revêt.[38]

We begin to perceive a basic difference in the way in which the
Neoclassics and the Romantics use the terms "real" and "ideal." The
Neoclassic says that the universe is real and imbued with meaning;
it contains or veils the ideal, which is an archetype of beauty, that
perfection to which we all aspire. Art, which communicates the meaning of the universe, is also called ideal (*le beau idéal des formes*). The
Romantic says that the universe is real and imbued with meaning
(I do not here include the illuminist view that the phenomenal universe
is only a reflection or an emblem of the higher spiritual realm, the
ideal which is the true reality). The conception in the artist's mind
is ideal (it is an idea), and the work of art is real and concrete. Romanticism is essentially spiritualist and Christian, says Desmarais; its so-
called materialism is only in its imagery.[39]

In a general way, the dominant spiritualist philosophy, reinforced
by a revival of Platonism on one hand and Christian inspiration on
the other, combine to encourage these changes in direction or emphasis: 1. The ideal exists in the spiritual realm and in the conception of the work of art rather than in the work itself. 2. Formal beauty, *le beau visible*, in art has diminished in importance, opening the
way to a more expressive form of art, even the ugly. 3. The work
of art is no longer primarily an imitation of sensible reality. 4. If the
form is a direct and faithful expression of the idea, then the real and
the ideal are closely joined.

Such is the new poetry conceived and proclaimed by the young
Romantics at the *Muse Française*: "... la poésie, âme de tout ce qui
doit vivre, réunion sublime de l'idéal et du réel, en un mot expression plutôt qu'imitation de la nature: car une copie, quelque exacte
qu'elle soit, ne rend pas la nature, si l'imagination n'a point pénétré
dans son esprit."[40] The ideal contains the real, it is "la matière soumise

---

[38] *Ibid.*, pp. lxxx-lxxxi.
[39] *Essai*, pp. 102, 118, 119.
[40] A. Guiraud, "Nos Doctrines," Marsan ed. (Paris: Cornély, 1907), II, 15.

à l'idee" (A. Garnier, quoted above), or "les croyances intimes de l'homme manifestées au dehors."[41] In the latter case the ideal is the poetic element within the writer which finds outer expression.

It is at this same time, during the 1820s, that the fantastic begins to lay claim to a place among artistic categories. Many of the arguments advanced by its partisans relate it to accepted values and criteria. The *merveilleux*, an accepted element of Classical literature, continues to have its place beside the ideal as a domain which lies beyond imitation. In a dialogue published in the *Mercure de France* in 1816, Lourdoueix assigns the *merveilleux* particularly to poetry: "Moi je soutins qu'on ne devait jamais s'unir à [la nature] que pour l'épurer et l'ennoblir; que l'idéal était l'âme des beaux-arts, et qu'il n'était pas de véritable poésie sans le merveilleux..."[42] He also follows Chateaubriand in disapproving of pagan myths, but he spiritualizes the marvelous even more than his great predecessor. According to *Le Génie du christianisme,*

> Chez les Grecs, le ciel finissait au sommet de l'Olympe, et leurs dieux ne s'élevaient pas plus haut que les vapeurs de la terre. Le *merveilleux* chrétien, d'accord avec la raison, les sciences et l'expansion de notre âme, s'enfonce de monde en monde, d'univers en univers, dans des espaces où l'imagination effrayée frissonne et recule. (II.iv.3)

Lourdoueix argues that pagan myths have impoverished our imagination by giving concrete form to our ideas. On the contrary, the modern soul is charmed by vague forms and attracted by the strange, the marvelous, the fantastic.

> Outre les sens extérieurs,... nous avons intérieurement une faculté de concevoir, qui est le plus noble attribut de notre âme; c'est une espèce d'instinct qui nous porte aux notions d'un monde intellectuel, dont nous ferons un jour partie; c'est par là que nous arrivent les idées du sur-naturel et du merveilleux; ces idées tiennent essentiellement à ce qu'il y a de plus noble en nous: pourquoi donc les abâtardir et les dégrader, en les revêtant de nos chaînes terrestres?

For a critic of the *Archives Philosophiques,* man gives to the fantastic or marvelous beings of any kind which he creates, a part in his own destiny.

[41] "De *La Confession...*" *Revue Française,* 15 (1830), 63.
[42] "Petite Débauche romantique," 25 May 1816, quoted in Eggli and Martino, *Le Débat romantique,* pp. 462-63.

[Ces créatures] ont été pour lui un moyen d'étendre son existence, de multiplier, dans le temps et dans l'espace, le nombre des points où il y avait quelque chose à aimer ou à craindre, quelqu'espérance à chérir, quelqu'intérêt à soigner, quelque portion de vie enfin à exercer hors de lui-même, tant il est vrai que l'homme ne réside pas tout entier dans l'individu, mais qu'il se sent vivre partout où il porte et unit son âme et sa pensée.[43]

Thus imaginary creatures open up to us the limitless reaches of any conceivable universe.

Quatremère de Quincy deals briefly with the *merveilleux* in the context of epic poetry. If generalization, the traditional means of idealizing, simplifies and concentrates in the least possible volume, transformation or transposition, the other means by which genius operates, is a kind of metaphorical recomposition. The marvelous, says Quatremère, is the most powerful agent of transposition. Human beings are also transformed by contact with the imaginary or the superhuman. In Quatremère's theory, the marvelous takes its place beside other ways of assuring the fictional character of literature, such as choosing subjects distant in time or space.[44]

In 1827 a critic of *Le Globe* links fairy stories of the past to religion, in that the *féerie* was the counterpart of Christianity in social life and played the first role in the world of poetry. He relates it to Romance languages and thinks it would be natural to attach it to recent works of Romantic literature.[45]

Thus by its links to literary tradition, to the ideal, and to religion, the marvelous retains a favored place among artistic modes. But when the imaginary or the supernatural takes other forms, it loses support among the critics. Baron Massias, for example, sounds very uncompromising: "L'art n'avoue point comme son oeuvre les rêves et les chimères et il répudie tout ce qui ne tourne pas au profit de l'intelligence."[46] Cyprien Anot, who stresses the religious character of Romanticism, rejects the spooky décor of the Gothic which some have tried to present as Romantic.[47] The diabolical and the *frénétique* find few defenders.

---

[43] Review of Lamotte-Fouqué, *Ondine*, 2 (1817), 220.
[44] *L'Imitation*, pp. 274, 277, 324-27.
[45] H., review of *Lettres sur les Contes de fées attribués à Perrault sur l'origine de la féerie*, 11 Jan. 1827.
[46] *Théorie du beau*, p. 245.
[47] *Essai sur les nouvelles théories littéraires*, in *Elégies rhémoises* (Paris: Amyot, 1825), p. 186.

Nicolas Artaud, however, accepts all manifestations of our belief in the invisible, religious or superstitious, divine or demonic, which have figured so largely in our past history:

> Douée d'une vertu créatrice, [la faculté religieuse ou superstitieuse] enfanta les dieux des antiques mythologies, personnifia les forces de la nature, anima les astres, mit les fleuves, les sombres forêts sous la garde de quelque génie tutélaire: ce fut elle encore qui, au moyen âge, peupla de démons et de fées les donjons, les vieux châteaux, asiles de la féodalité, les antiques manoirs de ces barons qui répandaient la terreur autour d'eux, et toutes ces créations fantastiques que la superstition avait si fort enracinées dans nos croyances.[48]

He deplores the fact that this faculty, which is an important part of poetic talent, is retreating before the advances of science, and he welcomes the reappearance of the *merveilleux* in the romances of Walter Scott.

The master romancer himself wrote an article in defense of the *merveilleux*, which was published in the newborn *Revue de Paris*. He, too, linked the marvelous to religion. As the best way of reviving it in contemporary literature, he recommended not exaggerating marvelous incidents in novels, as some had done unsuccessfully, but digging up old traditions and ballads. Though he praises Lamotte-Fouqué's *Ondine* and accepts *Le Diable amoureux* and *Trilby*, he cannot approve of the new fantastic genre from Germany, on the grounds that the writers let their imaginations run so wild that the reader can see nothing in their novels but bizarre and absurd tricks.[49]

But some French writers are willing to go farther than Scott. Duvergier de Hauranne protests against those who make fun of the supernatural of the Germans while accepting the classical *merveilleux*.[50] He seems to have a taste for the diabolical and for the "fantômes invisibles" which surround us and which he sees as a necessary enrichment for the poet. These "délégués du mal" are superior dramatic agents, and the Romantic poet has the great advantage of being able to draw upon evocation of the dead, magic, charms, and all sorts of Gothic superstitions to impress us with the presence of evil. "Placé

---

[48] *Essai littéraire sur le génie poétique au 19e siècle* (Paris: Rignoux, 1825), p. 6; reprinted from *Revue Encyclopédique*, 25 (1825), 601-19.
[49] 1 (1829), 25-33.
[50] "Du Robin des bois," signed O., *Le Globe*, 8 Feb. 1825.

au milieu de tous ces êtres, le poète étend son sceptre sur les deux mondes."[51] Thus the modern demoniac supernatural, like the traditional *merveilleux*, enlarges the poet's domain, which according to Audin, should include everything from the contemplation of the divine to the bloodcurdling to vulgar familiar reality.

Nodier, who was better qualified than anyone to speak of the supernatural, like others linked it to a venerable tradition. The history of the supernatural tale goes back to the most ancient times and belongs to all countries, for a penchant for the marvelous is innate in all men. "Il est l'instrument essentiel de sa vie imaginative, et peut-être même est-il la seule compensation vraiment providentielle des misères inséparables de la vie sociale."[52] Not only does Nodier follow this tradition in its various developments, he also relates it to the state of the society in which it flourishes. In 1819 he affects to deplore the current taste for vampires:

> L'idéal des poètes primitifs et des poètes classiques, leurs élégants imitateurs, était placé dans les perfections de notre nature. Celui des poètes romantiques est dans nos misères. Ce n'est pas un défaut de l'art, c'est un effet nécessaire des progrès de notre perfectionnement social. On sait où nous en sommes en politique; en poésie nous en sommes au *cauchemar* et aux *vampires*.[53]

In his important article, "Du fantastique en littérature" (1830), Nodier uses the word "fantastique" to emcompass all supernatural phenomena but groups them in various classes. In tracing the history of the fantastic, he assigns to it one of the three worlds frequented by men from ancient times:

> De ces trois opérations successives, celle du génie divinement inspiré qui avait deviné le monde spirituel, celle de l'imagination, qui avait créé le monde fantastique, se composa le vaste empire de la pensée humaine.[54]

Like the other two realms, the fantastic finds its culminating point in God. Etymologically, the word "superstition," i.e., "science des

---

[51] "Du romantique," pp. lx, lxiii.

[52] *Oeuvres*, 12 vols. (Paris: Renduel, 1832-1837), V, 102; originally published in *Revue de Paris*, 20 (1830), 205-26.

[53] Article on translation of *Le Vampire* by Byron (actually by Polidori), *Mélanges de littérature et de critique* (Paris: Raymond, 1820), I, 412.

[54] *Oeuvres*, V, 72.

choses élevées," retains its high place in human knowledge as a kind of adjunct to religion. This he calls the "fantastique religieux," of solemn and somber character. Purely rational man is at the bottom of the scale. As for the poet, he has his place on the second step from the top, in "la région moyenne du fantastique et de l'idéal." The "fantastique purement poétique" borrows magic and miracles from the fairies and beautifies the world. As for the horrible and the grotesque, for which many contemporary authors have a predilection, they may claim ancient models of the highest quality. "La descente du roi d'Itaque [Odysseus] aux enfers rappelle, sous des proportions gigantesques et admirablement idéalisées, les goules et les vampires des fables levantines, que la savante critique des modernes reproche à notre nouvelle école..."[55] (In the 1832 preface to *Smarra*, Nodier tells us that the Odyssey is "du fantastique sérieux.")

According to Nodier the fantastic flourishes when societies are in their infancy or on their deathbed. It seems to preside at the beginning of a new historical cycle. This rise and fall can be seen in antiquity, where after Homer, it declined until it was briefly revived by Lucian and Apuleius. After flourishing again in the Middle Ages, encouraged by the Moorish invasion, it faded away with the Renaissance, especially after the invention of printing, with a few isolated exceptions (Dante, Ariosto, Shakespeare, Perrault). We might hold Cervantes responsible for destroying the fantasies of the preceding centuries, says Nodier, but in fact the fables had grown old and it was time for a change and a new start for social life. It was natural that new generations of writers should hold past centuries in derision. The French became so accustomed to imitation that they forgot their own rich heritage.

> Nos fées bienfaisantes à la baguette de fer ou de coudrier, nos fées rébarbatives et hargneuses à l'attelage de chauve-souris, nos princesses tout aimables et toutes gracieuses, nos princes avenants et lutins, nos ogres stupides et féroces, nos pourfendeurs de géants, les charmantes métamorphoses de l'Oiseau bleu, les miracles du Rameau d'Or, appartiennent à notre vieille Gaule comme son ciel, ses moeurs et ses monuments trop longtemps méconnus.[56]

The post-Napoleonic period, a time of decadence or transition, has brought the fantastic back to popularity, which has been a good thing, since

---

[55] *Ibid.*, V, 72-73, 77.
[56] *Ibid.*, V, 99-100.

Nous devons même reconnaître en cela un bienfait spontané de notre organisation; car si l'esprit humain ne se complaisait encore dans de vives et brillantes chimères, quand il a touché à nu toutes les repoussantes réalités du monde vrai, cette époque de désabusement serait en proie au plus violent désespoir, et la société offrirait la révélation effrayante d'un besoin unanime de dissolution et de suicide. Il ne faut pas tant crier contre le romantisme et contre le fantastique. Ces innovations prétendues sont l'expression inévitable des périodes extrêmes de la vie politique des nations, et sans elles, je sais à peine ce qui nous resterait aujourd'hui de l'instinct moral et intellectuel de l'humanité.[57]

Rather than being corrupting and unworthy, Nodier tells us, this literature is what saves us. The richest source for the fantastic is the dream, and though in 1820 Nodier seems critical of the horrible and nightmarish, "ce genre de drame et d'épopée qui n'a point de modèle dans l'imagination des hommes éveillés,"[58] his own *Smarra* (1821), belies this attitude, and by 1830 he is openly committed to the genre. In *La Fée aux miettes* he wishes to study "le mystère des influences des illusions du sommeil sur la vie solitaire."[59] In the new preface to *Smarra* (1832) he reaffirms his belief in the dream as the spring of the *fantastique moderne*; the waking poet has not often enough drawn upon the fantasies of the sleeping poet.[60]

Such is Nodier's contribution to the theory of the fantastic at the period of its greatest popularity, around 1830. In the years following he will make even broader claims for the dream, not just that it nourishes the life of the imagination amidst the poverty of *la vie positive* but it has given rise to civilized social organization.[61]

Aside from the essays and prefaces of Nodier, the most interesting commentary on the fantastic at this period, is to be found in the articles appearing in *Le Globe* on the occasion of the publication of Hoffmann's *Tales* in France. As all students of the genre know, these tales were a revelation of what the true fantastic was. If Nodier had placed its best source in the dream, Duvergier de Hauranne found it not only there but in certain bizarre waking moments and especially

---

[57] *Ibid.*, V, 78-79.

[58] *Mélanges*, I, 413.

[59] Préface, *Contes*, Classiques Garnier (Paris: Garnier, 1961), p. 171.

[60] *Ibid.*, p. 38.

[61] "Le Pays de rêves," *Contes de la veillée* (Paris: Fasquelle, 1875), p. 215. See Roger Bozzetto, "Nodier et la théorie du fantastique," *Europe*, nos. 614-15 (1980), pp. 70-78.

in the area on the edge of sleep. Hoffmann halts the floating forms of this state of half-sleep and draws the figures.[62] What particularly struck both this critic and Jean-Jacques Ampère was the extent to which the German fantastic (which they more often called "merveilleux") was attached to ordinary daily life. Thus Ampère's remarks on Tieck: "Ce qui fait la puissance de ce merveilleux, c'est qu'il n'a rien de fantasmagorique et de puéril, qu'il est toujours lié à un sentiment vrai et profond de ce que les événements humains ont de mystérieux et pour ainsi dire de surnaturel."[63] We pass easily from a real to a fantastic world. And in Hoffmann, what grips us are the presentiments and strange events which happen to us, what Ampère calls "le merveilleux naturel." Or as Duvergier de Hauranne describes it,

> Supposez un récit naturellement enchaîné, des caractères finement tracés, des incidents réels et vraisemblables, en un mot une peinture spirituelle, touchante, de la vie humaine, de la vie bourgeoise surtout; puis, au milieu de tout cela, non de communes apparitions, ni des prodiges vulgaires, mais quelques merveilles bien neuves, bien inattendues, tantôt bouffonnes, plus souvent terribles, mais qui, terribles ou bouffonnes, font frissonner et pâlir.[64]

Only Cazotte's *Le Diable amoureux* can compare with Hoffmann in France, say both critics, passing over Nodier without a word. When you read Hoffmann, says Duvergier de Hauranne, you don't know if it is truth or fiction, and the author himself was sometimes not sure. It is magnetism in particular which occupies this shifting ground.

> Là vraiment se trouvent des faits, des faits incontestables et que la science humaine n'a pu encore expliquer; là disparaît en quelque sorte la limite qui sépare le naturel et le surnaturel, les lois de ce monde et celles d'un monde supérieur; là par conséquent existe une mine de vives émotions et un champ sans bornes pour l'imagination.

Jean-Jacques Ampère emphasizes the element of madness in these tales. Cazotte was thought to be a little mad, and Hoffmann was frightened by his own stories while writing them. "La liaison même du récit, son allure simple et naturelle, a quelque chose d'effrayant

---

[62] Review of *Contes fantastiques, Le Globe,* 26 Dec. 1829.
[63] Review of *Deux nouvelles et une pièce tirées des Oeuvres de L. Tieck,* 17 June 1829.
[64] 26 Dec. 1829.

qui rappelle le délire tranquille et sérieux des fous."[65] The bizarre and the terrible come out of everyday events. What better reunion of the real and the unreal? The *merveilleux* is set apart from reality but the new fantastic is incorporated into it.

[65] Review of *Aus Hoffmanns Leben und Nachlass*, 2 Aug. 1828.

8. The Real and the Ideal (II)

The 1820s are a time of growing preoccupation with reality in art, which many, especially its partisans, call "truth." Obviously, this is a different truth from that of the Neoclassics. These two words, "la réalité" and "la vérité," along with "le positif" appear with increasing frequency in the critical writing of the Restoration. Popular taste had always been more favorable to naturalistic representation than the critics, and the latter are, for the most part, reluctant to accept it. Even the most "advanced" critics have strong reservations, as we shall see. But the arts seem to be moving toward naturalism; the decline of the Davidian school in painting, the influence of English painters, and the vogue of Scott's historical novel are factors that push them toward naturalism. "Ce qui caractérise éminemment notre époque, c'est l'amour de la réalité," says Thiers in 1824.[1] The "besoin du vrai" is "le trait de caractère du siècle," says Le Globe.[2] As early as 1817 the *doctrinaire Archives Philosophiques* found that reality in fiction (the critic used "réalités," in the plural) was suitable to the seriousness of the times.[3] But it is in 1824, the year of the founding of Le Globe, that the word "réalité" begins to appear with noticeable frequency, particularly there and in some other liberal publications. The following year Sainte-Beuve speaks of "*ce besoin presque unanime de vérité qui se*

---

[1] *Revue Européenne*, 1:36; quoted in Pontus Grate, *Deux critiques d'art de l'époque romantique* (Stockholm: Almquist and Wiksell, 1959), p. 35.

[2] "*Etudes de littérature populaire* de Walter Scott et de Fauriel," 21 Sept. 1824.

[3] Review of Jebediah Cleishbotham [Walter Scott], *The Tales of My Landlord*, etc., *Les Puritains d'Ecosse* et *Le Nain mystérieux, Contes de mon hôte*, II, 25-26.

proclame hautement dans les arts de notre époque."[4] Again, Thiers: "La peinture participe au mouvement général des esprits... et le *goût de la vérité* s'y fait sentir comme au théâtre, comme en musique, comme partout."[5]

This "reality" can mean historical authenticity, a photographic eye, depiction of details, correctness of line, or naturalness of color. Perhaps most importantly, it means a wide choice of subject matter, from historical or present times, from any place or social milieu. This is a *nature* distinctly not *choisie*, but wide open: "L'art doit être libre et libre de la façon la plus illimitée," says Thiers. "Tout ce qui fait partie de l'univers, depuis l'objet le plus élevé jusqu'au plus bas, depuis la céleste Madone *di Sisto* jusqu'aux ivrognes flamands, est digne de figurer dans nos imitations puisque la nature l'a jugé digne de figurer dans ses oeuvres."[6] This sounds like the Hugo of 1827, but Thiers adds a precaution as to manner:

> La seule précaution à prendre, c'est de ne pas vouloir faire produire à un objet une impression qui appartient à un autre. Ne veuillez pas composer la tragédie avec des visages ignobles, de la bure et des sabots, mais faites avec cela des *farces*; et si elles sont comiques, spirituelles et vraies, vous aurez rempli l'un des mille objets que l'art doit se proposer.

Such a widening horizon is seen first of all in painting and is most readily accepted in the portrait, genre painting, and landscape, where naturalistic representation was traditionally more characteristic. E.-J. Delécluze attributes the popularity of genre painting to the fact that people like "la vérité," that is, an exact resemblance, to which the Davidian critic hardly concedes even a "beauté relative."[7] Thiers, on the other hand, favors genre painting because it is "celle où nous pouvons déployer le plus de vrai génie, parce que c'est celle où il nous est permis de peindre d'après nature et de rendre nos impressions personnelles."[8] Exact representation is not just mechanical copying but gives the artist the opportunity to express his own view of the world; he is freed from the conventions of history painting. Thiers also likes genre painting because it is accessible to and enjoyed by a wide public, not just an elite. Likewise, Arnold Scheffer saw in the

---

[4] "Petite Revue littéraire," *Le Globe*, 28 Dec. 1825.
[5] "Exposition de 1824," *Le Globe*, 26 Sept. 1824, signed Y—.
[6] *Le Globe*, 24 Oct. 1824.
[7] *Lycée Français*, 2, 236 (1819).
[8] *Constitutionnel* of 21 Sept. 1824, reprinted in *Salon de 1824*, p. 61.

development of genre painting a sign of the democratization of French society, in that the ordinary life and concerns of the common people could be an interesting subject for art.[9]

Landscape painting, which like genre painting has been relatively free of Neoclassic idealism, begins to come into its own during the Restoration, with strong help from the English, in particular Constable and Bonington, whose paintings were a sensation at the 1824 Salon. According to Thiers, the French landscape painters are inferior to the English and Dutch because they do not stay close enough to nature.[10] The Dutch and the English have not dreamed of a better world, unlike the French, who, not satisfied with their own land, are always going to Italy or Switzerland to look for beauty. Ludovic Vitet, who became art critic for *Le Globe* after Thiers, was what we might call a moderate liberal in matters of art. He finds that landscape painting, for all its relative independence of the *beau idéal*, has exhibited the same general tendencies as other types of painting: the expressiveness of the eighteenth century, the purity of line of the Davidian era, and now "la vérité de l'imitation." He fears, however, that this new tendency will be carried to excess, that painters will choose to depict any old shack or whatever is in front of them on the road.[11] According to P. Grate, "vérité" wins out definitively in the Salon of 1831.[12]

Though Stendhal's preferences lie with the *beau idéal* of Raphael and Correggio, he expresses great esteem for what he calls "*peintres-miroirs*." He explains better than anyone else the charm of those landscape paintings which reproduce nature exactly enough to make him react as he would to a real landscape. He seems to enter into the painting. "On se sent tout à coup plongé dans une rêverie profonde, comme à la vue des bois et de *leur vaste silence*. On songe avec profondeur à ses plus chères illusions; bientôt on en jouit comme de réalités... Voilà les sentiments que me donne une promenade solitaire dans une véritable forêt."[13] Whereas only the greatest painters can succeed in the *beau idéal*, lesser talents may perform very creditably in naturalistic painting or literature. A great virtue of this kind of art, says Stendhal, is that it may reveal aspects of reality of which the artist himself

---

[9] Quoted in Pontus Grate, *Deux critiques d'art*, p. 36.
[10] *Constitutionnel*, 18 Sept. 1824.
[11] "Exposition des tableaux au profit des Grecs (III)," *Le Globe*, 24 June 1826.
[12] *Deux critiques d'art*, p. 81.
[13] *Racine et Shakespeare*, p. 258.

is not aware: "La nature a des aspects singuliers, des contrastes sublimes; ils peuvent rester inconnus au *miroir* qui les reproduit, sans en avoir la conscience." When Thiers says that he who paints after nature can best express his personal impressions, he is stressing the freedom of the artist; Stendhal, always the psychologist, has touched upon the more mysterious inner world, the unconscious.

In his articles on the 1824 Salon, originally published in the *Journal de Paris*, Stendhal responds to the "truth" in landscape painting. He greatly admires Constable's *Hay Wain*, though with some reservations. "La vérité saisit d'abord et entraîne... La négligence du pinceau de M. Constable est outrée, et les plans de ses tableaux ne sont pas bien observés, d'ailleurs il n'a aucun idéal; mais son délicieux paysage, avec un chien à gauche, est le miroir de la nature..."[14] Despite his admiration, he cannot help wishing that Constable had treated a more grandiose subject.[15] This is far from the "âpre vérité" of the epigraph to *Le Rouge et le noir*. As Georges Blin has pointed out, his praise for direct imitation is largely an attack on Academism.[16] He mocks the formulas of David's school unmercifully,[17] and prefers "la vérité trop crue" (as in Scheffer's *Mort de Gaston de Foix*) to "l'abus du style" (those pictures that are like frozen theatrical scenes); the raw truth is the lesser of two evils.

For Stendhal a good likeness of persons or places is just a point of departure toward higher expressive values.[18] The truth that counts is "*la vérité dans les sentiments du coeur.*" He responds to the *pathétique* of the *tableau de genre*, and if the subject of a painting moves him, he forgets all about drawing, color and chiaroscuro.[19] Before the supposedly nobler types of painting, his response is both emotional and esthetic and he recommends classic moderation. "Il y a une belle femme noyée dans le *Déluge* de M. Girodet qui m'a toujours fait le plus vif plaisir; c'est qu'elle est fort belle, et la beauté ôte l'*horreur* à ma sensation: il ne me reste que de la douleur noble et *un peu consolée*, la seule que les *beaux-arts* doivent chercher à produire."[20]

---

[14] *Mélanges*, III, 47.

[15] *Ibid.*, III, 54.

[16] *Stendhal et les problèmes du roman* (Paris: Corti, 1954), p. 22.

[17] See his funny, and outrageous, article of 12 Sept. 1824, reprinted in *Mélanges*, III, 25-29.

[18] G. Blin has summarized this aspect of Stendhal's thought, pp. 21-34.

[19] *Mélanges*, III, 31.

[20] *Ibid.*, III, 36.

As Stendhal's comment attests, exact representation was less readily accepted in "la grande peinture," that with historical and religious subjects; here the *classiques* stood fast and the moderates, though they liked the subjects, often disapproved of the manner of execution. In 1827 David's *Les Sabines* still has many defenders, including a critic of the *Revue Encyclopédique*, who defends Neoclassic truth in art: David wished to paint a *tableau d'histoire*, says he, so what he had to paint was not the scene as it must have taken place, if it did take place, but rather "les circonstances extraordinaires, le grandiose, le merveilleux."[21] The *tableau d'histoire* is to painting what the epic poem is in literature. "Servile" imitation should be found only in genre painting. "Le peintre d'histoire doit, au contraire, rendre, [par ses inventions et par le caractère de son dessin], les impressions, les idées les plus nobles, les plus poétiques, que la vue de la scène, la connaissance de ses causes et de ses résultats auraient pu réveiller dans l'esprit d'un spectateur éclairé." "Eclairé," not "naïf." The truth of a familiar scene can immediately be grasped, but not that of a great historical event, which must be rendered coherent by the painter. As we see, Neoclassic intelligibility is still indispensable in this type of art, and changes will be most difficult to make here.[22] Delécluze, for example, unlike those who insist on authentic details in a battle scene, prefers the *idea* of a battle. On the other hand, Stendhal remarked, a propos of *Les Sabines*, how absurd it really is for soldiers to engage in combat in the nude.[23]

As for sculpture, the critics seemed to have changed few of their ideas about it in the last thirty years, and there is still a distinct difference between what they expect of sculpture and of painting. The taste for reality has not extended to sculpture, which, according to L. Vitet, is the least popular of the arts in France during the 1820s.

> Si nos jeunes peintres d'aujourd'hui montrent quelque dédain pour la pureté des formes, s'ils courent de préférence après l'expression et la naïve imitation de la nature, il faut les laisser faire; mais il faut tâcher qu'à côté d'eux s'élèvent des sculpteurs qui sans s'inquiéter de leurs idées, s'attachent avec rigueur à la perfection des formes et à cette régularité de contours qui est la première loi de leur art.[24]

[21] J.-R. A., "Quelques vues sur l'école de David, et sur les principes historiques," 24 (1827), 586.

[22] *L'Artiste*, I (1830), 2.

[23] *Mélanges*, III, 14.

[24] Review of Clarac, *Musée de sculpture ancienne et moderne*, *Le Globe*, 25 July 1826. Cf. this comment from the *Annales de la Littérature et des Arts*: "...la peinture, plus

As this comment testifies, Neoclassicism maintains its hold on sculpture, which lags by about ten years behind the new movement in painting; it will come to life in the Salon of 1833.[25] Stendhal too is concerned about the future of sculpture; it is not of excessive realism that he complains, but rather of exaggerated expression. He holds to his old idea that sculpture should depict only "les habitudes de l'âme," eschewing ephemeral passions; sculptors should not depart from "cette *modestie raphaelesque*, de cette *tranquillité* des statuaires grecs sans laquelle il n'y a rien de sublime en sculpture."[26] What could be done to increase public interest in sculpture? It can be accomplished by avoiding theatricality, which is even worse in sculpture than in painting, says he, and by following the example of the Greek sculptors, not by copying their works, but "en choisissant, comme les sculpteurs grecs parmi les traits que présente la nature, en choisissant ce qui peut nous toucher au dix-neuvième siecle..."[27]

Quatremère de Quincy steadfastly maintains his opposition to naturalistic representation, which results in "le désenchantement de la réalité, substitué au charme de l'imitation."[28] Every poet and painter has two models, of which one is the soul of the other (as Cousin spoke of two beauties, one the expression of the other). He distinguishes a "vérité de réalité" for the senses and a "vérité d'abstraction" for the mind.[29] This "vérité de réalité" is quite unlike what others call "la vérité toute crue."

Though it is acknowledged that each person has a slightly different view from everyone else, there is a central agreed-upon reality common to all. What is chiefly under discussion is what aspects of this reality are suitable content for art, where to look for meaning, and how to convey it in the work of art.

The principal objection aimed at the current depiction of reality in the beaux-arts, not only by the *classiques* but also by the moderate Romantics, such as the *Globe* writers, is that it is ugly. The most frequent protests come from Etienne Delécluze, who was a moderate

---

variée dans ses effets, et forcée d'en produire un plus grand nombre, que la sculpture, a pu, jusqu'à un certain point, négliger le beau idéal, pour s'en tenir à l'imitation de la nature positive, mais toujours plus ou moins choisie... ." Especially in sculpture, minute and "servile" imitation should be avoided, says the critic P— (VII [1822], 200).

[25] See R. Baschet, *E.-J. Delécluze*, p. 265.

[26] *Mélanges*, III, 65.

[27] *Ibid.*, III, 86.

[28] *L'Imitation*, p. 104.

[29] *Ibid.*, pp. 212-13.

Classic. Robert Baschet tells us that he was particularly sensitive to visual beauty and that ugliness became his *bête noire*.[30] A brief reading among his articles (chiefly in the *Journal des Débats* during the 1820s), his Journal and his books amply verifies this: "C'est une vérité incontestable que, dans un art comme la peinture, où les dix-neuf vingtièmes du plaisir qu'il nous donne sont communiqués par la vue, il faut ménager cet organe [l'oeil]."[31] He adversely criticizes a painter who has chosen to depict "la vérité abjecte" of poverty and ugliness. In another article on the 1824 Salon, he chides the young generation of painters: "La recherche de la vérité exacte et démontrée est le défaut que la nouvelle Ecole de peinture doit redouter."[32] He attributes this system of exact imitation to the influence of current literary doctrines. Among the arts, says Delécluze, only music is holding to standards of beauty. Years later, in his *Souvenirs de soixante années* he will lay much of the responsibility on the writers of *Le Globe*:

> Les questions de tout genre passaient par la coupelle d'une théorie assez abstraite, et grâce à un éclectisme qui permettait d'admettre le laid auprès du beau, sous prétexte que dans la nature l'ombre opposée à la lumière donne plus de relief et d'éclat aux formes, les beaux-arts, en vertu de cette doctrine complaisante, étaient poussés dans la voie du réel qui, aujourd'hui, est devenu cette monstruosité que l'on nomme *réalisme*.[33]

It is true that the eclecticism of Cousin was the dominant doctrine at *Le Globe* in the middle 1820s; it led this group to try to find a middle ground between *classiques* and the *romantiques* of the Cénacle. But their stance is not what Delécluze remembered. Though Thiers sometimes made statements urging liberty and innovation, such as that quoted earlier in this chapter, he invariably pulled back to a moderate stand, and Vitet was even more moderate, not to say conservative. He reproached Delacroix with having "sacrificed art to reality" and gone too far toward the vulgar (*trivial*) and ignoble; the senators in *Marino Faliero*, says Vitet, are so ugly that they are grotesque.[34] Charles Magnin sounds like a true middle-of-the-roader:

> Longtemps les poètes soi-disant classiques et les peintres académiques nous ont donné pour beaux des ouvrages où le vrai manquait si ab-

---

[30] *Etienne Delécluze*, pp. 164, 271.
[31] *Journal des Débats*, 8 Sept. 1824.
[32] 9 Oct. 1824.
[33] *Souvenirs de soixante années* (Paris: Michel Lévy Frères, 1862), p. 264.
[34] *Le Globe*, 3 June 1826.

solument, qu'ils nous ont obligés à rappeler de toutes nos forces le vrai, banni de la poésie et des arts. Mais il ne s'ensuit pas que l'imitation du vrai seule soit un but d'artiste. Les scènes qui blessent la pudeur... blessent un sentiment naturel, le laid et l'horrible en blessent un autre.[35]

He does, however, admit the ugly and the atrocious into art, not as an end but as a means, as in Greek tragedy and Shakespeare; like Lessing, he draws the line at the visual arts.

Stendhal too complains of the ugliness of contemporary painting; of the 1824 Salon he says, "Jamais le laid n'a été en aussi grand honneur que dans la présente exposition."[36] He is repelled by the dead and dying Greeks in the *Massacre de Scio* who, says he, look like plague victims. But here the ugly is not equated with the real but comes rather from "l'exagération du triste et du sombre."[37] Like Magnin, he sees the depiction of the ugly and the repelling as an excessive swing of the pendulum away from the academic: "Mais le public est tellement ennuyé du genre académique et des copies de statues si à la mode il y a dix ans, qu'il s'arrête devant ces cadavres livides et à demi terminés que nous offre le tableau de M. Delacroix." We see here what we may note in many criticisms, that the ugliness lies not just in the subject but in the technique of the painting. Others speak of gaudy colors and incorrect drawing; they miss the smoothness of academic painting. Stendhal, though more open-minded than most, is not ready for such loose brushwork, though he recommends "le pinceau heurté de Salvator Rosa" to depict a hideous character.[38] He does appreciate the expressive powers of execution, but lags behind some painters of the 1820s. Such comments as those of Stendhal are exceptional. As P. Grate points out, almost no one grasped the relationship between expressivity of subject and expressivity of execution; in the name of truth and verisimilitude they condemned what they saw as sketchiness, incorrect drawing, and clashing colors.[39]

Some others besides Stendhal find that ugliness is the result not only of a too-faithful depiction of some unattractive aspects of reality but, as before, may come from an excess of expressiveness. Guizot's complaint of 1810 is reiterated, but the change in the object of the

---

[35] *Le Globe*, 26 July 1827.
[36] *Mélanges*, III, 41.
[37] *Ibid.*, III, 12.
[38] *Ibid.*, III, 35.
[39] *Deux critiques d'art*, p. 39.

criticism (from Girodet's *La Révolte du Caire* to Delacroix's *Le Massacre de Scio*) shows how painting has changed in fifteen years. Painters are now less timid about showing ugliness, and conservative critics object to it more and more. The time now comes when Hugo openly proclaims its place in art, but many refuse to follow him. In 1829 Duvergier de Hauranne, one of the regulars at *Le Globe*, has this view of the changes that have recently taken place: a few years ago, says he, what was lacking in works of art was reality; it was summoned, and it came and invaded everything.

> Il est tout simple que, sans repousser la réalité, on veuille aujourd'hui lui associer l'idéal. Il y a quelques années, préoccupés d'une idée abstraite, d'une forme immuable du beau, peintres et poètes négligeaient l'expression. On a appelé l'expression, et bientôt elle a introduit le laid. Il est tout naturel que, sans bannir l'expression, on la prie aujourd'hui de mettre le laid à la porte.[40]

The taste for reality is as evident in literature as in painting, and here too the response to faithful depiction of the real world is mixed. The word "réalisme" dates, as far as I know, from 1826, when it is proposed in *Le Mercure du 19e Siècle*, a periodical now turning toward Romanticism, to describe not just naturalistic representation but the rejection of imitation of artistic models:

> Cette doctrine littéraire qui gagne tous les jours du terrain et qui conduirait à une fidèle imitation, non pas des chefs-d'oeuvres de l'art, mais des originaux que nous offre la nature, pourrait fort bien s'appeler le *réalisme*; ce serait, suivant quelques apparences, la littérature dominante du dix-neuvième siècle, la littérature du vrai.[41]

Not that all writers of the *Mercure* were favorable to this "réalisme": "Jusqu'ici [le romantisme] a un peu trop sacrifié peut-être le beau au vrai, l'idéal au réel," says one.[42] And another protests against "la réalité textuelle" of some speeches of *Cromwell*.[43] It is not surprising that the illuminist Edouard Richer should complain, "On ne veut que du réel dans l'acception triviale du mot..."[44] Cyprien Desmarais recognizes

[40] "Lettre d'un abonné," *Le Globe*, 15 April 1829. This "letter," as a matter of fact, is principally an answer to Sainte-Beuve's *Joseph Delorme*.
[41] Avant-propos for the 13th volume, 13: 6.
[42] S. M., review of Manzoni, *Les Fiancés*, 20 (1828), 269.
[43] 20 (1828), 37.
[44] *Du genre descriptif* (Nantes: Mellinet-Malassis, Paris: Raynal, 1822), p. 17.

that Romanticism takes its subjects from all of nature, not just a *nature choisie*; he adds, "La poésie romantique... peint les objets tels qu'ils se présentent à l'intelligence humaine; elle est donc pleine de contrastes heurtés, comme la nature."[45] On the other hand, J.-J. Ampère in 1830, while praising the charms of the imaginary worlds of the 1820s, thinks that works with a "cachet de réalité" will be the most successful and the most durable.[46]

Le Globe writers, though they often tempered their remarks with reservations, were among the first to call for reality in literature, as we have seen. Their repeated urging of direct observation, physical or human, was a step in that direction. Their great interest in history is another: it is the literary genre which is the most concerned with the exact truth. When historical subjects are treated in works of literature, critics seem to demand historical accuracy more than in painting, no doubt because of the lingering classical tradition in historical-mythological painting. Historical truth is not only more convincing, says Thiers, it is dramatic and poetic:

> ... le goût de la vérité historique... est l'un des plus nobles penchants de notre époque. L'esprit humain veut être ému aujourd'hui, mais il veut être instruit; il veut la pensée, mais il la cherche dans l'histoire, car le monde réel a sa poésie, et c'est la seule véritable.[47]

Historical truth also makes literature instructive; utilitarian and didactic aims often encroach upon esthetic aims, years before the *saint-simoniens* take over *Le Globe*. It is unlikely that such serious-minded young critics would escape the all-pervasive utilitarianism of the times; at *Le Globe* it was at least leavened by libertarianism. In novels it reached such a point that Philarète Chasles was moved to protest: "Bizarre destinée de la littérature! ce n'est pas comme littérature qu'on l'aime et qu'on la recherche; on ne lui demande qu'une image des réalités de la vie, un répertoire de faits inconnus, de vérités utiles, de leçons éternelles."[48] An image of reality, along with instruction, would appear to be outside of art.

Walter Scott was much admired for the accuracy of his historical depiction; this admiration was not always justified, but the French did not know it at the time. Reading Scott led many people to an

---

[45] *Essai*, pp. 118, 119.
[46] Review of Mérimée, *Théâtre de Clara Gazul*, *National*, 23 Oct. 1830.
[47] "Salon de 1824," *Le Globe*, 26 Sept. 1824.
[48] Review of *Romans* of Vandevelde in *Mercure du 19e Siècle*, 14 (1827), 306.

interest in history and even influenced the writing of history. (A. Thierry paid tribute to Scott's part in the formation of his own perspectives on history.) His novels also appealed to the growing desire for reality, as the *Mercure du 19e Siècle* attested in 1825: "Ce qui peut paraître singulier d'abord, c'est que ce soit un romancier qui le premier ait satisfait au besoin que nous éprouvions tous de voir succéder des tableaux vrais et dégagés de toute personnalité à ces esquisses incomplètes où l'auteur ne montrait les choses que du côté qui flattait son imagination ou ses préjugés."[49] This is to say that the illusion of reality required completeness and impartiality, qualities one could more readily expect of an historian.

For Hugo Scott furnishes a model of historical fidelity and shows what the novel should be by bringing it close to nature. The novelist's aim, says he, is to express a useful truth in an interesting story, and to do this he must find "un mode d'exécution qui rende son roman semblable à la vie, l'imitation pareille au modèle."[50] It is true that Hugo had a very personal view of real life: for him it was a "drame bizarre" (of this more later). The action of the dramatic novel which he envisaged was to unfold in "tableaux vrais et variés, comme se déroulent les événements réels de la vie." Hugo is really more interested in moral truth than historical truth, and the dramatic effect is the most important of all. A novel laid out in dramatic scenes without the intervention of a narrator should give an illusion of reality impossible in first-person or epistolary narrative.

In the midst of the enthusiasm for historical exactitude, Vigny swims against the current, adhering to the classic virtues of "la vérité choisie" and the superiority of general human truth.

> Si donc nous trouvons partout les traces de ce penchant à déserter le POSITIF, pour apporter l'IDÉAL jusque dans les annales, je crois qu'à plus forte raison l'on doit s'abandonner à une grande indifférence de la réalité historique pour juger les oeuvres dramatiques, poèmes, romans ou tragédies, qui empruntent à l'histoire des personnages mémorables. L'ART ne doit jamais être considéré que dans ses rapports avec sa BEAUTÉ IDÉAL. Il faut le dire, ce qu'il y a de VRAI n'est que secondaire; c'est seulement une illusion de plus dont il s'embellit, un de nos penchants qu'il caresse. Il pourrait s'en passer, car la VÉRITÉ dont il doit se nourrir est *la vérité d'observation sur la nature humaine*, et non *l'authenticité du fait.*[51]

[49] J— Jph V—e, "De la réalité en littérature," 11 (1825), 507.
[50] Review of *Quentin Durward* in *Muse Française*, 1823. *Oeuvres complètes*, II/1, 433.
[51] "Sur la vérité dans l'art," *Oeuvres complètes*, II, 25.

Despite some differences in emphasis, he and Hugo are not far apart.

The impersonality invoked by Hugo and the writer of the *Mercure* is already considered a quality desirable in novels dealing with real life, just as it is later found characteristic of the realistic novel. Other references to impersonality of the author appear fairly frequently in the 1820s: of Scott, Ph. Chasles comments, "Le romancier s'efface dans ses fictions, ou plutôt il n'existe pas."[52] Sainte-Beuve objects to Vigny's presence in *Cinq-Mars*: "... lorsque Cinq-Mars et Marie de Gonzague s'entretiennent, on s'aperçoit trop que M. de Vigny est en tiers avec eux."[53]

The question of impersonality and objectivity extended to the tone and style of the narration, as Théodore Jouffroy points out in his comparison between Lesage and Scott. In the satire of *Gil Blas*, so carefully written, the author is always present:

> Non seulement Lesage ne dort jamais, mais il ne se néglige pas un seul moment: l'intention de l'artiste transpire jusque dans le moindre détail; tout mot porte et vous avertit qu'il porte; vous ne sauriez vous dérober un moment à la compagnie de l'auteur ni oublier en contemplant le spectacle le *cicerone* qui vous le fait voir.[54]

In a true novel a writer could allow himself a little more negligence: "... l'art, lorsqu'il paraît trop, peut nuire à l'effet des peintures les plus vraies, tandis qu'un certain abandon donne une dernière touche de naturel à la vérité même, comme la grâce est le parfum de la beauté." Sainte-Beuve, in his criticism of *Cinq-Mars* came even closer to the heart of the matter, not only in regard to care in writing, but in the arrangement of the whole work:

> M. de Vigny a une imagination de poète, et c'est une arrangeuse systématique à sa manière, que l'imagination: elle symétrise en se jouant, et, de la vie, elle a bientôt fait un drame. Le romancier n'est rien, au contraire, qu'un praticien consommé dans la science de la vie, s'accommodant à tout ce qu'elle offre d'irrégulier, et d'ordinaire s'y tenant.

Real life for Sainte-Beuve is not a drama, as it is for Hugo, and his realism comes closer to being a "slice of life" in the naturalist manner.

---

[52] *Mercure du 19e Siècle*, 14:306.
[53] *Le Globe*, 8 July 1826.
[54] Review of Scott, *Les Chroniques de la Canongate*, *Le Globe*, 1 Dec. 1827.

This insistence on reality in the mid-1820s coincides with the vogue of the *scène de moeurs* (including the early sketches of Balzac) which flourished from 1823 on, and the Restoration *romans de moeurs* of which Picard's *Le Gil Blas de la Révolution* (1824) is the best known. Though these tableaux dealt with contemporary life and ordinary people, they were often inspired by Scott; and so fixed was the public's eye on Scott that they did not evoke as much comment about reality as the historical novel. What seems to be important is the illusion of reality, even of a time long gone. It is not until the 1830s, when the historical novel has receded and the *roman de moeurs* decidely dominates the field, that realism will be attached only to contemporary subjects.

The theater also called upon historical subjects, and the 1820s saw a proliferation of *scènes historiques* as well as full-length plays. Postrevolutionary audiences required that historical drama show men and women of the past in all the dimensions of their real existence, said some forward-looking critics. This meant opening up the Classical system of dramaturgy and admitting both comic and tragic elements. Duvergier de Hauranne argues for this in *Le Globe* a year before Hugo's famous "Préface de *Cromwell*."

> Il est des siècles dont les contrastes forment le principal caractère. Les effacer, c'est affaiblir l'art et mentir à la nature; c'est, au lieu d'un corps plein de vie, ne plus présenter qu'un automate dont les mouvements mécaniques peuvent occuper l'attention, mais sans jamais toucher le coeur.[55]

In 1821 Guizot too had advocated a drama which combined the comic and the tragic, elements basic to our nature and particularly characteristic of modern man.[56]

Whether dealing with historical subjects or modern, the theater, say many writers, should tend toward the real. Of all literary genres, says Audin, drama is most characterized by reality, which pleases spectators hungry for emotion. He agrees with the *Globe* critic that Romantic drama gives us characters which seem of flesh and blood, able to

---

[55] "Du mélange du comique et du tragique," 10 June 1826.

[56] In his introduction to Shakespeare, *Oeuvres complètes* (republication of Letourneur's translation) (Paris: Ladvocat), I, p. LXVI. For an account of what Hugo's "Préface de *Cromwell*" owed to Guizot, see Claude Duchet, "Victor Hugo et l'âge d'homme," Hugo, *Oeuvres complètes*, III/1, 30-31.

live apart from the work, as opposed to ancient drama, whose characters were symbols.[57]

Théodore Jouffroy sets drama apart from other literary genres because it presents speech delivered directly by living people, accompanied by gestures and varying intonations. Words are then not just literary signs but also natural signs. When literature reproduces speech, says Jouffroy, it is like the plastic arts, in that it shows the soul directly. Drama acts immediately on our senses, whereas literary art must pass through the imagination and the memory; dramatic art presents reality directly, whereas literary art evokes the memory of reality.[58] It is this direct impact of the dramatic genre that Hugo wished to approach in the novel.

The call for reality which comes from Romantic writers of varying tendencies is central to the attack on many Classical theatrical conventions. In addition to the mixing of comic and tragic, other changes for which the young writers strove: abolition of the unities of time and place, increased richness of detail in added circumstances of time and place, a new flexibility for the alexandrine or drama in prose, rejection of the Classic *bienséances* — these all tend toward greater naturalness and an approximation of reality. Stendhal recommends dramatic works in prose and presents a summary of a play entitled *Lanfranc* as an example of Romantic comedy; it is Romantic in that its events resemble what happens every day and it is less affected than Classical comedy.[59] Even Vigny, who has so stressed his idealism in the novel, foresees a theater where "l'art sera tout semblable à la vie, et dans la vie une action entraîne autour d'elle un tourbillon de faits nécessaires et innombrables."[60] Vigny particularly stresses the importance of escaping from "la politesse" of Classical tragedy which so limits drama on all sides, the poetic as well as the real: "Elle seule était capable de bannir à la fois les caractères vrais, comme grossiers; le langage simple, comme trivial; l'idéalité de la philosoohie et des passions, comme extravagance; la poésie comme bizarrerie."[61] In the new poetic drama a handkerchief may be shown and named.

Duvergier de Hauranne argues in *Le Globe* that the unity of impression insisted on by the *classiques* is to be replaced by the unity

---

[57] "Du romantique," pp. li-lii.

[58] *Cours d'esthétique,* pp. 228-29.

[59] *Racine et Shakespeare,* p. 84.

[60] "Lettre à lord - - -," 1829, Preface to *Le More de Venise, Oeuvres complètes,* I, 337.

[61] *Ibid.,* I, 338.

of interest, which allows both laughter and tears. "Qu'est-ce en effet que le drame? Une représentation de la nature humaine, idéale et poétique il est vrai, mais de cet idéal qui n'efface pas la réalité, de ce poétique qui n'en est que l'expression vive et claire."[62] Drama should show real people, not ideas, man complete and full of contrasts. "La nature, la nature, c'est toujours là qu'il en faut revenir." This reality is not opposed to the ideal, it is reality presented poetically.

The drama should encompass all reality, and it was at the center of the hopes of the new generation for the transformation of literature. "Le drame est la poésie complète," says Hugo. "L'ode et l'épopée ne le contiennent qu'en germe; il les contient l'une et l'autre en développement; il les résume et les enserre toutes deux."[63] He sees no limits to its domain, nor to that of any art. "Tout ce qui est dans la nature est dans l'art." Two years later he will reiterate this idea in the preface to *Les Orientales*: "Tout est sujet, tout relève de l'art, tout a droit de cité en poésie... L'art n'a que faire des lisières, des menottes, des bâillons; il vous dit Va! et vous lâche dans ce grand jardin de poésie où il n'y a pas de fruit défendu" (*OC*, III.1, 495-96). Had he not said in 1822: "La poésie c'est tout ce qu'il y a d'intime dans tout"? Hugo finds a source for the contrasts inherent in drama in the Christian dualism of body and soul, the struggle between two opposing principles. This dualism corresponds particularly well to his own esthetic of contrasts. "La poésie née du christianisme, la poésie de notre temps, est donc le drame; le caractère du drame est le réel; le réel résulte de la combinaison toute naturelle de deux types, le sublime et le grotesque, qui se croisent dans le drame, comme il se croisent dans la vie et dans la création" (*C*, 60). This is obviously a very personal point of view of one for whom life is a "drame bizarre"; others find real life more "quotidienne."

Hugo calls on the principle of reality particularly in his arguments against the unities of time and of place. The *décor unique* of French Classical drama cannot be justified by the principle of verisimilitude put forth by Boileau as one basis for the unities; reality actually destroys the unities.

Quoi de plus invraisemblable et de plus absurde, en effet, que ce vestibule, ce péristyle, cette antichambre, lieu banal où nos tragédies

---

[62] "Du mélange du comique et du tragique," 6 May 1826.
[63] "Préface de *Cromwell*," *Oeuvres complètes*, III/1, p. 58. Future references to this work will be abbreviated *C* followed by the page number.

ont la complaisance de venir se dérouler, où arrivent, on ne sait comment, les conspirateurs pour déclamer contre le tyran, le tyran contre
les conspirateurs, chacun à son tour,... Quoi de plus contraire, nous
ne dirons pas à la vérité, les scolastiques en font bon marché, mais à
la vraisemblance? Il résulte de là que tout ce qui est trop caractéristi-
que, trop intime, trop local, pour se passer dans l'antichambre ou dans
le carrefour, c'est-à-dire tout le drame, se passe dans la coulisse. Nous
ne voyons en quelque sorte sur le théâtre que les coudes de l'action;
ses mains sont ailleurs. Au lieu de scènes, nous avons des récits; au
lieu de tableaux, des descriptions. De graves personnages placés, comme le choeur antique, entre le drame et nous, viennent nous raconter
ce qui se fait dans le temple, dans le palais, dans la place publique,
de façon que souventes fois nous sommes tentés de leur crier: "Vraiment! mais conduisez-nous donc là-bas! On s'y doit bien amuser, cela
doit être beau à voir!" (*C*, 62-63)

An exact locality, insists Hugo, is one of the first important elements
of reality, for the place itself contributes, along with the characters
speaking and acting, to the effect on the spectator. "Le lieu où telle
catastrophe s'est passée en devient un témoin terrible et inséparable;
et l'absence de cette sorte de personnage muet décompléterait dans
le drame les plus grandes scènes de l'histoire" (*C*, 63).

The famous preface starts with history and ends with the drama,
the complete literary genre, and between the two comes a direct attack not just on dramatic conventions but on the Neoclassic esthetic
as a whole. The ideal beauty which the Neoclassics adapted from antiquity has outlived its time and has become false and conventional.
"Le christianisme amène la poésie à la vérité" (*C*, 50). The modern
muse will have a higher and broader view of the universe. "Elle sen-
tira que tout dans la création n'est pas humainement *beau*, que le laid
y existe à côté du beau, le difforme près du gracieux, le grotesque
au revers du sublime, le mal avec le bien, l'ombre avec la lumière."
Neoclassic esthetics would not disagree with the premiss, but its conclusions, that the artist must either exclude or idealize the ugly, that
he must make the universe more coherent, that he must eliminate
and generalize, are the opposite of Hugo's.

La muse moderne se demandera si la raison étroite et relative de l'artiste doit avoir gain de cause sur la raison infinie, absolu, du créateur;
si c'est à l'homme à rectifier Dieu; si une nature mutilée en sera plus
belle; si l'art a le droit de dédoubler, pour ainsi dire, l'homme, la vie,

la création; si chaque chose marchera mieux quand on lui aura été son muscle et son ressort; si enfin, c'est le moyen d'être harmonieux que d'être incomplet.

The putative counter-protest leaves no doubt as to the answer: "Ne savez-vous pas que l'art doit rectifier la nature? qu'il faut l'*anoblir*? qu'il faut *choisir*?" (*C*, 51). What art must do is what nature does:

[La poésie] se mettra à faire comme la nature, à mêler dans ses créations, sans pourtant les confondre, l'ombre à la lumière, le grotesque au sublime, en d'autres termes, le corps à l'âme, la bête à l'esprit; car le point de départ de la religion est toujours le point de départ de la poésie. Tout se tient. (*C*, 50)

Hugo does not wish the artist to use any one of a pair of opposites alone, for then art would be incomplete. One element brings out the other, by contrast; specifically, the grotesque makes the sublime stand out more.

A number of observations may be made concerning these pages. One of the first things that strikes the reader is the multiple, imprecise, or shifting meanings of some key words: "beau" is not differentiated from "sublime," and the grotesque is associated with so many other concepts that it is hard to define its meaning. But Hugo is definite about one thing: even if "tout ce qui est dans la nature est dans l'art," he clearly differentiates between nature and art and usually makes clear about which one he is speaking. "La division du beau et du laid dans l'art ne symétrise pas avec celle de la nature. Rien n'est beau ou laid dans les arts que par l'exécution" (*C*, 51 [note]). On moving from the physical universe into the world of art, we may shift from ugliness to beauty or vice versa.

Beauty seems to be of several sorts: first it is the conventional Neoclassic exterior *beau* of the Davidian school, which he finds ugly: "… rien n'est plus laid que tous ces profils grecs et romains, que ce beau idéal de pièces de rapport qu'étale, avec ses couleurs violâtres et cotonneuses, la seconde école de David." The beauty which he places in contrast to the grotesque is a spiritual beauty:

En effet, dans la poésie nouvelle, tandis que le sublime représentera l'âme telle qu'elle est épurée par la morale chrétienne, [le grotesque] jouera le rôle de la bête humaine. Le premier type, dégagé de tout alliage impur aura en apanage tous les charmes, toutes les grâces, toutes les beautés… (*C*, 55)

But this spiritual beauty is essentially always the same; perfection can be monotonous. "Le beau n'a qu'un type; le laid en a mille."[64] Now he shifts to beauty as form, as it is perceived by human sensibilities, which in classic art is a purely human type, eliminating that which offends us: "C'est que le beau, à parler humainement, n'est que la forme considérée dans son rapport le plus simple, dans sa symétrie la plus absolue, dans son harmonie la plus intime avec notre organisation. Aussi nous offre-t-il toujours un ensemble complet, mais restreint comme nous." The ugly, on the other hand, is a detail of a great whole which eludes us and which harmonizes, not with man, but with all creation. Opening up art to the ugly opens up all of life to the artist.

In the long explanatory note on ugliness as a type to be imitated and the grotesque as an element of art, he espouses a broader type of beauty. It has already been made clear that in art inspired by the modern muse and executed by true genius, ugliness as such does not exist, it has become the grotesque. The grotesque may be a multitude of things: "... d'une part, il crée le difforme et l'horrible; de l'autre, le comique et le bouffon. Il attache autour de la religion mille superstitions originales, autour de la poésie mille imaginations pittoresques" (*C*, 52). In the "ideal", that is, imaginary, world, it is the horrible and the fantastic; in the real world it gives us parody, caricature, satire, farce. It can include the truly evil (Iago) and the merrily good-hearted (Figaro) (*C*, 55). "Une chose difforme, horrible, hideuse, transportée avec vérité et poésie dans le domaine de l'art, deviendra belle, admirable, sublime, sans rien perdre de sa monstruosité" (*C*, 51 [note]). In artistic representation the ugly becomes not only grotesque but sublime, beautiful, though still not pleasing to the eyes. As Claude Duchet puts it in his Presentation of *Cromwell*, ugliness is redeemed by art (*C*, 33). So the beautiful in art includes the grotesque and the monstrous; it includes not only the demoniac, but also what is physically repelling: "le mendiant rongé de vermine de Murillo," "Job et Philoctète, avec leurs plaies sanieuses et fétides."

These last examples show better than anything else how far Hugo has diverged from the proscriptions of Lessing, who, as we remember, wished to exclude extreme pain and suffering from the visual arts,

---

[64] During Raphaël's visit to the antique dealer in Balzac's *La Peau de chagrin*, a Chinese monster "réveillait l'âme par les interventions d'un peuple qui, fatigué du beau toujours unitaire, trouve d'ineffables plaisirs dans la fécondité des laideurs." (Classiques Garnier, p. 20.)

though he allowed them in literature. Philoctetes was the classic example. The old attitudes are still current, as we have seen in many comments on contemporary painting, Delacroix in particular. Murillo was also an exemplar for others besides Hugo, but seen from the opposite point of view: Salvandy, for example, would have preferred that Murillo show pain and suffering by facial expression and the presence of a comforting personage rather than by wounds exactly rendered.[65]

Moral ugliness was a staple element of great literature, for esthetic as well as moral reasons. As long as evil was not included in the hero's character, as long as it was morally instructive or picturesque, it did not seem objectionable, and in the 1820s we find fewer protests against ugliness in literature than in painting. It is after 1830 that protests about literary ugliness will multiply as realism gains a real foothold. Stendhal's mimetic justification of the morally ugly in *Le Rouge et le noir* ("un miroir qui se promène sur une grande route") did not prevent his readers from being shocked on finding immoral propensities in his sympathetic protagonists.

As often happens, theory did not go as far as practice. Hugo's defense of the monstrous and horrible, bold as it was for the time, hardly kept pace with some of the horrors already present in the novels of the 1820s. Before the end of the decade the sadism of the *roman frénétique* reached new heights (or depths) in Janin's satiric *L'Ane mort et la femme guillotinée* (1829) and it continued its morbid flowering in the 1830s. Hugo's illustrations are mostly drawn from the past, principally Shakespeare for literature (though he does mention Faust), and Callot rather than Géricault or Delacroix.[66]

Sainte-Beuve takes a more common, ordinary view of reality. He holds himself apart from the Cousinian spiritualism of most of the other Globe writers and maintains the "matérialisme tranquille" of his medical-student days.[67] We have seen that he was one of those who most stressed reality in the arts as well as in other fields, and in 1830 he reiterates this view of the years just past: "Il serait injuste

---

[65] Review of J. Janin, *La Confession, Journal des Débats*, 17 April 1830.

[66] For another approach to the ugly, through religion, see F.P. Bowman, *Le Christ romantique* (Geneva: Droz, 1973), Ch. 7, "Théologie et esthétique: le divin, le sublime et le laid."

[67] The expression comes from Victor Pavie in 1827 (quoted by G. Michaut, *Sainte-Beuve avant les "Lundis"* (Fribourg, 1903), p. 73.

de contester le développement mémorable de l'art pendant les der-
nières années, son affranchissement de tout servage, sa royauté intérieure bien établie et reconnue, ses conquêtes heureuses sur plusieurs
points non jusque-là touchés de la vie."[68] He is scrupulous about
historical authenticity in the novel and chides the Vicomte d'Arlin-
court severely for his falsification of history, and what was even worse,
his falsification of human nature.[69] We have seen that he liked a novel
that gives the haphazard effect of real life.

It is on the subject of reality in lyric poetry that Sainte-Beuve makes
his most original contribution.[70] In his *Pensées de Joseph Delorme* he
defends "la peinture d'un monde moins métaphysique et d'une vie
plus réelle" than Lamartine's, as another kind of poetry which also
has its place.[71] He has tried to be original, says he, in his humble
and bourgeois way, "observant la nature et l'âme de près, sans
microscope, nommant les choses de la vie privée par leur nom, mais
préférant la chaumière au boudoir, et, dans tous les cas, cherchant
à relever le prosaïsme de ces détails domestiques par la peinture des
sentiments humains et des objets naturels."[72]

A year later he has not changed his way of proceeding in his own
poetry: "...c'est presque toujours de la vie privée, que je pars,... je
ne cesse pas d'agir sur le fond de la réalité la plus vulgaire, et... en
supposant le but atteint... j'aurai seulement élevé cette réalité à une
plus haute puissance de poésie."[73] Everyday happenings of private
life thus combine the *intime* — a term Sainte-Beuve brought into vogue
around 1830 — and the real. It contrasts with the colorful, eloquent
poetry of his friend Hugo. If he wishes to lift reality to the poetic plane,
the poet must guard against slipping into the vulgar:

> ... c'est précisément à mesure que la poésie se rapproche davantage
> de la vie réelle et des choses d'ici-bas, qu'elle doit se surveiller avec plus
> de rigueur, se souvenir plus fermement de ses religieux préceptes, et

---

[68] "Mouvement littéraire après la Révolution de 1830," *Le Globe*, 11 Oct. 1830.
[69] *Le Globe*, 15 Jan. 1825.
[70] Review of A. Métral, *Le Phénix* in *Le Globe*, 30 Oct. 1824, unsigned but identified
by Michaut (p. 106) as the work of Sainte-Beuve.
[71] *Pensée* VII, *Vie, poésies et pensées de Joseph Delorme*, ed. G. Antoine (Paris: Nouvelles
Editions Latines, 1956), p. 143. The *Mercure du 19e Siècle* in 1829 called Joseph
Delorme the Géricault of the new school of poetry (quoted by Antoine, p. 237).
[72] *Pensée* XVII, 150.
[73] Preface to *Les Consolations* (Paris: Urbain Canel, Levavasseur, 1920), pp. xxxi-xxxii.

tout en abordant le vrai sans scrupule ni fausse honte, se poser à elle-même, aux limites de l'art, une sauvegarde incorruptible contre le prosaïque et le trivial.[74]

The distinction between "le prosaïsme," which is acceptable, and "le prosaïque," which is to be avoided, is a fine one. "Le prosaïsme" may perhaps be related to the form he wished to give to his verses, which should be simple and remain close to prose.

The growing insistence on the use of contemporary reality in art is also evident in the esthetics of Jouffroy, a partisan of spiritualism like most of the *Globistes*, but only moderately so.[75] His *Cours d'esthétique* not only theorizes about the ties between the visible and the invisible but emphasizes the necessity for the artist to show things and show them clearly and comprehensibly. He accentuates the outward manifestations of a spiritual world by means of objects which are symbolic but also real, concrete, and familiar. The difference between "l'école de l'idéal" and "l'école de la réalité" (or "de l'imitation de la nature"), represented by Molière, Lesage, and Scott, is the difference between the abstract and analytical on one hand and the concrete and outwardly active on the other. "Ainsi l'art, dans la route de l'idéal, ne peut reproduire que la passion et non l'homme passionné; il ne peut reproduire que la passion telle qu'elle est dans l'artiste et non la passion dans toutes ces modifications que mille circonstances lui font subir" (205). The passionate man's words and acts are the natural symbols of passion. Writers make a mistake when they reach for truth without looking for reality, says Jouffroy. Scientists analyse, philosophers seek to know inner workings, but "l'artiste, au contraire, ne connaît pas le fond, il connaît la surface, l'extérieur, il ne regarde que le symbole, il en apprécie la valeur, il considère comment le dehors exprime le dedans..." (158). He does not explain, he expresses, and in his depiction of the exterior, he is a painter. Because he does not explain, he must make himself understood by choosing easily understood natural and contemporary signs, "des signes naturels, ceux dont le sens n'échappe à personne au monde, et les signes habituels du pays et du temps où l'on vit" (214).

In another lesson Jouffroy carries the distinction between real and ideal a step further. There are two ways of idealizing, says he: first

---

[74] *Pensée* VII, 143.
[75] In his articles on materialism and spiritualism in *Le Globe* (27 and 31 Dec. 1828) he finds both systems incomplete.

by analysing a passion and giving a metaphysical (i.e., psychological) description of it, secondly by showing a man in the throes of passion but eliminating everything but the most significant expressions of this passion. On the contrary, Walter Scott (who epitomizes the real for most writers of the 1820s) includes extraneous details which individualize his characters (218-19). The emphasis on showing, and showing in detail, versus explaining, recalls Hugo's prescription for the dramatic novel, also inspired by Scott, and it is typical of a preference for the graphic over the analytical which is common during the Restoration.[76]

Though these writers recommend turning toward faithful depiction of the real world, specifically contemporary reality, they are careful not to confuse reality with art. Sainte-Beuve, the closest to everyday life, seems to be the most preoccupied with finding structures and styles suitable for translating the commonplace into artistic form. Stendhal, Hugo and others accept as evident that real life does not exist on the stage and that dramatic illusion does not lie in trying to reproduce it. For Stendhal it lies in the spectator's momentary response to certain gripping situations and thrilling words.[77] For Hugo it lies in a heightened impression of life ("cette vie de vérité et de saillie") communicated to the spectator through the enthusiasm of the poet. In the "Préface de *Cromwell*" Hugo explicitly distinguishes between "la réalité selon l'art" and "la réalité selon la nature" (*C*, 70). The truth of art cannot be *absolute* reality. (According to Hugo, some thought that it could, but it is hard to know who these people were.) "L'art, outre sa partie idéale, a une partie terrestre et positive." This is the artistic medium, the material and technical part of art. Like so many others before and since, he has recourse to the image of the *speculum*, "un miroir où se réfléchit la nature," but Hugo's mirror is not like Stendhal's:

> ... si ce miroir est un miroir ordinaire, une surface plane et unie, il ne renverra des objets qu'une image terne et sans relief, fidèle mais décolorée: on sait ce que la couleur et la lumière perdent à la réflexion simple. Il faut donc que le drame soit un miroir de concentration qui, loin de les affaiblir, ramasse et condense les rayons colorants, qui fasse d'une lueur une lumière, d'une lumière une flamme...

[76] See my book *The Idea of the Novel in France: The Critical Reaction 1815-1848* (Geneva: Droz, 1961), pp. 125-28.
[77] *Racine et Shakespeare*, p. 18.

Le théâtre est un point d'optique. Tout ce qui existe dans le monde, dans l'histoire, dans la vie, dans l'homme, tout peut et doit s'y réfléchir, mais sous la baguette magique de l'art. (*C*, 70-71)

Every artist has his own way of transforming reality, and this statement seems to characterize the flamboyant Hugo very well: he brings out forms and enhances lights and colors. It also fits a large proportion of artistic productions of the Romantic period, which often enhance to the point of exaggerating. Vigny complains of this in 1832: "On ne fait guère dans l'art à présent que ce que les peintres appellent *des charges*."[78] Painting and drawing, drama (including Hugo) and novel, all suffer so from heightened effects that they are like caricature, says he.

After that of the ordinary mirror, the image of the concave mirror, or the burning glass, is the most common one that I have found in the theoretical texts of the Empire and the Restoration, followed closely by that of the prism. In the first case rays of light, whether they pass through or are reflected, are concentrated, for a heightening of effect. The image of the prism is a little less clear: occasionally the refraction of light indicates the analytical eye, but usually the prism signifies the individual vision which colors reality. I have found the image of the Aeolian harp a number of times (in Joubert and Eckstein, for example), but that of the lamp, which, according to M. H. Abrams (*The Mirror and the Lamp*) is central to English Romanticism, not at all. Of the two French favorites, the prism is closer to conveying the projection of the individual artist's temperament indicated in the lamp image.

The image of the concave mirror, often called "miroir concentrique," is used by all kinds of writers, from Quatremère de Quincy through Delécluze to Hugo and Balzac, each using it to mean whatever he likes. Balzac tells us that it comes from Leibniz.[79] The flat mirror usually signifies a photographic reproduction of concrete reality; it is also used by the illuminists, who say that the physical universe is

---

[78] *Journal d'un poète, Oeuvres complètes*, II, 957.

[79] "Cette âme était enfin, selon la magnifique expression de Leibniz, *un miroir concentrique de l'univers.*" Quoted by J. Rousset, *L'Intérieur et l'extérieur* (Paris: Corti, 1968), p. 224. While Balzac speaks of the artist contemplating the universe within himself, the others are speaking of their work. Eggli tells us (*Le Débat romantique*, p. 100 n) that Schiller also used the image.

a mirror of the spiritual universe or of God.[80] Those who use the image of the "concentric" mirror are all opponents of a naturalistic representation of reality. For the moderate Neoclassics it means not a distortion of form or a heightening of color but a concentration of meaning, a more coherent depiction of the universe. Both Neoclassics and Romantics see the necessity of an interpretation and a development of reality in the work of art. There are mirrors for image makers of all tendencies.

[80] The mirror figures importantly in Saint-Martin in ways too numerous to be gone into here. Madame de Staël said that poetry should be the earthly mirror of the divinity (*De l'Allemagne*, II, 178).

9. *The Inner and the Outer*

During the Restoration theorists and critics continue as before to stress the importance of personal emotion in the artist as a wellspring of creativity. As before, the lyric impulse is found to be characteristic of primitive man. According to an article in *Le Catholique*, presumably by Baron Eckstein, lyricism followed directly upon the very first poetic manifestation of the earliest times:

> Lorsque l'ensemble des connaissances sur l'homme, sur Dieu, sur l'univers, fut déposé au sein d'une révélation primitive, la poésie, dans son premier période, fut religieuse, scientifique, philosophique. Ensuite, le sentiment individuel se manifesta, sous la forme lyrique, par la contemplation de cet ordre de choses.[1]

The most famous statement of the theory of primitive lyricism appears, of course, in the "Préface de *Cromwell*":

> Aux temps primitifs, quand l'homme s'éveille dans un monde qui vient de naître, la poésie s'éveille avec lui. En présence des merveilles qui l'éblouissent et qui l'enivrent, sa première parole n'est qu'un hymne. Il touche encore de si près à Dieu que toutes ses méditations sont des extases, tous ses rêves des visions. Il s'épanche, il chante comme il respire. Sa lyre n'a que trois cordes, Dieu, l'âme, la creation; mais ce triple mystère enveloppe tout, mais cette triple idée comprend tout... Voilà le premier homme, voilà le premier poète. La prière est toute sa religion, l'ode est toute sa poésie. (*C*, 45)

---

[1] "Des journaux littéraires considérés dans leurs rapports avec la poésie," 1 (1826), 423.

The lyric faculty is innate in man, says Eckstein, as long as he remains unspoiled, though in most people it remains latent.

> Chez le poète lyrique, ces accents inarticulés, ces doux accords qui sommeillent chez la plupart des hommes, et s'éteignent dans le chaos des intérêts et des passions, revêtent une forme sensible. Il compose comme la corde vibre; il livre ses accents, comme la harpe éolienne, au souffle inspirateur qui anime la nature.[2]

Civilization has killed this faculty, and anyone who is to be a lyric poet today must be a child of primitive times, in other words, recover some of the naïveté and spontaneity of those days.

The importance of personal emotion as an explanation for the existence of certain kinds of art in modern times has its counter-tendency, the habit of explaining them by the current truism, taken from Bonald, that literature is the reflection of society. These two dicta, along with the basic doctrine that art is an imitation of nature, are more or less in balance in the 1820s; the first two are not really brought into question by anyone, but they are stressed principally by the innovators. The mimetic doctrine is subject to considerable modification. A fourth principle, that of example and tradition within the arts ("imitation" in the other sense) is not often under attack in its broad sense; it is usually a question of being free to choose the most suitable and fruitful sources of inspiration, not Racine but Shakespeare, not David but Rubens. Not even those with the highest aspirations to originality wished to cut themselves loose from the past of their own art. Though these principles do not all work in the same direction, it is possible to conciliate them, as Nodier does: "Répétons ici le mot tant de fois répété: *la littérature est l'expression de la société.* Joignons-y cette axiome, qui ne paraît pas moins évidente: *la poésie est l'expression des passions et de la nature...*"[3] Starting from this all-inclusive view Nodier concludes that there is little difference between Classicism and Romanticism — which could be maintained in 1821 — and that Romanticism is perhaps the Classicism of the moderns. A critic of the *Annales*, Saint-Valry, (who also contributed to *La Muse Française*) in his turn finds a way to combine the two seemingly contradictory principles. He first enunciates the expression-of-society maxim, saying that it applies especially to poetry, then continues: "En effet, la poésie, qui doit être considérée

---

[2] "Le Peintre Muller," *Le Catholique*, 9 (1828), 41.
[3] Review of Spiess, *Le Petit Pierre*, *Annales* 2 (1821), 78.

comme la révélation toute en images de nos sentiments les plus intimes, excelle à peindre les passions et le coeur des hommes. La science même du moraliste n'a jamais plongé des regards aussi avant dans ce ténébreux labyrinth."[4] What counts here is not the poet's feelings but "le coeur *des hommes*." The poet is less the source of emotion in his work than a mirror for the emotions of others. In fact, poetry, according to Saint-Valry, follows "le mouvement des esprits" more closely than the other literary genres, so that poets of a certain period, in spite of their individual differences, all bear the imprint of the civilization surrounding them.

Lahalle, however, is not ready to apply the reflection-of-society axiom to music: "... les expressions musicales partent du fond des entrailles humaines; elles appartiennent à l'homme de toutes les époques, de tous les lieux."[5] Nor is music an art of imitation, says Fétis, the best music critic of the Restoration, it is an art of expression, and what it expresses is "les affections de l'âme." He does not claim that it is capable of conveying what a certain individual feels, but it does more, it moves the listener.[6]

According to Massias, a human being is necessarily expressive: "Il y a non seulement sympathie mais presque identité entre notre extérieur et notre intérieur. Lorsque celui-ci est pressé et agité par une surabondance de vie, elle s'échappe et se manifeste par le mouvement de toute l'organisation, comme dans une espèce d'enfantement."[7] This movement made measured and rhythmic, becomes dance.

Even more than music and dance, comment on the emotional sources of art refers to literature. To some extent, this predominance of literature is due to theories of primitive language. If the word coincides with the thing itself, verbal expression is the most direct of all. According to Bonstetten, all the arts are simply developments of the language of feeling:

La véritable parole de l'âme est dans les beaux-arts... Le langage parlé se compose de sons articulés et de mouvements plus ou moins lents ou accélérés; la musique n'est que le développement des sons parlés, de l'accent parlé, et des mouvements faiblement indiqués de la simple parole. Le langage écrit a commencé par une grossière peinture que

---

[4] Review of Jules Lefebvre, *Le Parricide*, 10 (1823), 257.
[5] *Essais sur la musique*, p. 56.
[6] *Revue Musicale*, 3 (1828), 510, 514-15.
[7] *Théorie du beau*, p. 67.

la véritable peinture n'a fait que développer. Qu'on ne s'y trompe pas: dans l'origine du langage, les sons écrits et parlés n'étaient pas des signes, mais la chose même qu'on voulait exprimer, comme le chant des oiseaux est le sentiment même qui parle, et non le signe de ce sentiment.[8]

Language has long since lost its original purity, but some critics see in the works of the Romantic poets a return to self-revelation. Whereas in Classical literature the author is almost always a narrator or interpreter of other persons or events, says Cyprien Desmarais, the Romantic writer turns the light upon himself:

... dans la littérature romantique... l'écrivain nous livre, pour ainsi dire, toute sa pensée et toute son âme; c'est en mettant sous nos yeux l'anatomie de son être, qu'il nous initie à la connaissance de l'homme: voilà pourquoi la littérature romantique a quelque chose de plus individuel et de plus intime; c'est pour cela encore qu'elle est moins propre à l'imitation, et que toutes ses productions ont un caractère particulier d'originalité et de nouveauté.[9]

Personal thoughts and feelings are not only the impelling force, they are the content of the work itself, which may be lyrical or analytical; indeed, this passage suggests the *roman d'analyse*, stressing at the same time the virtues of the Classical *moraliste* ("la connaissance de l'homme") and the Romantic values of originality and novelty. If applied to the novel, this principle stands at the opposite pole from Hugo's impersonal dramatic novel, as co-existing counter-tendency.

It is poetry, the queen of the arts, which is the emotional expression par excellence. For Lamartine, who first brought the new lyricism into France, poetry is "la respiration de l'âme." Victor Hugo and his friends at *La Muse Française* have no doubt of it. From his first critical writings in *Le Conservateur Littéraire*, Hugo stresses the emotional element in poetry. "Qu'est-ce... qu'un poète? Un homme qui sent fortement, exprimant ses sensations dans une langue plus expressive. La poésie, ce n'est presque que sentiment, dit Voltaire."[10] It is curious to see the adolescent Hugo citing Voltaire on this question, especially when Chénier, the poet under review, had already furnished the perfect motto, "le coeur seul est poète." The word "sensations" harks back to the eighteenth century, but it also announces *Les Orientales*.

---

[8] *Etudes de l'homme*, II, 251.
[9] *Essai*, p. 133.
[10] Article on André Chénier, *Oeuvres complètes*, I/1, 473.

Great passions make great men, says Hugo, and all the examples he gives are writers.[11] And in his ironic attack on Classical convention four years later, "Ce n'est point réellement aux *sources d'Hippocrène, à la fontaine de Castalie*, ni même au *ruisseau du Permesse*, que le poète puise le génie; mais tout simplement dans son âme et dans son coeur."[12]

Musset's direct outpouring of emotion in his poetry comes immediately to mind. "Ce qu'il faut à l'artiste ou au poète, c'est l'émotion," says he in a letter to his brother Paul (4 Aug. 1931). The importance of suffering in the creation of art is also often expressed by Musset in his poetry, in the famous pelican of "La Nuit de mai" or the injunction to the poet, in "Impromptu," to "faire une perle d'une larme." Many critics join the chorus in what is already becoming a Romantic cliché. *Le Globe* agrees that what we ask of poets today is "une peinture naïve et spontanée de leurs propres émotions."[13] Artaud, after singing the praises of a vivid imagination, still gives the first place to the emotions: "[La poésie] vit surtout de passions, d'émotions; c'est au coeur de l'homme qu'elle doit parler; autrement la brillante parure resterait froide et inanimée."[14]

In the 1820s many recognize that it is a time of a new upsurge of the lyric genre, and Lamartine is usually acknowledged as the greatest lyric poet of the day. Some *Globe* critics, however, being of philosophical bent, are too "reasonable" to share the fervor of the prophets of *La Muse Française*. Charles de Rémusat prefers Casimir Delavigne to Lamartine, and his lyric poet is less in tune with the universe than with the life of his own time.

La poésie lyrique sort de la pensée, tout empreinte du sentiment de celui qui l'a conçue, pour se porter successivement sur tous les objets. Monotone ou variée, détaillée ou vague, intime ou extérieure, elle a tous les caractères comme l'homme même...

Une telle poésie doit plaire à notre âge. En reproduisant des émotions personnelles, elle satisfait à ce besoin du naturel et du vrai, goût dominant de l'époque; et par son caractère de généralité, doué de la rapidité vagabonde de la pensée et même de la rêverie, elle répond singulièrement à cette disposition de doute et de contemplation où nous jettent les doctrines et les événements du siècle. L'univers et un seul

11 "Du génie," *ibid.*, I/1, 518.
12 Review of *Eloa, La Muse Française*, *ibid.*, II/1, 452.
13 Review of Ph. Chasles, *La Fiancée de Bénarès*, 10 Feb. 1825.
14 *Revue Encyclopédique*, 25 (1825), 603.

homme, l'infini et l'individu, tel est le contraste qui fait le fond de la poésie lyrique comme de la pensée humaine.[15]

On the whole, however, for most of those who speak of the subject, the lyric muse is "la muse de tous les temps."[16]

The mark of individuality which an artist leaves on his work comes not so much from emotional expression as from his sensibility and imagination, the quality of his vision. In the nineteenth century, critics were just beginning to deal with the question of originality, a quality which had always existed in great artists without their seeking for it. Even when aiming to reproduce nature exactly or when following the models of ancient art, geniuses of the past were original without knowing it. David, who encouraged his students to follow their own bent, told Delécluze, "... il n'y a rien de si traître que l'art de la peinture. Dans l'ouvrage se peint l'homme qui l'a fait."[17] It is one of those axioms that seems to generally accepted — within limits: the *Journal de Paris* says facetiously: "S'il était vrai, comme on le dit proverbialement, qu'un auteur se peignît dans ses ouvrages, M. Lacroix .[Delacroix]... aurait donc dans le masque des teintes un peu vertes et un peu jaunes..."[18] This cautious attitude is found everywhere, not just because something new and different shocks, but because an artist who disregards the rest of humanity to concentrate on his own individual feelings and ways of seeing the world is considered by many to be derelict in his duty toward his public, or selfish, or even ill. Thus Léon Peisse, a moderate critic, says reproachfully of Byron and E. T. A. Hoffmann that they speak only of their own impressions and not of ours, though he does concede that they represent their own generation, appealing to many, and have a powerful imagination.[19] Auguste Jal wryly comments in his *Esquisses* that originality seems to be considered a vice in France,[20] and, according to P. Grate, Arnold Scheffer, who wrote in *La Revue Française*, was the only art critic who really praised originality.

But some of the best writers claimed for artists the right to be themselves. Stendhal had from the beginning prized the unique

[15] "De l'état de la poésie française," 12 Feb. 1825.
[16] Guizard, review of P. Lebrun, *Le Voyage de Grèce*, *Revue Française* 1 (1828), 233.
[17] *Louis David*, p. 63.
[18] "Salon de 1827," 27 Oct. 1827.
[19] Review of Hoffmann, *Contes fantastiques*, *Le National*, 15 Jan. 1830.
[20] Quoted by P. Grate, *Deux critiques d'art*, p. 40.

character of each of his beloved Italian painters. What he wished to impart to the readers of his *Histoire de la peinture en Italie*, said he, was the ability to "reconnaître la teinte particulière de l'âme d'un peintre dans sa manière de rendre le clair-obscur, le dessin, la couleur."[21] Stendhal lays emphasis not on the content but on the execution, and in *Promenades dans Rome* he addresses the question of style:

> Le *style* en peinture est la manière particulière à chacun de dire les mêmes choses. Chacun des grands peintres chercha les procédés qui pouvaient porter à l'âme cette *impression particulière* qui lui semblait le grand but de la peinture. Un choix de couleurs, une manière de les appliquer avec le pinceau, la distribution des ombres, certains accessoires, etc., *augmentent le style* d'un dessin.[22]

And he repeats the same phrase about "la teinte particulière de l'âme." In 1824 he has already acknowledged the importance of brushwork as an expressive means.[23] And he is one of the few to befriend Delacroix. In 1827 he complains that individuality is what is lacking in most French paintings. Delacroix is not really a painter to his taste (he will later come to like him), and he has made derogatory comments about his work, but he admires the courage which has gained Delacroix the respect (if not always the liking) of the public. He may be wrong, says Stendhal, "mais [il] ose être lui-même" (*ibid.*, III, 92).

Sainte-Beuve also encourages the individuality of contemporary artists: "Géricault n'a pas imité Raphaël, et il a été Géricault. C'est bien assez. Eugène Delacroix et Louis Boulanger n'imitent pas Géricault, mais ils sont eux-mêmes... et ils ont raison, et nous devrions nous plaindre et nous affliger s'ils faisaient autrement."[24]

Delacroix himself felt keenly the need for personal expression through his painting. As a young man he copied parts of a speech on originality given in 1817 by Girodet, another artist who was intent on being himself and creating something new.[25] An entry in his *Journal* (14 May 1824) reveals this preoccupation: "Tu peux ajouter une âme de plus à celles qui ont vu la Nature d'une façon qui leur est propre... Ils ont peint leur âme en peignant les choses et ton âme

---

[21] *Histoire*, I, 134.

[22] *Promenades*, I, 83-84.

[23] *Mélanges*, III, 35.

[24] Article on Hugo, *Mercure du 19e Siècle*, 24 (1829), 465. See the Antoine edition of *Joseph Delorme*, p. LVII, for other examples of these sentiments from Sainte-Beuve.

[25] "De l'originalité dans les arts du dessin," *Oeuvres posthumes*, II, 185-204.

te demande aussi ton tour." The real creative impulse lies in the imagination, he tells us on another occasion: "Dimier pensait que les grandes passions étaient la source du génie! Je pense que c'est l'imagination seule, ou bien, ce qui revient au même, cette délicatesse d'organes qui fait voir là où les autres ne voient pas, et qui fait voir d'une différente façon."[26] At the same time, he wishes to communicate his own emotion to those who see his work: "Mais, du moins, que j'éprouve autant que possible, dans chacune de mes peintures, ce que je veux faire passer dans l'âme des autres!"[27] The characters portrayed in his paintings speak directly to the spectator: "Dans la peinture, il s'établit comme un pont mystérieux entre l'âme des personnages et celle du spectateur."[28]

If a poet goes back to the original sources of nature, says Hugo, his works will develop and emerge naturally from him: "Le poète est un arbre qui peut être battu de tous les vents et abreuvé de toutes les rosées, qui porte ses ouvrages comme ses fruits, comme le *fablier* portait ses fables" (*C*, 68).

Another champion of the individuality of talent in literature is Emile Deschamps, who, like Stendhal for painting, insists on the importance of style. "C'est l'ordre des idées, la grâce ou la sublimité des expressions, c'est l'originalité des tours, le mouvement et la couleur, l'individualité du langage, qui composent le style."[29] Style is indissolubly fused with content; they are one and the same.

Comme si on pouvait séparer l'idée de l'expression dans un écrivain; comme si la manière de concevoir n'était pas étroitement unie à la manière de rendre; comme si le langage enfin n'était qu'une traduction de la pensée, faite à froid et après coup! ces prétendues combinaisons ne produiraient que des choses monstrueuses ou insipides. On corrige quelques détails dans son style, on ne le change pas. Autant d'hommes de talent, autant de styles. C'est le son de voix, c'est la physionomie, c'est le regard. On peut préférer un style à un autre, mais on ne peut contester qu'il y ait cent façons d'écrire très bien. Il n'y a au contraire qu'une manière de très mal écrire littérairement; c'est d'écrire comme tout le monde...

[26] 27 April 1824; Ed. A. Joubin (Paris: Plon, 1955), I, 87.
[27] *Ibid.*, 25 April 1824, I, 85.
[28] *Ibid.*, 8 Oct. 1822, I, 17.
[29] *La Préface des Etudes françaises et étrangères d'Emile Deschamps*, ed. Henri Girard (Paris: Presses Françaises, s.d.), p. 58.

Imagination dominates in poetry, says Charles de Rémusat, and imagination is more individual than reason.[30] Speaking of Hugo and Sainte-Beuve, Charles Magnin says,

> Chacun d'eux parle sa langue; car, à titre de poètes, chacun d'eux a la sienne. Cette sorte de souveraineté sur le langage, ce droit de le refrapper à sa marque, n'a jamais été formellement reconnu par la critique, et a toujours été pris d'autorité par la poésie... Il faut une langue nouvelle à qui veut faire entendre des accents que nulle oreille humaine n'a entendus.[31]

While it is usually the Romantics and their sympathizers who stress the importance of individuality in art, one writer, Chauvet, who was often critical of them, agrees that the artist must first of all follow his own bent. Already before the end of the Restoration, neutral or anti-Romantic writers voice the complaint that will be so common in the 1830s, that the young writers in their eagerness to produce something new and original simply end up by gross exaggeration and false effects. According to Chauvet, the good qualities (energy, enthusiasm) of the Romantic poets are affected, and their work will not last. "En poésie surtout, l'individualité est indispensable. Certes, il est bon d'être neuf; mais il faut avant tout être soi."[32]

The modern poet may share with the primitive poet a general lyric propensity, but his works are not always naïve and spontaneous outpourings. The modern poet is also introspective and contemplative; he looks deep within himself, ponders, and brings forth new secrets.

> Nous autres modernes [says Artaud], ce que nous connaissons le mieux, c'est nous-mêmes, c'est-à-dire nos sentiments, nos passions, nos idées: nous allons de nous à la nature. Déjà les poètes modernes, pour rajeunir des similitudes usées, en renversent les termes, et comparent les phénomènes du monde physique aux sentiments de l'âme... Les régions de notre intelligence et de notre nature deviennent... l'asile de la poésie; elle s'y transporte tout entière, y découvre des trésors inconnus, et une mine féconde que les siècles exploiteront sans l'épuiser jamais.[33]

As science explains more and more of nature, says a critic of *Le Temps*, our imagination turns to the vague, the unknown, the infinite.

---

[30] *Le Globe*, 25 Aug. 1827.
[31] Review of *Vie, poésies et pensées de Joseph Delorme*, *Le Globe*, 11 April 1829.
[32] Review of *Odes et ballades* and *Les Orientales*, *Revue Encyclopédique*, 42 (1829), 133.
[33] *Revue Encyclopédique*, 25:607-08, article cited above, pp. 123, 157.

But there is one part of creation that man will never really know: himself. "C'est au fond de son propre coeur qu'il peut rencontrer encore tous les éléments de la poésie, le vague, l'inconnu, l'infini. La poésie, exilée du monde extérieur, trouve dans ce monde intime un inviolable asile, un domaine d'où rien ne la peut bannir." The elegy is an entirely personal poetry, as fresh in Lamartine's hands as it was for the ancients.

> C'est que le poète est lui-même son sujet; ses passions, ses sentiments, ses illusions, voilà l'objet de ses peintures; il nous fait descendre avec lui dans son âme;... il est neuf parce qu'il est lui; il est poétique parce qu'il s'ignore et s'étudie parce qu'il s'isole d'un monde trop expliqueé, ou ne s'en rapproche que pour mieux faire ressortir le mystère de lui-même.[34]

Hugo is another of these introspective poets, at least when he leaves the rich, picturesque, exotic world of *Les Orientales* for the inner world of *Les Feuilles d'automne*, which is even vaster than the outer universe: "Il est demeuré en lui, et c'est dans ce monde de l'âme, ce monde infini où le ciel est sans voûtes, qu'il se promène grave et solitaire, contemplant ces pensées éternelles qui circulent et gravitent parmi les ténèbres comme de grands astres."[35]

Hugo himself writes in *La Muse Française* of the process (he calls it a faculty) of meditation necessary for the work of inspiration to take place in the poet:

> Pour que la muse se révèle à lui, il faut qu'il ait en quelque sorte depouillé toute son existence matérielle dans le calme, dans le silence et dans le recueillement. Il faut qu'il se soit exilé de la vie extérieure pour jouir avec plénitude de cette vie intérieure qui developpe en lui comme un être nouveau; et ce n'est que lorsque le monde physique a tout à fait disparu à ses yeux, que le monde idéal peut lui être manifesté.[36]

In addition to the demythologization of the outer world, other explanations are offered for the tendency to turn inward. The Christian religion is sometimes seen as a determining factor, as it has been since the days of Chateaubriand, early in the century. Again, Lamartine furnishes the prime example of "une poésie rêveuse et méditative

---

[34] Review of Gaulmier, *Oeuvres posthumes*, 2 June 1830.
[35] J. R. [Jean Reynaud?], *Revue Encyclopédique*, 52 (1831), 170.
[36] *Oeuvres complètes*, II/1, 453.

qui, se separant du monde, demandait ses inspirations et ses succès à ce qu'il y a en nous de plus secret et de plus intime, mais peut-être de plus puissant, le sentiment religieux."[37] But the tendency is reinforced by the troubles of recent times, which have shut men up in the immovable forms of a new social order and turned them back into themselves.

> Prisonnier dans ces étroites classifications qui étouffent toute énergie individuelle et anéantissent les volontés particulières, l'homme a senti plus que jamais l'insuffisance de sa destinée ici-bas. Alors le retour sur soi-même est inévitable; alors on demande compte à la vie de tout ce qu'elle promet et donne si peu.[38]

The *mal du siècle* from which this generation suffers has led to an entirely personal poetry, whether it be an elegy or a philosophical meditation.

Cyprien Anot relates Romantic introspection not only to religion but to the influence of German philosophy, and in particular the doctrine of Kant, which has become known in France chiefly thanks to Victor Cousin:

> ... la philosophie des Allemands qui ont replacé la cause et le principe de nos actions dans l'âme elle-même, qui reconnaissent en elle une activité spontanée, indépendante des objets extérieurs... Kant a placé hors des atteintes du raisonnement les grandes vérités religieuses, l'existence de Dieu, l'immortalité de l'âme, la liberté de l'homme, en leur donnant une base inébranlable dans le sentiment qu'il prouve être le seul juge compétent et infaillible des vérités primitives... Dans la *Critique de la raison pratique* il ramène tout à la vie intérieure de l'âme...[39]

The works of Romantic writers (he is referring to the Germans) induce reverie in their readers because of their religious and spiritualist character. (We shall return to this question in chapter 10.)

In contrast to the flourishing of poetry encouraged by introspection, sculpture seems to be languishing, and this is no accident, according to L. Vitet. One of the reasons for its loss of popularity, says he, is the present primacy of spiritual values, "une supériorité plus

---

[37] H. Patin, review of *Harmonies poétiques et religieuses*, *Revue Encyclopédique*, 47 (1830), 129.

[38] Artaud in *Revue Encyclopédique*, 25:609, article cited above; see note 33.

[39] *Essai*, pp. 178, 180.

incontestable accordée à l'esprit sur la matière, à la nature interne sur le monde extérieur."[40]

Though description in prose fiction was in good repute (Scott's descriptions were much admired), most critics did not look upon descriptive poetry with favor. As we have seen, Delille's star had faded before the end of the Empire, but critics continued to speak of him, reminding readers that his genre was outmoded. Léon Thiessé, a *classique*, twice wrote articles attacking descriptive poetry, chiefly on the grounds that it pushed from the center of attention what should be the true subject of poetry, man and his feelings:

> ... il fut impossible de ne pas reconnaître que le génie descriptif était faux, parce qu'il avait pour fondement ce qui, dans tout ouvrage d'esprit, ne doit être que l'accessoire; on dut s'apercevoir bientôt que l'intérêt réel d'une production poétique ne peut reposer que sur les passions de l'homme. La nature est sans doute une vaste et brillante scène; mais elle a besoin d'être animée par la présence d'un acteur. C'est par les rapports que l'auteur de l'univers a établis entre elle et nous que la nature nous plaît, que nous aimons à en goûter les charmes; et l'art, qui n'est que l'expression des rapports des choses et des lois éternelles de la raison humaine, ne peut avouer tout ouvrage, quel que soit d'ailleurs le mérite de l'exécution, dans lequel l'homme est, pour ainsi dire, exilé de son propre domaine. Le poème descriptif, à cet égard, fait du monde une vaste solitude.[41]

The plaint is reiterated many times; for Artaud descriptive poetry is "un simulacre de poésie... un fantôme sans vie... un genre faux et plein de sécheresse,"[42] poetry deprived of its greatest charm, that which comes from the soul. According to Ed. Richer, moral philosophy is what makes the value of a poem. "La peinture des lieux n'est rien en elle-même. Il faut, pour qu'elle atteigne son but, qu'elle soit accompagnée des émotions qu'elle fait naître." Lamartine is the poet who accomplishes this ideal: "Après tant de vers purement descriptifs, nous avons pu voir enfin, dans notre langue, des tableaux de la nature, accompagnée de la peinture des sentiments qu'ils inspirent."[43]

[40] Review of Clarac, *Musée de sculpture ancienne et moderne, Le Globe*, 25 July 1826.
[41] Review of Viennet, *Epîtres et poésies, Revue Encyclopédique*, 10 (1821), 132. The second article, published in the *Mercure du 19e Siècle* in 1825 (1: 377-88), repeats the main points of this one.
[42] Article cited above, see note 33.
[43] *Du genre descriptif*, pp. 19, 27.

Some thought that descriptive poetry had become a Romantic genre. In fact, that is the way Quatremère de Quincy defines the new tendency in the early 1820s, when the term "romantique" is often applied by literary conservatives to any traits of new works that they do not like. Quatremère, armed with his strong belief in the *beau idéal* and the separation of the arts, attacks literary description, in poetry or prose, and his views are well known from pre-publication reading of excerpts from his book on *Imitation* (1823).[44] In his 1822 Preface to *Trilby*, Nodier answers Quatremère in his gently ironic way, not defending the Romantics but standing up for description:

> Une autre objection dont j'avais à parler… est celle qui s'est nouvellement développée dans les considérations d'ailleurs fort spirituelles sur *les usurpations réciproques de la poésie et de la peinture*, et dont le genre qu'on appelle *romantique* a été le prétexte. Personne n'est plus disposé que moi à convenir que le genre *romantique* est un fort mauvais genre, surtout tant qu'il ne sera pas défini, et que tout ce qui est essentiellement détestable appartiendra, comme par une nécessité invincible, au genre romantique; mais c'est pousser la proscription un peu loin que de l'étendre au style descriptif; et je tremble de penser que si on enlève ces dernières ressources, empruntées d'une nature physique invariable, aux nations avancées chez lesquelles les plus précieuses ressources de l'inspiration morale n'existent plus, il faut bientôt renoncer aux arts et à la poésie. Il est généralement vrai que la poésie descriptive est la dernière qui vienne à briller chez les peuples; mais c'est que chez les peuples vieillis il n'y a plus rien à décrire que la nature qui ne vieillit jamais.[45]

He invokes the examples of Virgil and Cicero to claim that poetry, i.e., literature, has as much right to be painterly as painting has to be literary:

> C'est pour un autre Chateaubriand, pour un Bernardin de Saint-Pierre à venir, qu'il faut décider si le style descriptif est une usurpation ambitieuse sur l'art de peindre la pensée, comme certains tableaux de David, de Gérard et de Girodet sur l'art de l'écrire; et si l'inspiration circonscrite dans un cercle qu'il ne lui est plus permis de franchir n'aura jamais le droit de s'égarer sous le *frigus opacum* et à travers les *gelidae fontium perennitates* des poètes paysagistes, qui ont trouvé ces heureuses expressions sans la permission de l'Académie.

---

[44] See Hugo's rather favorable comment on the excerpt read in the "Séance publique des quatre Académies" (1820), *Conservateur Littéraire, Oeuvres complètes*, I/1, 631-32.

[45] *Trilby*, ed. Castex (Classiques Garnier, 1961), pp. 97-98.

When he publishes his book in 1823, Quatremère seizes upon these passages by Nodier as corroboration of his own views of the deplorable practices of the Romantics. Quoting Nodier inexactly, he concentrates on the words "une nature physique invariable" as proof that description of physical nature is characteristic of the *genre romantique.*

> Comme les arts du dessin, ou ceux qui parlent aux yeux, ont besoin le plus souvent de traduire les idées morales en formes physiques, la poésie, qui peint à l'esprit, aime à convertir en impressions morales les sensations corporelles. Elle désigne les objets matériels, plutôt par leur effet sur l'âme que par leur action sur les sens, plutôt dans leur rapport avec les sentiments qu'ils produisent, que dans leur configuration visuelle. Son secret surtout est de transporter dans les espaces indéfinis de l'intelligence, qui en agrandit l'image, les sujets que l'art du dessin ne peut nous présenter que dans l'étroite enceinte d'un lieu donné.[46]

The Romantics seem to wish to borrow the painter's eyes to make an exact copy of material objects and thus are deserting the realms of the ideal. The Romantic writer is even encroaching on the technique of the visual arts:

> Son pittoresque est celui du crayon, ses descriptions sont formelles, ses métaphores sont techniques. Il allonge les corps en obélisques, les arrondit en coupoles, les creuse en calices. Il prétend modeler des formes, tracer des contours, profiler des lignes, projeter des ombres, grouper des masses. Il colore les fleurs de *minium*, peint le firmament d'outremer.[47]

An answer to Quatremère de Quincy comes from Cyprien Desmarais in his *Essai sur les classiques et les romantiques.* He does not agree that writers are drawing their inspiration from the procedures of painting nor that poets have deserted the ideal. On the contrary, the poet uses description of physical nature in order to explain moral nature, but has not learned how to do so effectively:

> Ce qu'on lui reproche avec juste raison, c'est la métaphysique de la pensée s'alliant sans ordre et sans choix dans ses tableaux à la peinture des objets matériels: sans cesse on le voit décrire des sites pittoresques, des solitudes majestueuses, moins dans l'intention d'en offrir seulement

---

[46] *L'Imitation*, p. 82. The second sentence seems to make of Quatremère a precursor of Mallarmé.
[47] *Ibid.*, p. 84.

le tableau à l'esprit du lecteur, et de l'étonner ainsi par le fini de l'imitation, qu'afin de produire sur l'âme les impressions tristes et rêveuses, que la vue réelle des objets aurait pu faire naître. C'est ainsi que sa muse tombe dans le vague, en voulant réunir des rapports trop éloignés et donner un corps à des idées trop subtiles, à des nuances de sentiments trop fugitives...[48]

The role accorded to description as such is one area where the *Globe* eclectics and the Cénacle clearly separate. (Desmarais is outside both groups.) In his well-known article "Du romantisme considéré historiquement," the *Globe* writer Després cites among other definitions that have been given of Romanticism, the *genre descriptif* (by which we may understand description for its own sake), which may not have been properly distinguished from another kind of depiction of nature.

Comme ces écrivains s'occupaient beaucoup du spectacle de la nature dans ses effets sur notre âme, nous en conclûmes que *la peinture du monde matériel était l'objet du romantisme, et nous le confondîmes avec le genre descriptif*, qui de tous est précisément celui qui a le moins de rapport avec cette littérature.[49]

According to Després, Romanticism is essentially spiritualist. Spiritualism does not banish the physical world from poetry, on the contrary, but it does lessen the importance of pure description. Poetry is an inner disposition, says Th. Jouffroy, and when poets try to speak of their poetic experience, they do so not by descriptions but by images and allegories.[50] Another eclectic, Garnier, picks up Quatremère's argument against excessive mixing of the arts: the risk of purely descriptive poetry, says he, is that it borrows too much from other genres; it shows poetry inferior to painting, and *l'harmonie imitative* shows poetry inferior to music.[51]

Matters come to a head in the late 1820s as Hugo more insistently defends description and Sainte-Beuve joins him. But the term "descriptif" is now replaced by the word "pittoresque," a change suggested by Sainte-Beuve and willingly adopted by Hugo in the "Préface de *Cromwell*." "Descriptive" poetry now means the dead poetry of Delille, "l'homme de la description et de la périphrase" (*C*, 73), whereas the

---

[48] *Essai*, p. 141.
[49] 1 Oct. 1825.
[50] Review of W. Scott, *Oeuvres complètes*, *Le Globe*, 13 Jan. 1827.
[51] "Observations sur le beau," *Revue Encyclopédique*, 30 (1826), 618.

new poetry which Hugo wishes to introduce into the drama is "picturesque." Hugo is not really talking about description in poetry but about a poetic style and verse form that will throw things into relief and bring to drama the life of its inexhaustible variety. It is Delille the versifier, "l'homme de la périphrase" who is the enemy now.

In the *Muse Française* Nodier had already pointed out the importance of the picturesque in the Romantics' attempt to renew the vocabulary and imagery of the Neoclassic descriptive style:

> L'esprit romantique est précisément de traduire les fables de l'ancienne poésie par des faits pittoresques, mais naturels. C'est la *pâle Phébé* avec son *char d'argent*, son disque d'argent, ses rayons d'argent et tout ce luxe d'orfèvrerie qu'elle traîne pesamment dans le ciel des païens, qui est du classique s'il en fut jamais.[52]

He thus places himself on Hugo's side in the latter's controversy with Hoffman (see above, p. 116).

Two years after *Cromwell* Hugo publishes *Les Orientales* and Sainte-Beuve his *Vie, poésies et pensées de Joseph Delorme*. The first is the most richly picturesque work of the Restoration, full of exotic fantasy. It is a splendid illustration of what Joseph Delorme shortly afterwards calls for in a few of his *Pensées*. Again the picturesque is in both the subject and the form, with special attention to vocabulary. Sainte-Beuve divides the Romantics into two principal camps, the descendants of Mme de Staël (*Globistes*) and of Chénier (*Cénacle*) (*Pensée* III). It is the latter who are preoccupied with matters of form, style, and technique. They are the poets and artists. The others prefer to speak of the conception of the work, of its emotional, moral, and intellectual content, to which questions of form are secondary; they are also alarmed at what they consider a new materialism in the new poetic picturesque (*Pensée* XV).

After Hugo, Sainte-Beuve levels an attack at Delille (*Pensée* XIII), who he is afraid is about to be rehabilitated.[53] He does not deny that Delille did write a few good lines.

> Mais que la manière de Delille ne soit pas radicalement fausse, que son badinage descriptif se puisse comparer à la profusion pittoresque

[52] "De quelques logomachies classiques," *La Muse Française*, 2:195.
[53] In Pt. II, Ch. 10 of *Le Rouge et le noir*, Julien Sorel, trying to make a favorable impression on the Academician who frequents the La Mole salon, professes to admire Delille's verses.

de nos jeunes modernes, que le lustre d'une miniature fardée ressemble à l'ardeur éblouissante du pinceau de Rubens ou de Titien, voilà ce qui est chose insoutenable selon moi, et ce qui marque un oubli complet du procédé des deux écoles.[54]

Though Delille was long out of favor, his poetic vocabulary lingered on; here Sainte-Beuve places him in direct opposition to Chénier and his disciples, and this is the reform he proposes:

Au lieu du mot vaguement abstrait, métaphysique et sentimental, employer le mot propre et pittoresque; ainsi, par exemple, au lieu de *ciel en courroux* mettre *ciel noir et brumeux*; au lieu de *lac mélancolique* mettre *lac bleu*; préférer aux *doigts délicats* les *doigts blancs et longs*.[55]

However, he does not limit the poet to adjectives of form and color but recommends that for contrast he mix with the "mots propres et pittoresques" a few indefinite adjectives such as "choisi," désiré," "souverain," "qui laissent deviner la pensée sous leur ampleur." (It is not clear why "jaloux," another word he proposes, is commendable while "fier," used by Delille, is not.)

In *Pensée* XV he defends "la splendeur de cette peinture inaccoutumée" of the new poets against the members of the "école genevoise" at the *Globe*. All through the *Pensées* he links the poet and the painter. Whether it is a question of true colors or of colors modified by the spectator's mood, the season of the year, the hour of the day, or the play of light, the eyes of the poet and of the painter are the same and they invent colors in the same way. Great painters, says Sainte-Beuve, know how to show subtle distinctions:

... ils démêlent ce qui est de l'heure et du lieu, ce qui s'harmonise le mieux avec la pensée du tout; et ils font saillir ce *je ne sais quoi* par une idéalisation admirable. Le même secret appartient aux grands poètes, qui sont aussi de grands peintres. Nous renvoyons les incrédules à André Chénier, à Alfred de Vigny, à Victor Hugo. Qu'on se tranquillise donc sur cette monotonie prétendue. Le pittoresque n'est pas une boîte à couleurs qui se vide et s'épuise en un jour; c'est une source éternelle de lumière, un soleil intarissable.[56]

There are certain inconsistencies in these last *Pensées*. After complaining in *Pensée* XIII about critics who advance three steps only to

---

[54] Antoine ed., *Pensée* XIII.146.
[55] *Pensée* XIV.146-47.
[56] *Ibid.*, p. 148.

retreat two, he does much the same thing. He mingles specific and picturesque adjectives with indefinite and abstract ones not very different from those he is criticizing; at the same time that he praises the bright new colors ("la splendeur de cette peinture inaccoutumée") which some writers have adopted, he shows that painters (and poets) attenuate these colors by idealizing. And aside from his few remarks on vocabulary, he does not sufficiently explain the link between visual effects and verse techniques which may help to suggest them.[57]

The response of the "Genevans" to this revival of *ut pictura poesis* is not long in coming. It is more mixed than Sainte-Beuve would lead us to believe. Charles Magnin is quite favorably impressed by *Joseph Delorme*, especially by the unity of idea and style, and he praises the efforts of the new poets to enlarge and develop poetic language (see quote, p. 161), though chiding them with being unduly fond of "la difficulté vaincue," in which, ironically, they resemble Delille. However, a few days later, another critic, identified by Sainte-Beuve as Duvergier de Hauranne, presenting his criticism as a letter from a *Globe* subscriber, takes quite a different tone as he concentrates on the criticism in the *Pensées*, especially the innovation proposed in the substitution of "bocage vert" for "bocage romantique." "Avant elle, c'était surtout à l'âme que la poésie s'adressait; la poésie parle maintenant aux yeux, toujours sans doute pour arriver à l'âme, mais pour y arriver par une voie détournée."[58] Hence too many minute descriptions.

> Aussi, pour prendre un exemple, à la vue d'un certain paysage, une certaine émotion naît dans l'âme. Par quelques mots larges et profonds, d'autres chercheraient à transmettre directement cette émotion; l'école nouvelle décrit le paysage avec toutes ses particularités, tous ses accidents, persuadée que l'émotion naîtra d'elle-même. Au premier coup d'oeil, cette manière paraît franche et vraie; cependant, poussée à l'extrême, elle me paraît manquer complètement son but.

The young poets, says the critic, could learn from the example of Scott, who does not try to make us see everything. In any case, the poet simply cannot find the nuances of color that a painter can.

---

[57] See comments by G. Antoine, *ibid.*, pp. 244-45.
[58] 15 April 1829. On January 21 of the same year, *Le Globe* had already said of *Les Orientales*: "C'est de la poésie pour les yeux."

Toutes ces couleurs si fines, si délicates, que Bonington trouve dans
sa palette, comment Hugo les trouvera-t-il dans sa plume? Pour rendre quarante nuances, la langue lui fournira-t-elle quarante mots?...
les arts, uns par le sentiment, uns par la pensée, diffèrent essentiellement par leurs moyens de rendre cette pensée, d'exprimer ce sentiment;
chacun a ses instruments, son domaine.

The emotional experience the spectator has before certain landscape
paintings cannot take place when the landscape is described in words.

La Revue Française, sister publication to *Le Globe*, reacts to Hugo's
poetry in a similar way.

Partant sans doute de l'idée que la forme est surtout le domaine de l'art,
et que la forme est nécessairement extérieure, M. Hugo le place tout
entier dans la reproduction des choses physiques, à l'exclusion des choses
morales. Le monde intellectuel, le monde des idées existe à peine pour
lui; le monde matériel, le monde des impressions fugitives et toutes sen-
suelles qui en procède, obtient tous ses hommages.[59]

Hugo runs over the surfaces, says the critic, without looking into the
"nature intime" of things. (He does not mention Hugo's earlier view
of poetry as "tout ce qu'il y a d'intime dans tout.") If the abbé Delille
adopted the procedures of the naturalist, who examines, analyses, and
recounts, Hugo has adopted those of the painter "qui, forcé de renoncer
à rendre la réalité de la nature extérieure, se contente d'en reproduire
l'ensemble et l'effet."[60] No art can truly render material reality; the
poet who limits himself to the world of appearances does not exploit
the advantage he has over the painter, that of looking into the world
of ideas. The critic also protests the linking of innovation in poetic
form with picturesque subject matter, independent of thought.

Le Mercure du 19e Siècle is moderately favorable to Hugo and *Les
Orientales*. The poems where imagination dominates, such as "Les
Djinns," have given rise to the criticism that Hugo writes only for
the eyes, says the critic.

On conçoit le reproche: la poésie d'imagination est à la fois celle qui
se comprend le moins, et qui se pardonne le moins. La poésie de sentiment, en nous retraçant les rêves du coeur, que nous avons nous-mêmes
éprouvés maintes fois, nous associe, en quelque sorte, au travail du

---

[59] De Guizard, "De la nouvelle école poétique, et de M. Victor Hugo," 7 (1829), 239.
[60] *Ibid.*, p. 242.

poète, et il nous semble que nous soyons pour quelque chose dans cette belle oeuvre qui nous émeut. Il en est tout autrement de l'autre espèce de poésie; elle nous accable et pèse sur nous comme un soleil; de là une sorte d'impatience et de révolte intérieure.[61]

In any case, says the critic, it is a mistake to think that Hugo neglects feeling and poetic idea just to dazzle us with color, and it is right that the image of Mazeppa tied to the runaway horse should strike us more strongly than the idea of genius which it symbolizes.

This is what strikes the critics and often displeases them: the predominance of the concrete and the colorful, even when used emblematically. According to Pierre Leroux, what has led to the reproaches of "poésie pour les yeux" and "matérialisme poétique" is Hugo's characteristic trait: "la force de représenter tout en emblèmes, exagérée jusqu'au point de ne pouvoir souffrir l'abstraction."[62] This produces the greatest beauties of his poetry, and also his faults.

In spite of these attacks on visual poetry, a certain "brotherhood of the arts" did exist in the last years of the Restoration and would continue strongly into the middle thirties. Poets and painters joined together in the Petit-Cénacle, where Gautier would rejoice over the "immixion de l'art dans la poésie" which he saw as "un des signes caractéristiques de la nouvelle école."[63] The new periodical *L'Artiste* (founded 1831) published reviews and criticism of all the arts.

But in the early 1830s Sainte-Beuve turns away from the picturesque toward the intime, and Victor Hugo in *Les Feuilles d'automne* and subsequent volumes becomes a "penseur," focusing more attention on the inner world. Charles Magnin declared that if poetry was to have a future, it must delve into secret regions: "Forcée de se retirer toujours plus avant dans les replis les plus reculés de la nature et du coeur humain, la poésie doit s'ingénier de plus en plus pour arriver à ces régions vierges et inexplorées, les seules où elle se complaise."[64] In the *Revue des Deux Mondes* Gustave Planche takes up the cudgels to attack, even more vigorously than his predecessors, "la poésie extérieure" and "l'art matérialiste."

The poet should find a middle path between an excessive preoccupation with the physicality of the universe and the inner world of

[61] 24 (1829), 201-02.
[62] "Du style symbolique," *Le Globe*, 8 April 1829.
[63] *Histoire du romantisme* (Paris: Charpentier et Fasquelle, 1895), p. 18.
[64] *Ahasvérus* et de la nature du génie poétique," *Revue des Deux Mondes*, 4 (2nd s.) (1833), 568.

the self. These two extremes are principles, more theoretical than actual, and there is always some interplay between internal and external stimuli.

Just as some think that modern civilization has dimished our lyric impulse, others say that it has also dulled our response to the world. Modern man, says a critic of the *Gazette Littéraire*, has lost the sensitivity that enabled the ancients to react spontaneously:

> ... à eux, le monde extérieur, c'est-à-dire, l'intelligence spontanée, le sentiment de la forme; notre sentiment à nous, émoussé qu'il est par l'amas des traditions, par une civilisation compliquée à l'infini dans ses éléments, se refuse à toute inspiration immédiate, nous avons besoin d'observer pour écrire, d'étudier pour sentir. Les anciens peignaient; nous méditons.[65]

The response is less pure but not necessarily less fruitful.

Sometimes the poet has the impression that he communicates directly with the divine, without communication with the world, as the ancient poet felt that he was being visited by the muse. "Il est certain," says Hugo, "que le véritable poète, s'il est maître du choix de ses méditations, ne l'est nullement de la nature de ses inspirations. Son génie, qu'il a reçu et qu'il n'a point acquis, le domine le plus souvent; et il serait singulier et peut-être vrai de dire que l'on est parfaitement étranger, comme homme, à ce qu'on a écrit comme poète."[66]

Poetry seems to come both from without and from within, to descend from some heavenly reaches and to well up from the innermost sources. The modern muse, says G. Desjardins in an exalted paragraph of the *Muse Française*, brings chords of celestial music to the ear and inspires a poetry which is the "nouvelle fille de l'harmonie universelle."

> Quand cette muse chante, ce ne sont pas seulement des sons cadencés, une douce euphonie qui flatte agréablément l'oreille; ce bruit terrestre et rapproché n'a rien de comparable à cette lointaine et céleste harmonie qui se fait alors entendre au dedans de nous... c'est l'âme tout entière qui se révèle... Un seul son de cette poésie divine touche plus que beaucoup de mots de l'ancienne poésie; son vers a contracté l'habitude du sentiment et du merveilleux: c'est la passion parlée.[67]

---

[65] Review of *Notre-Dame de Paris*, 2 (1831), 388.
[66] Review of *Eloa, Muse Française*, in *Oeuvres complètes*, II/1, 453.
[67] Review of Soumet, *Saül*, I, 129.

However, the outside world is seldom absent from poetry and even less so from painting. In particular, the *genre romantique* calls upon the most diverse inspirations, says Nodier.

> Des aspects encore inaperçus des choses, un ordre de perception assez neuf pour être souvent bizarre, je ne sais quels secrets du coeur humain dont il a souvent joui en lui-même sans être tenté de les révéler aux autres,... je ne sais quels mystères de la nature qui ne nous ont pas échappé dans l'ensemble, mais que nous n'avons jamais détaillés,...[68]

According to Lamartine, the inspiration for poetry and hence its character are all-encompassing:

> C'est l'incarnation de ce que l'homme a de plus intime dans le coeur et de plus divin dans la pensée, dans ce que la nature visible a de plus magnifique dans les images et de plus mélodieux dans les sons! C'est à la fois sentiment et sensation, esprit et matière; et voilà pourquoi c'est la langue complète, la langue par excellence qui saisit l'homme par son humanité toute entière, idée pour l'esprit, sentiment pour l'âme, image pour l'imagination, et musique pour l'oreille![69]

The world is what connects the self with the divine, says Massias: "La nature est le terme moyen, l'échelle mystérieuse, à l'aide de laquelle nous allons et venons de l'une à l'autre de ces grandes réalités."[70] He sets up a number of axioms concerning the different arts as products of the relationship of our faculties to our impressions of the object.

> On voit donc que tous les arts poussent l'homme de lui-même vers la nature et de la nature le ramènent vers lui-même: le faisant osciller perpétuellement entre deux infinis de divers ordres, le *moi* qui perçoit, et la *cause* de ses perceptions... Ainsi les beaux-arts prouvent et expliquent ce qui existe, le *moi*, le *non-moi* et leurs *rapports*;...[71]

Magnin too differentiates among the arts as to their relation to sensation, between the "sentiment du beau" and the "sentiment poétique." The mission of the plastic arts is to give us "l'impression du beau," but what moves us poetically is not direct sensation, "c'est une sensation occasionnelle, oblique, en quelque sorte, engendrée par de secrètes

---

[68] Article on *De l'Allemagne, Journal des Débats*, Nov. 1818; *Mélanges* (1820), I, 345.
[69] "Des destinées de la poésie," *Méditations poétiques*, ed. G. Lanson (Paris: Hachette, 1922), II, 387; originally published in 1834.
[70] *Théorie du beau*, p. 61.
[71] *Ibid.*, pp. 80-81.

affinités que notre imagination découvre… Ce que la poésie a le pouvoir d'exprimer ce n'est donc pas la sensation immédiate que nous recevons des objets: ce qu'elle est apte à exprimer, ce sont des rapports."[72]

[72] *Revue des Deux Mondes*, 4 (2nd s.) (1833), 573-74, article on *Ahasvérus* cited above.

10. The Symbolic Imagination

The symbolic conception of the universe which becomes common in the 1820s can be seen as the confluence of several currents:

1. First of all, the Neoclassic *beau idéal* is evolving toward new concepts of beauty or of expressiveness in art. The Neoclassic search for archetypes and essences behind physical appearances leads logically and without discontinuity to the concept of a spiritual world symbolically expressed by sensible phenomena. There is much of Quatremère de Quincy in Cousin.

2. The Christian tradition continues to play a role. Did not Saint Paul preach that the universe is a system of invisible things manifested visibly? Speaking of Chénier, Soumet comments, "Sa poésie, privée des images que fournit une religion spirituelle, ne peut se plonger comme la muse chrétienne dans ce vague de contemplation que fait naître en nous le pressentiment de l'invisible et de l'infini."[1]

3. Christianity joins hands with illuminism: Joseph de Maistre cites Saint Paul, as does the Swedenborgian Edouard Richer, one of the few illuminists writing during the Restoration who deals with esthetics in his work.[2] In an 1824 article Richer praises idealist philosophy, and even more the combination of idealism with the Scriptures, as practiced by Joseph de Maistre:

> En ne considérant plus le temps et l'espace, ces conditions nécessaires de toutes nos relations physiques, que comme des modes sensibles et

---

[1] *Lettres Champenoises*, 7, quoted by René Canat, *L'Hellénisme des romantiques*, I, 210.
[2] See A. Viatte, "Les Swedenborgiens en France de 1820 à 1830," *Revue du Littérature Comparée*, 11 (1931), 433, and P. Bénichou, *Le Sacre de l'écrivain*, pp. 265-73.

accidentels de notre entendement, [les philosophes] affranchissent totalement l'homme de l'influence des sensations, et le transportent dans cette sphère de l'invisible qui explique tout.[3]

An artist who approaches "ce monde immatériel, le seul qui soit vrai et où l'on ne peut arriver que par un détachement entier [du] moi" has become a passive vessel and has at least temporarily lost his powers. But the doctrine of correspondences, to which Richer subscribed, restores the physical world as a mirror and complete reproduction of the spiritual world. It enables the artist to translate the ecstatic vision and transmit a view of the immaterial world.

The belief in universal analogy most often associated with Swedenborg but common to illuminists of various stripes is spreading and is, as they say, in the air. If the illuminists do not often make the step into the realm of esthetics, the poets and some other writers influenced by them will do so. So many have written about the contributions of the illuminists since Auguste Viatte (*Les Sources occultes du romantisme*, 1928) and Jean Pommier (*La Mystique de Baudelaire*, 1932) that it is hardly necessary here to remind the reader of their importance. In this chapter we shall cite only a few examples of their direct influence as it is shown in some writers of the 1820s, on the eve of its flowering in Balzac, Nerval, and Baudelaire.

The Christian prophet Ballanche in his works of the late 1820s sees the physical universe not as a mirror but as an emblem ("L'ordre matériel est un emblème, un hiéroglyphe du monde spirituel") or a veil which hides the spiritual world.[4] Ballanche believes in the autonomous existence of ideas, "ces reines immortelles" which govern us;

lorsqu'elles viennent dans le monde réalisé, se saisir de l'empire légitime qui leur appartient, elles restent encore, pour le plus grand nombre, obscurément enfouies au fond des choses. C'est pourquoi le spectacle du monde réalisé ne dit rien à ceux qui n'ont pas pénétré dans le monde des idées: Platon le savait bien.[5]

Only the poet is able to perceive these hidden ideas and express the divine harmony which unites all things and links the physical and

---

[3] "De la philosophie idéaliste," *Lycée Armoricain*, IV, 319.
[4] *Palingénésie sociale, Oeuvres*, IV (1833), 212, 248.
[5] "Dédicace" to *Prolégomènes, Oeuvres*, IV, 6.

spiritual domains, since he receives the revelation of the world and of language. Orpheus asks,

> les objets de la nature, les arbres, les fleurs, les nuages, les parfums, la lumière, les vents sont-ils des emblèmes dont l'homme cherche l'explication après l'avoir perdue?... Y a-t-il une harmonie universelle dont l'homme puisse sentir tous les accords, deviner toutes les lois?[6]

Poets of various languages find in the universe images which can serve as symbols. "La poésie et les arts, comme la vie, sont symboliques; et c'est à ce caractère symbolique, qui est leur essence, qu'est due l'immortalité de leurs oeuvres."[7] The work of art, like physical appearances, may disappear, but the thought has a life of its own; having been communicated to others, simply from having been conceived, it is imperishable.

4. A new interest in Platonism, which is encouraged particularly by Cousin's new translation, combines with Christian spiritualism, often with an illuminist tinge, as in Ballanche, as well as with eclectic spiritualism.

5. The renewal of interest in pagan religions also plays a role, especially by the diffusion in French intellectual circles of Creuzer's *Les Religions de l'antiquité*, whose French translation by J. D. Guigniaut (Vol. I, 1825) was commonly known as *La Symbolique*. It was read in particular by Ballanche and Pierre Leroux, but Creuzer's disciple, Baron Eckstein, was principally responsible for spreading his influence in France. Creuzer defines symbols as "des idées pures, revêtues de formes corporelles."[8] A review in *Le Globe* of Guigniaut's translation, which B. Juden attributes to P. Leroux, characterizes *le symbolisme* (the word appears here for the first time in France):

> Les idées qui en font la base sont évidemment dérivées de cette philosophie nouvelle qui reconnaît Schelling pour son fondateur... Le sens du mot *symbole* présente à lui seul la définition entière. Le symbole est un signe, mais un signe qui non seulement rappelle, indique une pensée, c'est encore un signe qui l'*exprime* et la *contient* autant que ce qui est sensible peut exprimer et contenir ce qui ne l'est pas. Or c'est précisément le grand dogme de l'école actuelle, que la nature est le reflet

---

[6] *Orphée, Oeuvres*, V, 168.

[7] "Réflexions diverses," *Oeuvres*, VI, 296.

[8] I.1.26, quoted in D.O. Evans, *Le Socialisme romantique* (Paris: Marcel Rivière, 1948), p. 148.

ou, pour mieux dire, la forme vivante de la pensée de son auteur. Toute la matière est donc le symbole de Dieu qui vit en elle.[9]

6. As for philosophical, or secular, spiritualism, some commentators see it as merging with Christian doctrine, while for others it exists alongside it or supplants it. We have seen that for Anot and Desmarais spiritualism is characteristic of Romanticism, in contrast to the materialism of the ancients. They recognize that in the nineteenth century Cousin has accentuated a movement already initiated by Chateaubriand (and Mme de Staël). At *Le Globe*, Desprès in an often quoted article, "Du romantisme considéré historiquement," after rejecting several other definitions of Romanticism, decides that "*Le romantisme... est le transport du spiritualisme dans la littérature.*"[10] If literature is the expression of society, then Christianity, which in modern times is the common link among all Europeans, must be the fundamental principle of Romantic literature, by which he means literature since the Middle Ages: "toutes les compositions romantiques, quelle qu'en soit la forme, doivent être empreintes de christianisme, ou pour mieux dire du principe qui fait la base de cette religion: ce principe c'est le spiritualisme." This doctrine was rejected at the beginning of the nineteenth century because it was incompatible with the prevailing philosophical ideas in France, Desprès goes on to say. He makes no mention of Chateaubriand or of the religious revival in the early nineteenth century but gives the credit for the rise of French Romanticism to the recent philosophical movement: "Aussi, depuis dix ans que [les idées de la philosophie sensualiste] ont commencé à perdre de leur influence, la littérature romantique a-t-elle trouvé plus d'accès dans les esprits." A growing intellectual independence has helped free the French from literary dogmatism, says he, but it is not likely that those who questioned the foundations of sensualist philosophy would have taken to Romanticism if it had been based on material principles. Desprès concludes that the new literary school has been imported into France by the partisans of the new metaphysical doctrines. *Le Globe* does not elsewhere take such a limited view, ignoring all other influences, but does remain a stronghold of secular spiritualism.

In Lamartine also, spiritualism is a secular counterpart to Christianity which easily combines with it; he is directly inspired by Cousin's

[9] 27 Aug. 1825.
[10] 1 Oct. 1825.

translation of Plato to write *La Mort de Socrate*, whose "Avertissement" contains some passages reminiscent of *Le Vrai, Le Beau et le Bien* (at that time still unpublished lectures). Lamartine's Socrates is a spokesman for spiritualism and a precursor of Christianity.

When the word "expression" takes on a metaphysical dimension (by analogy with its theological meaning), as it does in Cousin's lectures, it has the enlarged meaning of material form by which the transcendental world manifests itself; this is also the meaning now commonly given to the word "symbol." Here again the eclectic view merges with the Christian view of the universe. The visible is the material part of things, the invisible is the spiritual part, says Jouffroy after Cousin. Everything is symbolic because everything we see excites in us the idea of something else that we do not see.[11] But Cousin's *vrai* is more metaphysical than religious, and Jouffroy is not a believer. The symbolic universe for Jouffroy is not religious but esthetic;[12] the symbol is what gives an esthetic dimension to things: "... nous connaissons la face esthétique des choses, nous savons que ce qui la distingue de leur face utile ou scientifique, c'est l'expression. Les objets et les événements sont esthétiques à titre de symboles."[13] The spiritualism of the eclectics is in part an outgrowth of the Neoclassical *beau idéal*, an esthetic, not a religious, doctrine. The eclectics, says Ph. Damiron, would found art in spiritualism but keep it free from mysticism. "[La poésie] en serait moins lyrique, elle aurait moins d'hymnes et de cantiques, elle aurait moins de méditations; mais elle serait mieux dans la nature, elle entendrait mieux l'expression; plus touchée des symboles, et plus sensible aux figures..."[14]

Artists of all nuances of opinion strove to penetrate the meaning of the universe, that is, to read the spiritual content of material objects which were its expression, or symbol. For some this receptivity was more important than the artist's creativity. If, in the theory of universal analogy, sensible signs of the spiritual world are absolute, they will be the same for all times and places for those who are able to decipher them. Revelation is what the believer aspires to. As Jean

[11] *Cours d'esthétique*, p. 132.
[12] P. Bénichou rightly stresses the fact that in secular spiritualism esthetic feeling takes the place of worship and prayer. (*Le Sacre de l'écrivain*, p. 258.)
[13] *Cours*, pp. 149-50.
[14] *Essai sur l'histoire de la philosophie en France du dix-neuvième siècle* (Paris: Ponthieu, 1828), p. xxviii.

Pommier points out, "La poésie devient une science au lieu d'un art, une réception au lieu d'une projection."[15] This is the common stance of the illuminists and sometimes others besides. A. F. Théry, a disciple of Cousin, sees the imagination as an enlightening faculty rather than a creative one; it reveals to us the analogies which exist between us and the spiritual world:

> L'imagination n'a pas mission de créer: elle colore, elle éclaire; c'est elle qui indique au poète les rapports secrets, les harmonies éclatantes qui unissent le monde des sens au monde des esprits. La rapidité des vues, la surabondance des idées et des sentiments du poète exigent que l'imagination lui prodigue sans retard et sans mesure toutes les brillantes analogies de l'ordre sensible.[16]

Receptivity is, for obvious reasons, stressed when speaking of the plastic arts, though it is of course only the first step. *L'Artiste* gives us a fairly typical comment: Delacroix is "un peintre qui n'a pas de genre, qui saisit ce qu'il voit dans la nature, et sait le poétiser... Dans ces ouvrages, nous n'avons toujours vu que l'intention de rendre la nature avec autant de vérité que de noblesse, et c'est là ce que nous demandons à la peinture..."[17] Delacroix himself thought that genius lay in seeing what others did not see and seeing in a different way (see passage quoted above, pp. 159-60).[18] The true artist, says Delécluze, cannot consider nature without seeking to penetrate her secrets. "Cette faculté de l'imagination, ce pouvoir intellectuel par lequel l'homme devient l'interprète de la nature à l'égard de ses semblables, est la qualité qui distingue essentiellement l'artiste..."[19] A good artist, says he, never descends from an abstract idea to real forms; his instinct leads him to go in the opposite direction.[20]

In the opinion of most critics, however, imagination plays an even more important role in creation than in perception.

---

[15] *La Mystique de Baudelaire*, p. 98.

[16] *De l'esprit et de la critique littéraires chez les peuples anciens et modernes* (Paris: Hachette, Locard et Davi, 1832), II, 370.

[17] V. Schoelcher, "MM Delacroix, Léon Cogniet, Decamps, etc.," 1 (1831), 226.

[18] *Journal*, I, 87. Baudelaire sees Delacroix's approach quite differently from Schoelcher: "Delacroix part... de ce principe, qu'un tableau doit avant tout reproduire la pensée intime de l'artiste, qui domine le modèle, comme le créateur la création...". ("Salon de 1846," *Curiosités esthétiques* [Conard ed.], p. 108).

[19] *Précis d'un traité de peinture*, pp. 5-6.

[20] *Ibid.*, p. 177.

C'est donc l'imagination qui saisit le lien entre l'idée et la matière, [says Ad. Garnier,] soit que, partant d'une expression, elle en trouve l'idée, soit que, partant d'une idée, elle en trouve l'expression. Mais dans ce dernier cas, son travail est plus difficile... Celui qui va de l'expression à l'idée ne fait que lire; celui qui va de l'idée à l'expression, compose.[21]

The artist both reads and composes; he starts with a model, chooses the traits he wishes to keep, then modifies them. The result of this, says Garnier, is *l'idéal*, or "la matière soumise à l'idée."[22] Whichever way one moves between the realms of idea and matter, it is the idea that dominates.

The artist who must make matter submit to his idea molds it, as God molds matter. He can be seen as competing with God, by creating a work of his own.

Il est dit dans le livre saint, [says Audin,] que Dieu fit l'homme avec un peu de boue: c'est donc avec un peu de boue que le poète romantique forme ses plus belles créations; dans toutes il entre de la matière; mais il faut avouer que cette matière sort souvent brillante de ses mains et que, semblable à la divinité, il sait répandre sur elle le souffle de la vie.[23]

Or, to reverse the comparison, God works as an artist does: "Dieu est descendu sur la matière; son monde idéal s'est abaissé sur elle; Dieu alors s'est emparé d'elle, comme le génie de l'artiste s'empare d'une masse inorganique d'où il fait sortir son chef-d'oeuvre."[24]

The parallel of God and man as creators may be carried further, to show the impossibility of actualizing a work which will equal the perfection of the original idea; expressed truth is less true than conceived truth. This idea, which runs through the Romantic period, has roots in Christianity and in Plotinus, according to whom creation took place by emanation. "Everything that reaches outwards is the less for it, strength less strong, heat less hot, power less potent,

---

[21] "Observations sur le beau," *Revue Encyclopédique*, 30 (1826), 611.

[22] *Ibid.*, 30:612. See above, Ch. 7.

[23] "Du romantique," preceding *Florence*, p. xxvi. Ervin Panofsky points out that such parallels suggest that the ideational faculty comes from divine knowledge. See his *Idea*, trans. Joseph J.S. Peake (Columbia: University of South Carolina Press, 1961), p. 91.

[24] Baron Eckstein, "Du beau," *Le Catholique*, 4 (1826), 517. According to Etienne Gilson, this is the original comparison, which theologians borrowed from art, not the other way around. See his *Painting and Reality* (New York: Pantheon, 1957), p. 121.

and so beauty less beautiful."[25] Victor Cousin teaches in his 1828 course that all creation is necessarily imperfect.[26] Incarnation means imperfection, with the exception, for Christian believers, of Jesus Christ. Vigny's struggle to keep purity of thought when conveyed in impure language is well known, as well as his dislike of incarnation on the religious plane. True feelings are inexpressible.

For the artist the problem is not only metaphysical but technical. Twice in the late 1820s Sainte-Beuve shows how the two are allied, first in his review of Hugo's *Odes et ballades*,[27] then in the first *Pensée* of Joseph Delorme:

> La vérité, en toutes choses, à la prendre dans son sens le plus pur et le plus absolu, est ineffable et insaisissable; en d'autres termes, une vérité est toujours moins vraie, exprimée, que conçue. Pour l'amener à cet état de clarté et de précision qu'exige le langage, il faut, plus ou moins, mais nécessairement et toujours, y ajouter et en retrancher; rehausser les teintes, repousser les ombres, arrêter les contours; de là tant de vérités *exprimées* qui ressemblent aux mêmes vérités *conçues*, comme des nuages de marbre ressemblent à des nuages. C'est souvent un peu la faute de l'ouvrier, c'est toujours et surtout la faute de la matière.[28]

The writer must always be conscious of the discrepancies between thought and expression, and the reader must learn to read between the lines.

In his 1830 article, "Des artistes," Balzac has some interesting remarks to make on the inner world the artist creates for himself and where his works germinate; he dwells on the pleasures of this world and the dangers of cherishing the conception of a work too long in his imagination:

> Or, pour l'homme plongé dans la sphère inconnue des choses qui n'existent pas pour le berger, qui, en taillant une admirable figure de femme dans un morceau de bois, dit: "Je la découvre!" pour les artistes enfin, le monde extérieur n'est rien! Ils racontent toujours avec infidélité ce qu'ils ont vu dans le monde merveilleux de la pensée... Quand un poète, un peintre, un sculpteur donnent une vigoureuse réalité à l'une

---

[25] *Ennead*, 5, 8, quoted in Frederic Will, *Intelligible Beauty in Aesthetic Thought* (Tübingen: Max Niemeyer, 1958), p. 28.
[26] I, 5th lesson, p. 29.
[27] *Le Globe*, 9 Jan. 1827.
[28] Antoine ed., p. 130.

de leurs oeuvres, c'est que l'intention avait lieu au moment même de la création. Les meilleurs ouvrages des artistes sont ceux-là, tandis que l'oeuvre dont ils font le plus grand cas, est, au contraire, la plus mauvaise, parce qu'ils ont trop vécu par avance avec leurs figures idéales.[29]

But in the late 1820s the Romantic writers were insisting that *fond* and *forme* are inseparable. We have seen that Deschamps insisted on it; Sainte-Beuve too in the fifth *Pensée* of Joseph Delorme. Modern poets do not lend undue importance to the form of the alexandrine and other technical matters, says he. "On a commencé par les accuser de mépriser la forme; maintenant on leur reproche d'en être esclaves. Le fait est qu'ils tiennent à la fois au fond et à la forme..." The rest of the passage continues the polemics with *Le Globe* of which we have spoken in the preceding chapter; the amusing thing is that Sainte-Beuve presents this union as now accomplished and the indispensable form found. Charles Magnin in reviewing *Joseph Delorme* credits Sainte-Beuve with having carried the reform of poetic style a step forward and brought the expression close to the thought. "Nous ne connaissons guère de livre où l'idée et le style soient plus intimement unis."[30] Each poet leaves his mark on the language. "Il faut une langue nouvelle à qui veut faire entendre des accents que nulle oreille humaine n'a entendus. Aussi les poètes, dans l'acception la plus large de ce mot, sont-ils, selon nous, les vrais artisans des langues; ce sont eux qui font et défont incessamment." Hugo, who in 1822 had said that poetry was not in the form of ideas but in the ideas themselves, in 1834 states emphatically: "Chez les grands poètes, rien de plus inséparable, rien de plus adhérent, rien de plus consubstantiel que l'idée et l'expression de l'idée."[31] He is evolving toward his famous "Qui délivre le mot délivre la pensée."[32]

The Belgian critic Alfred Michiels in 1842 gives an interesting aperçu of this question as it was debated in the 1820s and 1830s:

On se rappelle que dans les combats littéraires de notre siècle une des idées, le plus souvent émises peignait le romantisme comme un système d'art où le fond l'emportait sur la forme, l'esprit sur la matière. Aucun

---

[29] *La Silhouette*, 11 March 1830; *Oeuvres diverses*, Conard, I, 354.
[30] *Le Globe*, 11 April 1829.
[31] *Littérature et philosophie mêlées, Oeuvres complètes V/1, 30.*
[32] "Réponse à un acte d'accusation," *Les Contemplations*, I, 7.

des novateurs n'a explicitement professé, cette opinion; mais, outre le témoignage des souvenirs personnels, les journaux en offrent des traces nombreuses. Ainsi M. Delacroix passait pour négliger volontairement son exécution: l'enthousiasme poétique dont il était saisi, la crainte de perdre un moment de vue sa pensée, le forçaient, disait-on, de sacrifier le soin à la verve, le détail à l'ensemble... Les drames de M. Hugo et nombre de poèmes *échevelés* furent écrits sous son influence.[33]

Michiels attributes this idea directly to Cousin: "Il a soutenu avant tous les autres que la beauté de l'expression est la beauté supérieure, qu'elle efface ses rivales et ne leur laisse même qu'un charme d'emprunt. Ou elles n'existent pas, ou elles reflètent le beau spirituel." He quotes and summarizes: according to Cousin, beauty is expression and art the search for expression. Physical ugliness disappears in the radiance of spiritual beauty: Socrates' face (always Socrates!) becomes sublime when he speaks of the immortality of the soul.

C'est donc à peine si le laid existe; et dans tous les cas, pour le rendre agréable, il suffirait de lui adjoindre une beauté spirituelle ou même un sentiment énergique de la vie, quelle que fut sa nature. Le lecteur reconnaît, sans doute ici une des opinions les plus fameuses de nos romantiques. Elle a produit Quasimodo. Nous ne pouvons nous empêcher de faire à ce sujet un rapprochement singulier, mais dont l'exactitude nous paraît évidente. Les théories, soit justes, soit fausses, que nous venons d'exposer ont toutes été mises sur le compte de Victor Hugo; quoiqu'il ne les ait jamais ouvertement défendues, on ne peut regarder cette imputation comme tout à fait chimérique; elles se trouvent dans ses préfaces et dans ses ouvrages à l'état latent. Il a donc eu, en partie du moins, pour père intellectuel le traducteur de Platon. Les idées de M. Cousin, qui obtenait alors une grande vogue, circulant au milieu du public, frappèrent l'auteur d'Hernani et le convertirent un des premiers.[34]

Michiels perhaps overstates his case, but given the popularity of Cousin's ideas in the 1820s, they may well have made their mark on the young Hugo.

Jouffroy has a broader conception of beauty than Cousin, since he recognizes several kinds (see above, p. 113), but he finds that the *beau de l'invisible* is the principle of them all. He poses the question "Does

[33] *Histoire des idées littéraires en France au dix-neuvième siècle* (Paris: Coquebert, 1842), I, 105.
[34] *Ibid.*, pp. 106-07.

content act upon us esthetically without form?" but cannot answer.
If it is true that content without form cannot give esthetic pleasure,
one consequence is that art must be as much concerned with form
as with content. "L'artiste ne doit pas tant faire comprendre l'invisible que la montrer, et le montrer, c'est le revêtir de formes
matérielles."[35] No matter how well a person knows the deepest cor-
ners of the soul, he must know its outward manifestations to be an
artist.

There is general agreement that the idea comes first, then the form
follows. "L'idée préside à la naissance de la forme et la façonne en
quelque sorte; la forme révèle l'idée d'une manière sensible, et la fait
passer de l'état d'abstraction à celui de réalité," says Adolphe Pictet.[36]
The two are perfectly fused in classical art, but when the artist inspired by Christianity aspires to make form approach the infinite, his
problem is well-nigh insoluble.

> Ou bien, effaçant et reculant les limites dont elle ne peut jamais se
> dépouiller entièrement, elle devient gigantesque, vague, indéfinie, ou
> bien, elle se brise en quelque sorte, et s'efforce d'exprimer par la variété
> ce qui s'échapperait toujours au cercle borné d'une forme simple... Quel-
> que vaste que soit la forme, quelle que soit la richesse de ses transfor-
> mations, toujours l'infini la déborde, et l'idée ne trouve pas son entière
> expression.

The general effect of this kind of beauty, says Pictet, is one of mystery
and melancholy. The contrast between the finitude of form and the
infinity of idea has led artists to abandon sculpture for painting, less
palpable and material, and it has brought a mysterious immensity
in architecture. Poetry becomes intellectual, melancholy, and introspective; imagination is vague.

Pictet does not believe that beauty can come out of a preponderance
of form over idea. But the reaction against this spiritualist doctrine
by the partisans of *l'art pour l'art* will soon reverse the priorities of spirit
and matter. It does not matter what subject is treated, says F. Soulié
in *L'Artiste*, "c'est le pinceau que je viens étudier, c'est le ciseau que
j'admire; c'est le style, c'est exécution... qui me semble prodigieux."[37]

---

[35] *Cours d'esthétique*, p. 191.
[36] "Quelques idées sur la distinction des genres classique et romantique," *Bibliothèque Universelle (Littérature)*, 33 (1826), 233.
[37] Review of J. Janin, *Barnave*, 2 (1831), 88.

Everybody has ideas, says Jules Janin, but only art knows how to use them.

> [Le vrai connaisseur] aime la peinture pour la peinture: quand il regarde un tableau, il veut voir un tableau et non un mélodrame; pour lui, la peinture ne se fait qu'avec de la couleur et non pas avec des idées:... [le peintre] peint d'abord; il sait que la couleur seule est immortelle, il sait que l'art du peintre est uniquement dans les formes.[38]

The artist is a creator of forms, but not *ex nihilo*; most often he is presented as a collaborator with God. The Neoclassics said that he completes God's work, by making the elements of the universe more coherent. By so doing, said Cousin, he actually comes closer to carrying out God's conception than God himself. Pierre Leroux carries this idea a large step further by showing how man's art is incorporated into the universe, forming a new unity between man, God, and nature. Man was placed on earth to finish God's work, says he; his hand is God's and the earth is his work as well as God's. Man continues God's work by industry or by art. Art does not consist in trying to remake the mountain, reproduce it on a smaller scale, or copy its forms and colors in a picture.

> Mais tirer de la vue des forêts et des montagnes une inspiration créatrice, donner à l'habitation où les hommes se réunissent pour adorer le Dieu infini quelque chose de l'aspect de ces sublimes montagnes, et élever des temples qui s'harmonisent avec nos grands végétaux comme les petits temples de la Grèce s'harmonisaient avec les lentisques et les orangers, voilà l'*art*. C'est la montagne et la forêt changées en temple par l'homme, et reproduits par lui comme il convient de les reproduire. La forêt, la montagne étaient des monuments de la nature: le temple, inspiré par elles est un monument de l'homme. Et alors s'établit dans le monde une nouvelle harmonie: l'homme ne peut plus voir les colonnades des forêts et les autels des montagnes, sans que l'idée d'un temple à l'Eternel lui revienne en mémoire. C'est ainsi que le monde tout entier, en y comprenant l'art, qui en fait partie au même titre que les monuments naturels auxquels il s'ajoute, devient *symbolique*.[39]

If nature is a temple, it is because man by his creative efforts has transformed it into one. The monument created by man, himself a part of nature, is reintegrated into nature, to which it gives symbolic

---

[38] 7 (1834), 294-95.
[39] "De la poésie de notre époque," *Revue Encyclopédique*, 52 (1831), 404.

meaning.[40] But since man is God's hand, God is working through him, and one might say that God needs man, His own creation, to give symbolic meaning to the rest of the universe.

This is what happens when the artist creates, whether or not he considers himself the instrument of God: he sees in nature an analogue of his own feeling or idea which he then utilizes to express this feeling or idea. The impulse comes first from within, and the choice of the symbol is made by the artist. Leroux himself says that art, unlike industry, is "l'expression de la vie qui est en nous." During our lives we have assimilated impressions and images from the outer world, so that they are now part of our inner life. "Or, l'homme ne crée rien, en prenant le mot de création dans un sens absolu. Il n'a donc pas d'autre moyen de réaliser le produit de sa vie intérieure que de l'incarner dans ce qui existe déjà. De là il suit que le principe unique de l'art est le *symbole*."[41]

Imagination, which reveals hidden meanings behind objects, also incarnates the thought in material form, without which there is no art. Joubert had said years earlier: "J'appelle imagination la faculté de rendre sensible ce qui est intellectuel, d'incorporer ce qui est esprit; en un mot, de mettre au jour, sans le dénaturer, ce qui est de soi-même invisible."[42] Vigny's conception of the role of the imagination is quite similar: "... l'imagination donne du corps aux idées et leur crée des types et des symboles vivants qui sont comme la forme palpable et la preuve d'une théorie abstraite."[43]

By the 1820s such statements have become quite frequent; a few examples will serve as illustration. We will note that this incarnation of the spiritual is taken sometimes as a description, sometimes as a program, of the new poetry. First, two illustrious ancestors: Népomucène Lemercier says a propos of Chénier that no poet has a greater tendency to translate his ideas into images, which is the true way of poetry.[44] Audin does not seem fully to approve what he sees as a consequence of the influence of Schiller and his school: "... une sorte d'artifice poétique, qui consiste à matérialiser en quelque sorte les conceptions de l'intelligence, à enchaîner l'idéal sous des formes

[40]   See B. Juden, "L'Esthétique: 'l'harmonie immense qui dit tout,'" *Romantisme*, no. 5 (1973), p. 13.
[41]   *Revue Encyclopédique*, 52 (1831), 407.
[42]   *Pensées et lettres*, I, 61.
[43]   *Journal d'un poète, Oeuvres* II, (1824), 880.
[44]   *Revue Encyclopédique*, 4 (1819), 90.

corporelles, et en revêtir jusqu'aux abstractions de la pensée..."[45] On the other hand, *La Muse Française* in an exposé of its doctrines, quotes Schiller with full approval: "... il est accordé ou plutôt il est imposé à l'art idéal de saisir l'esprit de chaque chose et de l'enchaîner sous une forme matérielle..."[46]

In *Le Globe*, Charles de Rémusat contrasts English poetry, which has turned toward description of nature and the countryside, with German poetry, a contemplative poetry where outer objects play only a small role, and this role is symbolic: "elle n'emprunte du monde extérieur que des images et des couleurs pour figurer et peindre des idées."[47]

Baron Massias sees this contrast between Romantic and older poetry:

> Le romantisme qu'on pourrait définir, *poésie de la métaphysique*, doit tendre sans cesse à fixer, à colorer, à rendre palpable ce qui de soi est confus, fugitif, intangible et inapercevable, en opposition à l'ancienne poésie qui cherchait avec un soin tout particulier à donner une vie, une âme, un esprit, des affections aux choses qui tombent sous le sens.[48]

Actually, the Romantics do both; the two processes are corollary, and so the critic says, but maintains emphasis on materializing the spiritual.

Images are essential to Romantic poetry if it is to make its thought understood, says C. Desmarais:

> La littérature romantique sera plus aérienne et plus idéale que la littérature classique; et, toutefois, elle abondera davantage en comparaisons et en images: c'est que la poésie a bien plus besoin de traduire la pensée en images, lorsque la pensée est si vaporeuse et si déliée, qu'elle risquerait sans ce secours de n'être ni exprimée ni comprise.[49]

The more subtle and intellectualized the thought, the greater is the necessity for imagery. So it has always been with the great mysteries: "Le poète présente les faits divins sous la forme accessible du symbole," says Ballanche.[50]

---

[45] "Du romantique," preceding *Florence*, p. xxx.
[46] A. Guiraud, "Nos Doctrines," II, 15.
[47] "De la poésie anglaise et de la poésie allemande," 25 Aug. 1827.
[48] *Théorie du beau*, pp. 240-41.
[49] *Essai sur les classiques et les romantiques*, p. 97.
[50] "Dédicace" to *Palingénésie sociale*, *Oeuvres*, IV, 7.

It is possible for the poet to see analogies between the universe and himself (outer and inner universes) based solely on his emotional sensitivity and imagination; he may project his feelings onto the world in a purely subjective fashion and see in nature a reflection of his mood. Some of the passages quoted above seem to indicate this, others present the choice of images as a kind of intellectual process. But most often the poet sees himself, or the critic sees him, as both an interpreter and a creator: he sees hidden meanings behind phenomena, and he also invents. P. Leroux's article quoted above shows man's creation mingling with that of God and becoming part of it. This is possible because the whole universe is imbued with the spirit of God. Alexandre Soumet, who sprang to the defense of Mme de Staël during the polemic surrounding the publication of *De l'Allemagne*,[51] again expounds her message a few years later. The mind either contemplates the spheres and their harmony, or "il cherche dans le monde moral le type du monde physique et n'aperçoit que des symboles de l'âme humaine dans les phénomènes les plus cachés de la nature."[52] When Soumet joins the group of *La Muse Française*, he and his colleagues speak of the harmony of man with the universe and the symbolic character of this universe, developing these principles in their own way and expressing themselves in a poetic and exalted tone. Here Soumet sums up in a few sentences the visionary character of the poet:

> Le poète est essentiellement l'interprète de la nature et de la destinée, et la poésie n'a été appelé le premier des arts que parce qu'elle explique et achève, pour ainsi dire, l'oeuvre du Créateur. Elle dépouille les êtres de leur enveloppe vulgaire, pour les forcer à livrer à nos regards tous les secrets de leur merveilleuse existence. Tout est symbolique aux yeux du poète,... il devine que sous les différents objets dont il est environné il existe autre chose que ces objets eux-mêmes.[53]

The poetic enthusiasm of the *Cénacle* goes beyond Cousin's spiritualism, fervent as it may have been. (Joseph Delorme will a few years later remark on this difference between the poets and the philosophers. And Vigny the same year [1829] comments in his Journal: "L'éclectisme est une lumière sans doute, mais une lumière comme celle de la lune,

---

[51] In *Les Scrupules littéraires de Madame de Staël* (Paris: Delaunay, 1814).
[52] Review of Portalis, *De l'usage et de l'abus de l'esprit philosophique durant le 18e siècle*, *Conservateur Littéraire*, 3 (1820), 217.
[53] Review of Baour-Lormian trans. of *La Jérusalem délivrée*, *La Muse Française*, I, 296.

qui éclaire sans réchauffer. On peut distinguer les objets à sa clarté, mais toute sa force ne produirait pas la plus légère étincelle.")[54]

According to Nicolas Artaud, man is touched by nature and in turn animates it:

> ... la nature a un langage qu'elle adresse à l'homme, et il y reconnaît de mystérieuses analogies avec ses émotions antérieures... Dans cette alliance secrète de notre être avec les phénomènes de l'univers, n'y a-t-il pas déjà une sorte de poésie naturelle, qui semble attester et rétablir l'harmonie du monde physique avec le monde moral? Cette faculté qui réfléchit comme une glace fidèle les impressions du monde sensible, et y voit les symboles des affections de notre âme, qui trouve pour produire nos sentiments et nos pensées le tour le plus vif et l'image la plus transparente, c'est l'imagination; elle colore et anime tout ce qu'elle saisit; elle donne une forme sensible aux conceptions les plus abstraites et aux sentiments les plus intimes.[55]

For illustrations of their theories, which are at the same time the basis of the theories, the critics sometimes look to English nature poetry. Here Sainte-Beuve sees the interaction between nature and the poet's feelings which the critics so often remark upon: at the end of the eighteenth century, while French poets were describing the surfaces of things, in England "on s'avisa... d'associer à ces peintures les impressions qu'elles faisaient naître et de les vivifier par un reflet des sentiments humains."[56] In France this was done by some great prose writers (Jean-Jacques Rousseau, Bernardin de Saint-Pierre, Chateaubriand) but no poet attempted it before Lamartine. The English Lake poets have gone farther, they have identified themselves with the landscape, as Pichot has shown; Sainte-Beuve quotes a passage from the book under review:

> Dans ces solitudes muettes, sur le sein de ces lacs, dans le demi-jour de ces forêts, il leur semble que leur âme se fond avec l'âme universelle; ils sentent une influence invisible et ineffable qui les exalte, les ravit et les purifie. C'est un mysticisme qui a quelque rapport avec le panthéisme de Pythagore. Pour eux, tout ce qui est visible, tout ce qui est doué de mouvement ou d'une voix, n'offre plus seulement des symboles obscurs ou des emblèmes fantastiques, mais de véritables révélations.

---

[54] *Oeuvres*, II, 897-98.
[55] "Sur le génie poetique au 19e siècle," *Revue Encyclopédique*, 25 (1825), 603.
[56] Review of A. Pichot, *Voyage littéraire et historique en Angleterre et en Ecosse, Le Globe*, 15 Dec. 1825.

These poets are true seers; they see in nature not just a meaning their imagination has projected upon it, but what is really there. Sainte-Beuve thinks that some of this is exaggerated.

He does not elaborate on what Lamartine has accomplished in French poetry, but a few years later Henri Patin sees in the poet's work this vital interchange: "Partout vous trouvez chez M. de Lamartine cette même confusion de la nature et du monde invisible, se servant l'un à l'autre d'explication et d'emblème. Ainsi, chez lui la pensée prend toujours un corps, une figure, et la matière, à son tour, une âme et une voix."[57] Shortly thereafter Lamartine himself expounded in prose what was evident in his poetry:

> Il y a des harmonies entre tous les éléments, comme il y en a une générale entre la nature matérielle et la nature intellectuelle. Chaque pensée a son reflet dans un objet visible qui la répète comme un écho, la réfléchit comme un miroir, et la rend perceptible de deux manières: aux sens par l'image, à la pensée par la pensée; c'est la poésie infinie de la double création! Les hommes appellent cela comparaison: la comparaison c'est le génie. La création n'est qu'une pensée sous mille formes. Comparer, c'est l'art ou l'instinct de découvrir des mots de plus dans cette langue divine des analogies universelles que Dieu seul possède, mais dont il permet à certains hommes de découvrir quelque chose.[58]

The most extensive philosophical discussion of this correspondence between the invisible and the phenomenal is to be found in Théodore Jouffroy's *Cours d'esthétique*. According to his teachings, what lies behind and at the source of phenomena is an active force, in the universe and in us. Like Cousin, he believes that the same spirit is in all things. As smaller units combine to form the great unity of the whole universe, Jouffroy sees that all things are related, like different branches of the same trunk. "Une fois sur cette route, nous ne nous arrêtons plus; nous finissons par concevoir que ce vaste univers n'est qu'une seule substance, animée par un seul principe et tendant à une seule fin, au sein d'un espace et d'une durée infinis et indécomposables" (102). The animating principle is a universal force (Jouffroy also calls it "l'invisible" or "la nature active") which may be cosmic or moral. (The

---

[57] Review of *Harmonies poétiques et religieuses*, *Revue Encyclopédique*, 47 (1830), 134.
[58] *Voyage en Orient*, 2 vols. (Paris: Hachette, Furne), I, 30. Dated 11 July 1832. See commentary by Christian Croisille in "L'Harmonie lamartinienne," *Colloques Sainte-Beuve et Lamartine*, 8 Nov. 1968 (Paris: A. Colin, 1970), pp. 86-101.

context usually tells us whether Jouffroy is speaking of the self or the not-self when he says "l'invisible," but sometimes the distinctions are blurred.) Phenomena are its expression. "Or, les phénomènes et les qualités des corps qui sont des effets d'un principe en sont conséquemment les expressions ou les signes; et ce principe, c'est la force, ou c'est nous; car nous aussi nous sommes force, et toute force est identique, toute force est un principe actif"(114). But all we can perceive is phenomena and qualities of objects. "Ainsi le monde est pour nous l'expression de notre nature, le symbole de la force."

We who are spirit do not directly perceive spirit, nor does force perceive force. They cannot perceive each other or communicate except through an aggregation of matter.

> La matière, les qualités de la matière sont donc là comme des langues pour les forces qui veulent se percevoir, se toucher, se comprendre. Ce sont des truchements qui leur servent à faire mutuellement connaissance; les forces prennent la matière, la conforment et s'annoncent en se peignant à sa surface par leurs effets, se signifient et s'interpénètrent par les qualités qu'elles imposent à la matière. Le monde n'est qu'un symbole matériel qui permet aux forces de se parler et de converser entre elles, de s'exprimer à sa faveur dans quelque langage et de communiquer les unes avec les autres.
>
> Ainsi la matière est à la fois obstacle et moyen; la matière empêche les forces de s'approcher, et les aide à se montrer les unes aux autres. (145)

When an artist looks at an object, he is seeking the meaning of the symbol, not its manner of being or purpose; he looks for what it expresses. In theory, everything is expressive, though in practice we often discover meaning in objects with difficulty or not at all. The coherence of an object generally corresponds to its place in the chain of being: "Informe et mal taillée, la pierre ne dit rien de la force; du moins nous ne trouvons pas le sens de sa couleur, de sa forme. La figure humaine, au contraire, par ses traits, par ses regards, nous parle évidemment de la force ou de la vie qui l'anime intérieurement" (153). Jouffroy believes that the force is there behind every existing thing, but the knowledge of this force in objects where it is hidden ("obscurément enfouie," as Ballanche says) comes not from an illumination but by collaboration from the artist who by his work discovers it and makes it visible. He gives it form. The meaning of a stone does not appear to us, says Jouffroy, because its form is imprecise and its color indefinite; it lacks meaningful symbols of sound and movement.

La pierre exprimera, quand vous changerez sa forme et sa couleur, quand vous la sculpterez, même quand vous vous contenterez uniquement d'en régulariser la figure, quand vous lui donnerez l'éclat du diamant. La pierre ne dit pas grand'chose, parce que ses signes élémentaires ne ressortent pas assez; c'est un mot griffonné, mal écrit; il y a là des lettres, nous le savons; nous ne pouvons pas néanmoins les déchiffrer. (165)

The invisible hidden by matter is communicated to us through sympathy; this principle is at the heart of Jouffroy's esthetics. "Le sentiment esthétique fondamental, c'est le sentiment sympathique" (256).

Le fait esthétique résulte toujours du rapport de deux termes différents, l'objet et le sujet: l'objet qui, par l'expression, agit sur le sujet ou le spectateur; le sujet ou le spectateur qui, par la sympathie, reçoit l'action de l'objet. L'expression, c'est dans l'objet, la manifestation d'un certain état d'âme. La sympathie, c'est, dans le sujet, la répétition d'un certain état de l'âme que l'objet manifeste. (263)

According to Jouffroy, a moment of hesitation always precedes sympathy (or esthetic feeling), because our intelligence is at first unsure of the meaning of the expression of the object. Esthetic feeling may be slow to come, or weak, or not be produced at all, for various reasons: it may be that nature is imperfectly developed, that the outer signs of the object are indefinite, as in the case of the rough stone discussed above. Or the fault may lie with the viewer, who may be distracted by other things, or perhaps he is looking for too much precision of expression, in music, for example.

The sympathetic state differs from personal feeling in three ways: 1. in the sympathetic state, the sensations accompanying the principal fact are much less vivid; 2. when we feel sympathetically, our judgment falls on the outside object; 3. all circumstances which accompany a personal state (such as hopes, fears, agitations) disappear in the sympathetic state. The processes of expression and sympathy produce a pleasure which is independent of the state being reproduced or of the state in which the viewer finds himself. Thus we can take (sympathetic) pleasure in reproducing a state which in itself is disagreeable.

Expression and sympathy operate in the same way on the two levels of creation, nature and art. The invisible forces of nature (the object) act upon the artist (the subject) through expression and he receives this action by the operation of sympathy. The artist's work in its turn becomes the object which expresses the invisible; this meaning is sympathetically grasped by the spectator/listener/reader. Both nature and art are symbolic, both are expressive.

In art, Jouffroy departs farther from the *beau idéal* than his mentor Cousin. The latter had defined art as the expression of moral beauty with the aid of physical beauty. Jouffroy starts by saying that beauty is invisible and poses the question of whether material beauty exists. For him, expression, i.e., the concrete work of art, is subordinate or, as he says, accessory to the meaning. A person looking at nature or at a work of art is less struck by the expression than by the meaning. "Le signe et le perfectionnement du signe ne frappent pas autant [que le sens]" (238). (Another example of the predominance of *fond* over *forme*.) At the same time, the artist must be preoccupied with concrete expression. He is not a philosopher who delves into inner workings; he works with surfaces and tries to see how the outside expresses the inside (158; cf. 191). The expressive virtue of objects is not called beauty or ugliness; these words are applied only to moral, invisible nature, expressed by material forms. Beauty (or ugliness) is not in the expression, but art is (237-38). Meaning and beauty or ugliness are invisible; the work of art is, as Delacroix said, a bridge between souls, the matter by which they communicate.

Sainte-Beuve attended Jouffroy's lectures, and his erstwhile mentor's emphasis on sympathetic response is echoed a few years later in the *Pensées de Joseph Delorme*. Sainte-Beuve has considerably evolved since the days when he expressed reservations about the English poets. (Things moved fast in the 1820s, and in any case Victor Hugo has intervened, as well as Jouffroy.) He now sees the artist entering into an ecstatic communion with the world, leaving the philosopher far behind:

> Le sentiment de l'art implique un sentiment vif et intime des choses. Tandis que la majorité des hommes s'en tient aux surfaces et aux apparences, tandis que les philosophes proprement dits reconnaissent et constatent un *je ne sais quoi* au delà des phénomènes, sans pouvoir déterminer la nature de ce *je ne sais quoi*, l'artiste, comme s'il était doué d'un sens à part, s'occupe paisiblement à sentir sous ce monde apparent l'autre monde tout intérieur qu'ignorent la plupart, et dont les philosophes se bornent à constater l'existence; il assiste au jeu invisible des forces et sympathise avec elles comme avec les âmes; il a reçu en

naissant les clefs des symboles et l'intelligence des figures: ce qui semble à d'autres incohérent et contradictoire, n'est pour lui qu'un contraste harmonique, un accord à distance sur la lyre universelle. Lui-
même il entre bientôt dans ce grand concert, et, comme ces vases
d'airain des théâtres antiques, il marie l'écho de sa voix à la musique
du monde.[59]

This is particularly true of the lyric poet, says Sainte-Beuve, and it
places him above the level of trivial public debate. The artist is in
the center of the universe as in a vast theater where he is surrounded
by the concert, which he then joins. Like Hugo, he is an "écho
sonore."[60] Sainte-Beuve places the emphasis on revelation; the cen-
tripetal impulse dominates the centrifugal.

In one of the last poems of *Les Feuilles d'automne* Hugo places primary
emphasis on the poet's inner world which is enriched by moving
outward:

> Si vous avez en vous, vivantes et pressées,
> Un monde intérieur d'images, de pensées,
> De sentiments, d'amour, d'ardente passion,
> Pour féconder ce monde, échangez-le sans cesse
> Avec l'autre univers visible qui vous presse!
> Mêlez toute votre âme à la création![61]

When the artist's creation fuses with God's creation and becomes
part of the general harmony, as Sainte-Beuve and Leroux see it, it
shows their common source. As Leroux says, "nous puisons vie à la
vie universelle."[62] Hugo has said it, Leroux says it again, everything
that exists serves as a source of art, the ugly and the horrible along
with the beautiful: they are all parts of universal life. He chooses the
same image of the musical chord as Sainte-Beuve but interiorizes it:
we are in the universe of the soul:

---

[59] *Pensée* XVIII, 150.

[60]
> Tout souffle, tout rayon, ou propice ou fatal,
> Fait reluire et vibrer mon âme de cristal,
> Mon âme aux mille voix, que le Dieu que j'adore
> Mit au centre de tout comme un écho sonore.

"Ce siècle avait deux ans," *Les Feuilles d'automne* (June 1830).

[61] "Pan" (November 1831).

[62] *Revue Encyclopédique*, 52, 406; see note 39.

La poésie est cette aile mystérieuse qui plane à volonté dans le monde entier de l'âme, dans cette sphère infinie dont une partie est couleurs, une autre sons, une autre mouvements, une autre jugement, etc., mais qui toutes vibrent en même temps suivant certaines lois, en sorte qu'une vibration dans une région se communique à une autre région, et que le privilège de l'art est de sentir et d'exprimer ces rapports, profondément cachés dans l'unité même de la vie. Car de ces vibrations harmoniques des diverses régions de l'âme il résulte un *accord*, et cet accord c'est la vie; et quand cet accord est exprimé, c'est l'art; or, cet accord exprimé, c'est le symbole; et la forme de son expression, c'est le rythme, qui participe lui-même du symbole; voilà pourquoi l'art est l'expression de la vie, le retentissement de la vie, et la vie elle-même.[63]

The principle of *l'accord* is the same for all the arts, and they all merge into art *tout court*, all poetries into music.

For Desjardins, one of the collaborators of *La Muse Française*, the heavenly harmonies of the song of the Muse mark a new union between poetry and music:

Celui qui écoute les mélodies de cette ravissante muse, doute longtemps si les sons qu'il entend lui viennent du dehors et par l'intermédiaire des sens, ou ne s'élèverait pas du fond de son âme, où comme de vives et douces vibrations se font sentir; accords harmonieux, non pas de sons, mais de délicieuses sensations qui l'avertissent en effet qu'une alliance nouvelle entre la musique et la poésie est consommée, et que la lyre et les harpes de la poésie des anciens sont descendues aux profondeurs de l'âme du poète moderne.[64]

Even when the artist does not "hear" the universe, he must "donner une voix aux harmonies mystérieuses, qui unissent la pensée à la matière, et les choses de la terre aux choses du ciel."[65] Many of the comments (Leroux's in particular) bear traces of the mythic and primitivist theories we are already familiar with: the Pythagorean theories of celestial harmony in which music gives a revelation of the relationships of all things, and the myth of the poet-musician, Orpheus, privy to the secrets of the universe. For the poet of primitive times, as for Orpheus, poetry and music are inseparable. Lamartine also seeks this "new alliance," descended from the old, in a passage

---

[63] *Ibid.*, 52, 407-08.
[64] Marsan ed., I, 131-32 (same article quoted above, p. 173).
[65] Théry, *De l'esprit*, p. 316.

from his "Avertissement" to *La Mort de Socrate* which is reminiscent of Fabre d'Olivet: "Si la poésie n'est pas un vain assemblage de sons, elle est sans doute la forme la plus sublime que puisse revêtir la pensée humaine: elle emprunte à la musique cette qualité indéfinissable de l'harmonie qu'on a appelée céleste…"

Most music critics of the time were more down-to-earth, partly no doubt since they were dealing with heard melodies, not supposedly sweeter unheard ones. (Berlioz himself said in a letter to Victor Hugo, "Les *Poètes Littérateurs* ont de si étranges idées sur la musique…")[66] The long-standing debates continue, the first as to whether instrumental music can rank with vocal music, the other as to whether words or music should dominate in singing, specifically in opera. The supporters of instrumental music gain some ground in the late 1820s. Fétis explains the power of instrumental music to move the educated ear by the fact that the emotions it arouses are vague and have no determinate object. "Moins l'objet est évident, moins l'esprit est occupé, plus l'âme est émue, car rien ne la distrait de ce qu'elle éprouve."[67] On the other hand, in opera it is well to be occupied with words, says Fétis, for concentrated emotion is tiring and we need moments of rest. This critic definitely does not believe that poetry and music must exist together, on the contrary, one diminishes the effect of the other. Words effectively sung can move the listener, says Fétis, but they weaken the action of the music, for we cannot perceive several sensations at once by the same sense, hence words and music alternate in their effect. Fétis is preponderantly interested in the emotional effect of music; in his view, verbal expression appeals only to the mind and hence is not the essential object of music.

It is unanimously agreed in the 1820s that Rossini has greatly advanced the art of the opera, and his popularity remains firm. However, the young Berlioz has already started attacking him and his admirers,[68] and by 1830 even some of these admirers would like to see opera go beyond the "sensual" Rossini and the Italian school in general.[69] In

---

[66] *Correspondance générale*, ed. Pierre Citron (Paris: Flammarion, 1972-), I, 508; 10 Dec. 1831.

[67] "Sur la philosophie et sur la poétique de la musique,"*Revue Musicale*, 3 (1828), 515.

[68] In *Le Corsaire*, 10 Aug. 1823 and 11 Jan. 1824. In his *Mémoires*,2 vols. (Paris: Garnier-Flammarion, 1969), I, 142, he calls Rossini a composer of "musique sensualiste."

[69] See Joseph d'Ortigue, "Palingénésie musicale," *L'Artiste*, 6 (1833), 237. D'Ortigue was a friend of Berlioz.

late 1831 the Parisians are impatiently awaiting Meyerbeer's grand opera *Robert le Diable*, and Berlioz's orchestral music is making its mark.[70] Moreover, the song which accomplishes the perfect fusion of poetry with music is at hand: around 1830 the German *Lied* is being discovered in France, and the French art song, fathered by Berlioz, is just being born.[71]

Not unexpectedly, the theory of music lags behind that of the other arts. In 1828 Fétis points out the need for an esthetics of music. He outlines the salient questions which should be solved[72] but does not himself long persist in the effort to solve them. In the early 1830s, *L'Artiste* also often complains of the dearth of competent music criticism. Berlioz will soon step in to fill part of the gap, particularly after accepting the post of music critic at the *Journal des Débats* in 1835.[73]

The picture of the poet vibrating sympathetically with the universal lyre serves to remove us even farther from the conception of art as an imitation of nature. Bonstetten, who was so sensitive to music and devoted so much attention to it, was one of the first to say emphatically that art was not an imitation of nature (see above, p. 41). Nor is *La Muse Française* satisfied with imitation: "la poésie, âme de tout ce qui doit vivre, réunion sublime de l'idéal et du réel, en un mot expression plutôt qu'imitation de la nature..."[74] Now Leroux attacks "les absurdes théories qui ont pris pour base l'imitation de la nature, même en indiquant pour but l'aspect du beau." Art is "le développement de la nature sous un de ses aspects à travers l'homme."[75] As Frenhofer says in *Le Chef d'oeuvre inconnu*, "La mission de l'art n'est pas de copier la nature mais de l'exprimer."

---

[70] See Jacques Barzun, *Berlioz and the Romantic Century*, 2 vols. (Boston: Little, Brown, 1950), I, 214.

[71] See Frits Noske, *La Mélodie française de Berlioz à Duparc* (Amsterdam: North Holland Publishing Co., 1954), pp. 82-83.

[72] *Revue Musicale*, 3 (1828), 415-16.

[73] We should note one particularly pertinent article on imitation in music, "De l'imitation musicale," *Gazette Musicale*, 1 and 6 Jan. 1837. Berlioz, though he rejects traditional theories of imitation (Carpani, Lacépède), does accept it as legitimate on certain conditions: 1) it should be the means, never the end, 2) it must be worthy of holding the listener's attention, 3) it must not ape reality but be close enough to avoid misconceptions, 4) physical imitation should not occur in a spot where *emotional* imitation (expressiveness) is called for. This article is discussed by Barzun, *Berlioz*, I, 172-81, in a chapter on program music.

[74] A. Guiraud, "Nos Doctrines," II, 15.

[75] *Revue Encyclopédique*, 52, 409.

Among the arts, poetry is the privileged domain of symbolic expression because of the special powers attributed to the word by theorists of various nuances, from eclectics to illuminists. Writers, literary critics, and theorists naturally accord great importance to language and often see it as the superior medium of expression. Sainte-Beuve and Hugo, as we have seen, insisted on the inseparability of *fond* and *forme* and worked for the reform of poetic vocabulary and versification; Leroux, Deschamps, and Magnin foresaw that poets would form their own special language. Poetic language would be different from common language, sometimes obscure, even hermetic, and would require an effort, even a special gift, for comprehension by the reader.

For the eclectics too, we recall the pre-eminent place of the word: for Victor Cousin it is "le symbole le plus vaste et le plus clair" which gives poetry its privileged place, and for Jouffroy it sets literature off from the other arts. Language, says Jouffroy, is made up of conventional signs which cannot reproduce directly the natural expression of the invisible, as other arts do. "Mais la littérature ne peut se faire comprendre que par des mots, par des sons qui n'ont en eux-mêmes aucune vertu esthétique, qui ne viennent que d'une convention." Some might argue that music and painting are superior to literature as direct communication, that they operate as Delacroix's "bridge between souls," since no words impede the passage of the vague message, which is on a higher plane than thought.[76] But according to Jouffroy, literature is saved by the evocative power of words, conventional signs though they may be.

> Alors elle prononce des mots qui rappellent à notre mémoire l'invisible tel que nous l'avons vu sous ses signes naturels... elle emploie un signe qui réveille dans l'imagination l'image du signe naturel... C'est avec les sens que nous percevons les différents objets qui nous donnent ou peuvent nous donner l'émotion esthétique; pour éprouver cette émotion, il faut qu'avec leur secours nous saisissions hors de nous l'objet complexe composé de l'invisible et du visible, qui seul nous émeut esthétiquement... quand la littérature éveille des souvenirs sensibles dans l'imagination, l'image, rappelant l'objet, produit le même effet que l'objet sur la sensibilité, c'est-à-dire, l'émotion esthétique. (226, 227)

Once this image has been found, literature is placed on the same line as the other arts, except that it acts through an image instead of through

---

[76] See E. Gilson, *Painting and Reality*, p. 128.

natural signs. Jouffroy thus pulls literature back into his general esthetic system, though it operates in a special way.

A return to the primitive language, to which the illuminists and their sympathizers aspired, would lead to a transparent symbol. This "langue de la nature," which existed before that spoken by man, was a hieroglyphic language in which each image represented an idea. In Christian doctrine it corresponds to "le Verbe," as distinguished from "la parole" of physical human language, the Word by which God accomplished creation and drew form from chaos.[77] Material languages spring from and draw upon this divine language, "âme et génie de la parole." They express the idea of things by their form (words), just as the material world is an expression of the suprasensible world. The poet supposedly has the power to go through the material language to reach the "natural" language and his work partakes of both, as his vision encompasses both sensible and suprasensible worlds. This is exactly the way that Alexandre Soumet defines the poet's search: "Tout est symbolique aux yeux du poète, et, par un échange continuel d'images et de comparaisons, il cherche à retrouver quelques traces de cette langue primitive révélée à l'homme par Dieu même, et dont nos langues modernes ne sont qu'une ombre affaiblie."[78] Richer is impatient of constraints and inveighs against the rules of the grammarians; language (at this level) is only an instrument, says he; the future poet will draw upon the metaphors of the "natural" language.[79]

Language itself leads to an understanding of the universe. If all objects of nature are emblems whose explanation man has lost, says Ballanche, "... cette explication ne doit-il pas la trouver dans la parole, révélation qui ne finit point, chaîne éternelle dont tous les anneaux, attachés entre eux, sont d'indestructibles traditions."[80]

Though belief in symbolic expression is widespread, there is little theoretical discussion of any extent on what characterizes symbolic language. It is agreed that it communicates knowledge that cannot be expressed any other way. But distinctions are not consistently made between "symbol," "metaphor," "emblem," "allegory," and "hieroglyphic". (Creuzer distinguished between allegory, which indicates a general idea distinct from it, and symbol, which is "l'idée

---

[77] See Eckstein, review of Constant, *De la religion*, *Le Catholique*, 1 (1826), 103-04.
[78] Review of Baour-Lormian trans. of *La Jérusalem délivrée*, *La Muse Française*, I, 296.
[79] See A. Viatte, "Les Swedenborgiens en France de 1820 à 1830," *Revue de Littérature Comparée*, 11 (1931), 439, 442.
[80] *Orphée*, *Oeuvres*, V, 168.

même rendue sensible et personnifiée.")[81] "La métaphore est le *trope*, le *symbole* universel," says Baron Massias. "Renfermant un double objet, celui qui *figure* et celui qui est figuré, elle donne un double plaisir en donnant une double connaissance."[82]

In one of the few articles on the subject, entitled "Du style symbolique," Pierre Leroux includes the words "symbole," "emblème," and "allégorie" in the general "métaphore"; all these tropes (figures) fulfill the function of "faire entendre au lieu de dire," which a simple comparison (simile) is incapable of accomplishing.[83] The artist, like most men, substitutes the sensible for pure conceptions, whereas the mathematician works in the opposite direction. The metaphorical method consists of not developing the idea but only the image, which becomes a true emblem. He gives as examples Hugo's "Les Deux Iles" and *René's* birds of passage. This kind of allegorizing, says Leroux, is the great invention of the last fifty years, the trope having been out of use for two hundred years. In an historical sketch of its recent development, Leroux begins with Bernardin de Saint-Pierre and advances through writers French and foreign up to the contemporary school. Byron is a particularly clear case of a poet who conceives ideas already in sensible form: "les idées ont, pour ainsi dire, des pieds et des bras,..." Hugo is the most audacious of all; he does not seem to be able to tolerate abstraction, but sometimes presents a whole poem as a symbol. Leroux cites as particularly admirable examples the description of the Spanish city in the Preface to *Les Orientales* and "Mazeppa." Unlike the Neoclassic Jean-Baptiste Rousseau, who proceeded by dispersion, Hugo proceeds by concentration. (Once more the image of the "miroir de concentration" is applicable.)

Though comment on the question is rather sparse, there seem to be two schools of thought on whether the symbol should be clear or obscure, precise or vague. According to C. Desmarais, imagery serves to clarify cloudy thought.[84] Taking the symbol in its broad sense of sensible aspect, Jouffroy classes the arts according to the character of the symbol: since sound is a vague symbol, music is a vague art; since form is a precise symbol, painting is a precise art. The sounds

---

[81] Guigniaut translation, I.i.30, quoted in D.O. Evans, *Le Socialisme romantique*, p. 152.

[82] *Principes de littérature*, p. 168.

[83] *Le Globe*, 8 April 1829.

[84] *Essai*, p. 97.

of language reproduce in our minds natural symbols, which may be vague or precise, hence poetry may be as vague as music or as precise as painting (136). He sees the difference between Classicism and Romanticism as preference of the former for the clear and the latter for the vague. He opts for clarity and intelligibility and stresses the importance of the natural sign (217). He gives as an example of the natural symbol the natural physiognomy, which is a symbol of the soul (the human face is the most expressive of all objects). In writing, this would be a portrait in words of a living person in action, represented as exactly as possible. Jouffroy by his emphasis on the natural and the contemporary is a kind of realist. His examples are drawn not from poetry but from fiction and drama. But the choice of the symbol is more complicated than that, for signs, which have a natural meaning, also acquire meaning through imagination, association of ideas, and convention (as in the case of religious symbols) (138).

The feeling for the infinite, says Eckstein, can be contained in a limited form: "On ne doit pas oublier qu'à travers la beauté antique perce comme une vague et légère sensation de l'infini, et que la beauté moderne peut de son côté trouver ses bornes et se renfermer dans ses limites."[85] This corresponds to Creuzer's "plastic symbol" (as opposed to the "mystic symbol"): the statues of the Greek gods, with their precision of form, summoned the spectator to a meditation on the infinite.[86]

On the other hand, Pierre Leroux defends the vague and suggestive forms corresponding to the "mystic symbol." It is important, says he, that the metaphor, which is the very life of poetry, move us out of the realm of discursive thought: when the image replaces the abstract term and the vague expression replaces the proper term, then abstraction disappears and mystery is born.[87] Moreover, vagueness is unavoidable when treating certain subjects: modern poets, like idealist metaphysicians, are often (unjustly) criticized for vagueness, says E. Richer; [88] if Lamartine appears vague, says H. Patin, it is for good reason: "C'est la condition du sujet, mystérieux, obscur, comme l'infini, qui est bien une conception de notre esprit, mais non pas une idée claire."[89]

---

[85] "Du beau," *Le Catholique*, 11 (1828), 348-49.
[86] Cf. Ancillon, *Mélanges*, p. 21; passage quoted on p. 84.
[87] "Du style symbolique," *Le Globe*, 8 April 1829.
[88] "Du vague en littérature," *Lycée Armoricain*, 3 (1824), 371.
[89] Review of *Harmonies poétiques et religieuses*, *Revue Encyclopédique*, 47 (1830), 133.

For the illuminists, and others who share some of their ideas, the poetic symbol may be not so much vague as obscure for the uninitiated, who do not have access to the "natural" language. Perhaps it is because the symbol accedes to the divine and is found through revelation that the illuminist theoretician cannot define the form it may take in the poem. It is true that Ballanche says, "Notre poésie est un symbole, et c'est ce que doit être toute vraie poésie, car la parole de Dieu, lorsqu'elle se transforme en la parole de l'homme doit se rendre accessible à nos sens, à nos facultés, s'incarner en nous, devenir nousmêmes…"[90] But is it really "accessible à nos sens"? He goes on: "Au fond, le symbole est une vérité que la langue de l'homme ne peut dire à l'oreille de l'homme, et que l'esprit dit à l'esprit." Behind the symbolic language is a truth that is communicable only from one mind to another, but the nature of this language remains mysterious.

The symbol can be anything drawn from our common life, says Leroux: "Le poète ira puiser dans le monde extérieur, à la source commune des impressions, dans l'océan de vie où nous sommes tous plongés, des images capables de donner par elles-mêmes les sensations, les sentiments et jusqu'aux jugements qu'il veut exprimer."[91]

Whether mystic or plastic, vague or precise, the symbol should not be immutable but constantly shifting. Charles Magnin warns against its being fixed by ideological or artistic dogma.[92] It changes with time; we recall Jouffroy's insistence on the contemporary. At the opposite ideological and religious pole, Ballanche too (in a relatively unobscure moment) says that the symbol must keep pace with historical changes:

> S'il fut donné au Dante de se rendre l'expression puissante de son temps, qui me donnera d'être l'expression vraie du mien?… qui me présentera les faits divins sous la forme accessible du symbole? Toutefois le symbole actuel ne peut plus être le symbole primitif, les condescendances divines devant changer selon les progrès du genre humain.[93]

Ballanche looks forward, not back to some inaccessible primitive language.

It is generally true that for all nuances of spiritualism, the symbol has a special resonance, communicating the mystery of the invisible

---

[90] *Orphée, Oeuvres*, VI, 82.
[91] *Revue Encyclopédique*, 52 (1831), 407.
[92] Review of Viollet-le-Duc, *Précis d'un traité de poétique et de versification*, *Le Globe*, 7 Oct. 1829.
[93] *Prolégomènes, Palingénésie sociale, Oeuvres*, IV, 7.

and the transcendent. "Par la voie du symbole," says Ballanche, "le poète essaie de communiquer aux hommes ce que le langage ordinaire est impropre à exprimer."[94] It is the only way of communicating the feeling for the infinite or the divine, concepts otherwise impossible to represent; here religious and artistic symbols meet. The symbol may be vague and enigmatic, but generally the artist chooses natural phenomena that open vast spaces, suggest elevation or induce dizziness. The sea and the sky are the most common symbols for the infinite, as everyone knows, but the critics of the 1820s seldom expound upon this, though, like P. Leroux and Baron Massias, they sometimes themselves make metaphorical use of these phenomena. "Le propre du sublime," says Massias, "est de porter notre sensibilité au-delà de ses limites, et de la perdre dans l'océan de la beauté absolue, ou dans les profondeurs les plus secrètes de notre infini relatif..."[95]

As opposed to the ancient symbol, plastic and precise, characteristically presented in a precise form, contemporary artists often give preference to the vague or obscure, couched in a medium of imprecise contours. It is less likely to be sculpture than painting, less likely to be painting than literature. Whatever the medium, form is sometimes ill-defined. Does this represent a dominance of *fond* over *forme*, as Pictet claimed? Does it show the inevitable imperfection of the incarnation of the idea? Does the sketchiness of form reflect the artist's spontaneous effort to capture a fleeting inspiration? All of these things, no doubt. Or is a vague, ill-defined form the most suitable expression of a thought that is vague or elusive, a concept accessible to the mind but that the senses cannot grasp? Then *fond* and *forme* would find a new balance. A few passing remarks suggest that this is so. C. Desmarais connects Romanticism with "ébauches sublimes";[96] H. Patin sees the rapport between vagueness of expression and the infinite in the poetry of Lamartine; according to Eckstein, "le beau moderne imparfait mais immense offre une idée d'infini."[97] These are fragmentary mentions of the elements of a new Romantic esthetic.

Whatever the differences of emphasis among writers of varying tendencies, the conception of the symbol as it developed through the

---

[94] *Ibid.*, IV, 7.
[95] *Théorie du beau*, p. 15.
[96] *Essai*, p. 91.
[97] *Le Catholique*, 11 (1828), 347.

Restoration, is a duality within a unity, or a duality striving to become a unity. The sensible world as material expression of the spiritual world, sense impressions as the route to spiritual revelation, the concrete work of art springing from an idea—these are dualities. The fundamental unity and harmony of the universe, a single divine force behind all things, intuitive communication of the artist with the divine through phenomena, man's creation as a continuation and completion of God's creation, the primitive language where the sign is identical with the thing signified, the inseparability of *fond* and *forme*—these are unities. The symbol, sensible expression of an idea, should be a fusion of the two universes. The poets in particular are eager to mingle their souls with all creation and join in the universal harmony. The poet-seers before all others lay claim to the symbol.

Conclusion

If we seek to define the evolution in the conception of the proper representation of the world in the work of art during the thirty-year period we have examined, we can perhaps best do so by following the changes in the meaning of the word "expression." The principle of art as self-expression, widely accepted in the period of Neo-classical dominance, is reinforced and extended in the search for individuality and originality. But what renews the lyric impulse is not only deeper introspection but a stronger sensibility and an interchange with outer forces, natural or human.

Expression is also traditionally linked to the mimetic, and it remains so, but it increasingly detaches art from the strictly imitative. In Davidian Neo-classicism it follows certain accepted forms. A decisive change takes place when expression is extended beyond human beings, and to a lesser extent animals, to encompass all phenomena. Victor Cousin's definition of expression as the outer manifestation of an inner essence fits the Neo-classic conception, but it also goes beyond reference to physical and moral qualities into a transcendental domain.

Cousin sometimes uses the words "expression" and "symbol" synonymously, and others will follow him. It is surely an excessive ambiguity of vocabulary to equate two fundamentally different concepts. An expressive image shows the thing itself, pointing up some significant characteristics. A symbolic object in the traditional sense, as Quatremère de Quincy defines it, represents a concept, but does not, cannot resemble it. It often takes the form of allegory: a blind-

207

folded woman holding scales symbolizes justice. This conventional symbol still has an abstract character, but it is clear and universally understood, and it is selective.[1] When a symbol not only represents but coincides with an inner essence, symbolic meaning is everywhere, in all objects, diffused throughout the universe. The symbol has become vague, suggestive, often difficult to grasp. The artist's task is made immeasurably more difficult, not only in vision but in execution, and the spectator/reader must also bring great sensitivity to his encounter with the work of art. Jouffroy's natural symbol for justice, the portrait of a just man, which is to replace the traditional allegorical figure, shows the merging of the expressive and the symbolic. In practice it may not be intelligible to others than the artist.

French painting of the period tends to remain close to traditional concepts of the symbol, but renews and extends them. Delacroix's figure leading the people is at the same time a robust young Parisian woman and, as the title indicates, an allegory of freedom. As for Mazeppa, a subject so often treated by painters of the time (Géricault, Delacroix, Horace Vernet, Louis Boulanger, later Chassériau), as well as by Byron, Hugo, and later Liszt, it too constitutes a renewal of an old symbol, in this case, unbridled passion or genius represented by the mythic Phaethon, whose chariot is dragged off by runaway horses (see use of this symbol by Girodet, p. 79). Portrait, still life, and especially landscape are better able to convey the pervasive and vague symbolism described by the theorists. It is present in many French paintings, though less obviously so than in the haunting, mysterious landscapes of Caspar David Friedrich or in the dizzying abysses and immense spaces of Turner and John Martin. The critics of the time, however, did not remark upon it.

The word "symbol" also sometimes comes to mean not only the person or thing represented but the concrete elements of the artistic medium. Jouffroy speaks of words, forms, and sounds as symbols. Heinrich Heine also, in the early 1830s, says that the means by which the artist realizes his idea are symbols, and the arts he refers to are the plastic arts and drama, which are closest to the mimetic.

> In the recitative arts, these means consist of intonations or sounds and words. In the representative arts, they are supplied by color and form.

[1] The distinction between allegory and symbol is central to German Romantic esthetics. For a discussion of writings on this subject by Goethe, Schelling, and others, see T. Todorov, *Théories du symbole* (Paris: Eds. du Seuil, 1977), pp. 235-59. The French are less precise in their distinctions than the Germans.

Sounds and words, colors and forms, that above all which appeals to sense, are, however, only symbols of the idea — symbols which rise in the soul of the artist when it is moved by the Holy Ghost of the world, for his artworks are but symbols, by which he conveys his ideas to others.[2]

But this is uncommon in France, where most critics and theoreticians see symbols, in this sense, only in literature, rather than placing all artistic media on the same plane. They give a special status to the word, a sign which can become a symbol. A visual representation of the visual, or a verbal representation of the verbal, does not have the same power of transformation as a verbal representation of the nonverbal.

If we started the period with an opposition between naturalistic representation and ideal beauty, we may see the opposition after thirty years as between the expressive or picturesque representation of reality and an effort to impart to the work of art a transcendental significance, the life force in the universe, which most would call divine, responding, through phenomena, as Jouffroy says, to the life force within. The difference between naturalism and the ideal beauty of the Neoclassics was a difference not only between ways of seeing the world but between styles in the plastic arts. This difference in styles is not so evident in 1830. Color, movement, and picturesque detail may serve to dazzle the senses or to give us a glimpse of a spiritual realm. A symbol may be extraordinary, even fantastic, or it may be a natural symbol, an ordinary, everyday object. Forms and styles are fluid, they vary greatly, but the differences are individual rather than corresponding to marked differences in the conception of art. The correspondence between *fond* and *forme* increasingly preoccupies theorists as well as the artists themselves, but it remains characteristic of the 1820s that the idea should dominate over the manifestation of the idea.

What then of the frequency of the image of the concave mirror? It indicates dominance of the representation of the real world; the subjectivity of the artist is manifested in the personal way in which reality is concentrated. In spite of the insistence on the transparency of the symbol, the artist remains firmly attached to the real world, to represent it, to transform it, to penetrate beyond it. He uses the elements to convey his own inspirations.

[2] "The Salon: The Exhibition of Pictures of 1831," *Morgenblatt*, literary supplement of *Augsburger allgemeine Zeitung*, quoted in Elizabeth Gilmore Holt, ed., *The Triumph of Art for the Public* (Garden City: Anchor Press/Doubleday, 1979), p. 304.

Of the two great movements or dominating tendencies which are an outgrowth of the esthetic principles we have discussed, realism will come before symbolism, and in 1830 we are on its threshold. But nascent realism is still tinged with spiritualism (*pace* Stendhal); positivism is yet to come. Who better embodies Jouffroy's theories than Balzac? The artist should not forget the spirit behind the matter; when Victor Hugo is seen to do otherwise, he is taken to task.

Whether the artist gives dominance to the visible world or the invisible, the two are inseparably joined, and the work is expressive, to one degree or another, in one sense or another that the critics of the time gave to the term.

Selected Bibliography

Primary Sources

A. BOOKS

Ampère, Jean-Jacques. *De l'histoire de la poésie* (Athénée de Marseille). Marseille: Feissat aîné et Demonchy, 1830.

Ancillon, F[rançois]. *Mélanges de littérature et de philosophie.* 2 vols. Paris: H. Nicolle et F. Schoell, 1809

André, Yves-Marie (Père). *Essai sur le beau.* In *Oeuvres philosophiques.* Introduction de Victor Cousin. Paris: Charpentier, 1843; rpt. Geneva: Slatkine, 1969.

Anot, Cyprien. *Essai sur les nouvelles théories littéraires.* In *Elégies rhémoises.* Paris: Amyot, 1825, pp. 153-201.

Arsenne, L.C. *Manuel du peintre et du sculpteur.* 2 vols. Paris: Librairie Encyclopédique de Roret, 1833.

Artaud, Nicolas. *Essai littéraire sur le génie poétique du 19e siècle.* Paris: Rignoux, 1825.

Audin, J.M.V. *Du romantique.* In *Florence.* 2 vols. Paris: Pigoreau et Ponthieu, 1822, pp. i-cxxiii.

Ballanche, Pierre Simon. *Du sentiment considéré dans ses rapports avec la littérature et les arts.* Lyon: Ballanche et Barret; Paris: Calixte Volland, An IX-1801.

_____. *Oeuvres.* Paris: Bureau de l'Encyclopédie des Connaissances Utiles, 1833; rpt. Geneva: Slatkine, 1967.

Balzac, Honoré de. *Oeuvres diverses.* Paris: Conard, 1935. T. I (1824-1830).

Barthez, P.J. *Théorie du beau dans la nature et les arts.* 2nd ed. Paris: Vigot Frères, 1895. [1st ed. 1807.]

Batteux, Charles. *Les Beaux Arts réduits à un même principe.* Paris: Saillant et Nyon, Veuve Desaint, 1773; rpt. Geneva: Slatkine, 1969.

Berlioz, Hector. *Correspondance générale*. Ed. Pierre Citron. 3 vols. Paris: Flammarion, 1972.

Bonstetten, Charles-Victor de. *Etudes de l'homme*. 2 vols. Geneva: Paschoud, 1821.

_____. *Recherches sur la nature et les lois de l'imagination*. 2 vols. Geneva: Paschoud, 1807.

Cabanis, [Pierre Jean Georges]. *Oeuvres complètes*. Vol. V. Paris: Bossange, Didot, 1823-1825.

[Castelnau, Junius]. *Essai sur la littérature romantique*. Paris: Le Normant père, 1825.

Castil-Blaze [Blaze, F.H.J.]. *De l'opéra en France*. 2 vols. Paris: Janet et Cotelle, 1820.

Chabanon, Michel. *De la musique considérée en elle-même et dans ses rapports avec la parole, les langues, la poésie et le théâtre*. Paris: Pissot, 1785.

Chateaubriand, François-René Vicomte de. *Le Génie du christianisme*. 2 vols. Paris: Flammarion, 1948.

_____. "Lettre sur l'art du dessin dans les paysages." In *Oeuvres complètes*. Vol. I. Bruxelles: Weissenbruch, 1829.

Chénier, André. *Oeuvres complètes*. Bibliothèque de la Pléiade. Paris: Gallimard, 1958.

Chénier, Marie-Joseph. "Essai sur le principe des arts." In *Oeuvres diverses et inédites*. Vol. X. Bruxelles: Weissenbruch, 1816, pp. 91-130.

Condillac, Etienne de. *Essai sur l'origine des connaissances humaines*. In *Oeuvres complètes*. Vol. I. Paris: Lecointe et Durey, 1821-1822; rpt. Geneva: Slatkine, 1970.

Cordier de Launay, Louis-Guillaume-René. *Théorie circonsphérique des deux genres du beau avec application à toutes les mythologies et aux cinq beaux-arts*. Berlin: Imprimerie de Louis Quîen, 1806.

Cousin, Victor. *Cours d'histoire de la philosophie*. Vol. I. Paris: Pichon et Didier, 1828-1829.

_____. *Cours de philosophie. Du vrai, du beau et du bien*. Publié par Adolphe Garnier. Paris: Hachette, 1836.

_____. Manuscript Notes for his Courses 1817-1829. Bibliothèque Victor Cousin.

Damiron, Philippe. *Essai sur l'histoire de la philosophie en France au dix-neuvième siècle*. Paris: Ponthieu, 1828.

Delacroix, Eugène. *Correspondance générale*. Ed. André Joubin. 4 vols. Paris: Plon, 1936-1938.

_____. *Journal*. Ed. André Joubin. Vol. I (1822-1852). Paris: Plon, 1950.

Delécluze, Etienne J. *Louis David, son école et son temps*. Paris: Didier, 1855.

_____. *Précis d'un traité de peinture*. Paris: Bureau de l'Encyclopédie portative, 1828.

_____. *Souvenirs de soixante années*. Paris: Michel Lévy Frères, 1862.

Delestre, J.B. *Etudes des passions appliquées aux beaux-arts.* Paris: Joubert, 1833.

Delille, Jacques. *L'Imagination.* 2 vols. Paris: Giguet et Michaud, 1806.

Deschamps, Emile. *La Préface des Etudes françaises et étrangères d'Emile Deschamps.* Introduction and notes by Henri Girard. Paris: Presses Françaises, 1923.

Desmarais, Cyprien. *Essai sur les classiques et les romantiques.* Udron: Vernarel et Tenon, 1824.

Diderot, Denis. *Oeuvres.* Bibliothèque de la Pléiade. Paris: Gallimard, 1946.

Droz, Joseph. *Etudes sur le beau dans les arts.* Paris: Renouard, 1815.

Dubos, Jean-Baptiste. *Réflexions critiques sur la poésie et sur la peinture.* 7th ed. Paris: Pissot, 1770; rpt. Geneva: Slatkine, 1967.

Dussault, Jean-J.-F. *Annales littéraires.* 5 vols. Paris: Maradan et Lenormant, 1818-1824.

Emeric-David, Toussaint-Bernard. *Recherches sur l'art statuaire.* Paris: Nyon aîné, An XIII-1805.

Fabre d'Olivet, Antoine. *La Musique.* 2nd ed. Paris: Chacornac, 1910.

Fauriel, Claude. *Réflexions préliminaires.* In Baggesen, *La Parthénéide.* Paris: Treuttel et Würtz, 1810.

Fétis, François-Joseph. *La Musique mise à la portée de tout le monde.* 2nd ed. Paris: Duverger, 1834.

Flocon, Ferdinand et Aycard, Marie. *Salon de 1824.* Paris: Leroux, 1824.

Gautier, Théophile. *Histoire du romantisme.* Paris: Charpentier et Fasquelle, 1874.

Girodet-Trioson, Anne Louis. *Oeuvres posthumes.* 2 vols. Paris: Renouard, 1829.

Grétry, André-E.-M. *Mémoires, ou Essais sur la musique.* 3 vols. Paris: Imprimerie de la République, An V.

Guizot, François. *Etudes sur les Beaux-arts en général.* Paris: Didier, 1852.

—————. "Vie de Shakespeare." In Shakespeare, *Oeuvres complètes.* Vol. I. Trans. Letourneur, F. Guizot. 13 vols. Paris: Ladvocat, 1821, pp. i-ciii.

Hegel, G.W.F. *Aesthetics.* Trans. T.M. Knox. 2 vols. Oxford: Clarendon Press, 1975.

Hoffman, François-Benoît. *Oeuvres.* Vol. VII. Paris: Lefebvre, 1829.

Hugo, Victor. *Oeuvres complètes.* Vols. I/1, II/1, III/1. Ed. Jean Massin. Paris: Club Français du Livre, 1967-1969.

Ingres, Jean-Auguste-Dominique. *Ecrits sur l'art.* Preface by Raymond Cogniat. Paris: La Jeune Parque, 1947.

Ingres raconté par lui-même et par ses amis. Introduction by Pierre Courthion. Vésenaz-Geneva: Pierre Cailler, 1947.

Jal, Auguste. *L'Artiste et le philosophe.* Paris: Ponthieu, 1824.

—————. *Esquisses, croquis, pochades.* Paris: Ambroise Dupont, 1828.

Joubert, Joseph. *Carnets.* Ed. A. Beaunier. 2 vols. Paris: Gallimard, 1938.

Jouffroy, Théodore. *Cours d'esthétique.* Preface by Ph. Damiron. Paris: Hachette, 1843.

Kant, Immanuel. *Critique of Judgement.* Trans. by James C. Meredith. Oxford: Clarendon Press, 1952.

Kératry, Auguste-Hilarion. *Du beau dans les arts d'imitation.* 3 vols. Paris: P. Audot, 1822.

Lacépède, Etienne, comte de. *La Poétique de la musique.* Paris: A l'Imprimerie de Monsieur, 1785.

Lahalle, P. *Essai sur la musique.* Paris: Rousselon, 1825.

Lamartine, Alphonse de. "Avertissement" à *La Mort de Socrate.* In *Oeuvres choisies.* Ed. Maurice Levaillant. Paris: Hatier, 1925.

_____. *Correspondance.* 2nd ed. 4 vols. Paris: Hachette; Furne: Jouvet, 1881-1882.

_____. "Des destinées de la poésie." In *Méditations poétiques.* Grands Ecrivains de la France. Vol. II. Paris: Hachette, 1922.

_____. *Voyage en Orient.* 2 vols. Paris: Hachette, Furne, 1887.

Lemercier, Népomucène. *Cours analytique de littérature générale.* Vol. I. Paris: Nepveu, 1817, pp. 7-55.

Lessing, Gotthold Ephraim. *Laocoön.* Trans. E. A. McCormick. New York: Bobbs-Merrill, 1962.

Maine de Biran, François-Pierre. *Influence de l'habitude sur la faculté de penser.* Vol. II of *Oeuvres.* Ed. Pierre Tisserand. Paris: F. Alcan, 1922.

Massias, Nicolas, baron de. *Principes de littérature, de philosophie, de politique et de morale.* 4 vols. Paris: F. Didot, 1826.

_____. *Théorie du beau et du sublime.* Paris: F. Didot, 1824.

Michiels, Alfred. *Histoire des idées littéraires en France au dix-neuvième siècle.* 2 vols. Paris: Coquebert, 1842.

Morel, Alexandre-Jean. *Principe acoustique nouveau et universel de la théorie musicale,* ou *Musique expliquée.* Paris: Bachelier, 1816.

Nodier, Charles. *Contes.* Classiques Garnier. Ed. Pierre-Georges Castex. Paris: Garnier, 1961.

_____. *Contes de la veillée.* Paris: Fasquelle, 1875.

_____. *Mélanges de littérature et de critique.* 2 vols. in one. Paris: Raymond, 1820; rpt. Geneva: Slatkine, 1973.

_____. *Oeuvres.* 12 vols. Paris: Renduel, 1832-1837; rpt. Geneva: Slatkine, 1968.

Pichot, Amédée. *Voyage historique et littéraire en Angleterre et en Ecosse.* 3 vols. Paris: Ladvocat et Charles Gosselin, 1825.

Pictet, Adolphe. "Quelques idées sur la distinction des genres classique et romantique." In *Bibliothèque Universelle (Littérature),* 33 (1826), 217-44.

Ponce, Nicolas. *Mélanges sur les beaux-arts.* Paris: Leblanc, 1826.

Quatremère de Quincy, Antoine Chrysostome. *Considérations morales sur la destination des ouvrages de l'art.* Paris: Crapelet, 1815.

_____. *Essai sur l'Idéal dans ses applications pratiques aux oeuvres de l'imitation propre des arts du dessin.* Paris: Adrien Leclère, 1837.

_____. *Essai sur la nature, le but et les moyens de l'imitation dans les beaux-arts*. Paris: Didot l'aîné, 1823.

Richer, Edmond. *Du genre descriptif*. Nantes: Mellinet-Malassis; Paris: Raynal, 1822.

_____. *Le Livre de l'homme de bien* suivi de *La Visite de Gustave*. Paris: Treuttel et Würtz; Nantes: Mellinet, 1832.

Rousseau, Jean-Jacques. *Essai sur l'origine des langues*. Ed. Charles Porset. Bordeaux: Guy Ducros, 1970.

Sainte-Beuve, Charles Augustin de. *Les Consolations*. Paris: Urbain Canel, Levavasseur, 1830.

_____. *Vie, pensées et poésies de Joseph Delorme*. Ed. Gérald Antoine. Paris: Nouvelles Editions Latines, 1956.

Saint-Martin, Louis Claude de. *De l'esprit de choses*. 2 vols. Paris: Laran, Debrai, Payolle, An 8.

_____. *Des erreurs et de la vérité*. Vol. I of *Oeuvres majeures*. Ed. R. Amadou. 3 vols. Hildesheim and New York: Georg Olms Verlag, 1975.

_____. *L'Homme de désir*. Lyon: n.p., 1790.

_____. *Oeuvres posthumes*. Vol. II. Tours: Letourmy, 1807.

Senacour, Etienne Pivert de. *Obermann*. Ed. critique publiée par G. Michaut. 2 vols. Paris: E. Cornely, 1912-1913.

_____. *Rêveries sur la nature primitive de l'homme*. Ed. J. Merlant and G. Saintville. 2 vols. Paris: Droz, 1940.

Sobry, Jean-François. *La Poétique des arts*. Paris: Delaunay, Brunot-Labbe, Colnet, 1810.

Staël-Holstein, Anne-Marie-Germaine (Necker) baronne de. *De l'Allemagne*. Grands Ecrivains de la France. 5 vols. Paris: Hachette, 1958-1960.

_____. *De la littérature*. Ed. Paul Van Tieghem. 2 vols. Geneva: Droz; Paris: Minard, 1959.

_____. *Oeuvres complètes*. Vols. II, VIII, IX. Paris: Treuttel et Würtz, 1820-1821.

Stendhal (Pseudonym of Beyle, Henri Marie). *Oeuvres complètes*. Ed. V. del Litto and E. Abravanel. 47 vols. Geneva: Edito-Service, S.A., 1967-1974.

Théry, Augustin François. *De l'esprit et de la critique littéraires chez les peuples anciens et modernes*. 2 vols. Paris: Hachette, Locard et Davi, 1832.

Vigny, Alfred comte de. *Oeuvres complètes*. Vol. II. Bibliothèque de la Pléiade. Paris: Gallimard, 1948-1950.

Villoteau, G.A. *Recherches sur l'analogie de la musique avec les arts qui ont pour objet l'imitation du langage*. 2 vols. Paris: Imprimerie Impériale, 1807.

Viollet-le-Duc, Emmanuel. *Précis d'un traité de poétique et de versification*. Paris: Bureau de l'Encyclopédie portative, 1829.

Winckelmann, Johann Joachim. *History of Ancient Art*. Trans. G. Henry Lodge. 4 vols. in two. New York: Frederick Ungar, 1968.

————.*Writings on Art*. Ed. David Irwin. London: Phaidon, 1972.

B. PERIODICALS CONSULTED

Annales de la Littérature et des Arts. 1820-1829.
Archives Littéraires de l'Europe. 1804-1808.
Archives Philosophiques. 1817-1818.
L'Artiste. 1830-1834.
Le Catholique. 1826-1829.
Le Constitutionnel. 1822-1824.
Le Courrier Français. 1820-1828.
La Décade Philosophique, Littéraire et Politique. 1796-1807. (Files incomplete.)
Gazette Littéraire. 1830-1831.
Le Globe. 1824-1830.
Journal des Débats. 1814-1828.
Journal de Paris. 1816-1827.
Lycée Français. 1819-1820.
Mercure du 19e Siècle. 1823-1830.
La Minerve Française. 1818-1820.
La Minerve Littéraire. 1820-1821.
La Muse Française. 1823-1824. Ed. J. Marsan. 2 vols. Paris: Cornély, 1907.
Le National. 1830.
La Quotidienne. 1823-1827.
La Revue de Paris. 1829-1832.
La Revue des Deux Mondes. 1831-1835.
Revue Encyclopédique. 1819-1831.
Revue Française. 1828-1830.
Revue Musicale. 1827-1830.
Le Temps. 1830.

Secondary Sources

Abraham, Pierre et Desné, Roland, eds. *Manuel d'histoire littéraire de la France*. Vol. IV, 1789-1848. Paris: Editions Sociales, 1965-.

Abrams, Meyer H. *The Mirror and the Lamp*. Oxford, London, New York: Oxford University Press, 1953.

Baldensperger, Fernand. *Sensibilité musicale et romantisme*. Etudes Romantiques. Paris: Presses Françaises, 1925.

Barzun, Jacques. *Berlioz and the Romantic Century*. 2 vols. Boston: Little, Brown, 1950.

Baschet, Robert. *E.-J. Delécluze témoin de son temps 1781-1863*. Paris: Boivin, 1942.

————. "Ingres et Delacroix: Une esquisse de leur doctrine artistique." In *Revue des Sciences Humaines*, 34, no. 136 (1969), 625-43.

Bénichou, Paul. *Le Sacre de l'écrivain 1750-1830*. Paris: Corti, 1973.

Benoît, François. *L'Art français sous la Révolution et l'Empire*. Paris: L.-Henry May, 1897.

Bertrand, Louis. *La Fin du classicisme et le retour à l'antique*. Paris: Hachette, 1897.

Birkett, Mary Ellen. "*Pictura, Poesis* and Landscape." In *Stanford French Review*, II (1978), 235-46.

Blin, Georges. *Stendhal et les problèmes du roman*. Paris: Corti, 1954.

Boas, George. *French Philosophies of the Romantic Period*. Baltimore: Johns Hopkins University Press, 1925.

Boime, Albert. *The Academy and French Painting in the Nineteenth Century*. London, New York: Phaidon Press, 1971.

Bosanquet, Bernard. *A History of Aesthetic*. London: Macmillan, 1932.

Bowman, Frank Paul. *Le Christ romantique*. Geneva: Droz, 1973.

Bozzetto, R. "Nodier et le théorie du fantastique." *Europe*, no. 614-15 (1980), pp. 70-78.

Canat, René. *L'Hellénisme des romantiques*. 2 vols. Paris: Dider. Vol. I: *La Grèce retrouvée*, 1951. Vol. II: *Le Romantisme des Grecs 1826-1840*, 1953.

_____. *La Renaissance de la Grèce antique (1820-1850)*. Paris: Hachette, 1911.

Cartwright, Michael T. *Diderot critique d'art et le problème d'expression*. Diderot *Studies*, XIII. Geneva: Droz, 1969.

Cassagne, Albert. *La Théorie de l'art pour l'art en France*. Paris: Hachette, 1906.

Chouillet, Jacques. *L'Esthétique des lumières*. Paris: Presses Universitaires de France, 1974.

Coleman, Francis X.J. *The Aesthetic Thought of the French Enlightenment*. Pittsburgh: University of Pittsburgh Press, 1971.

Croisille, Christian. "L'Harmonie lamartinienne." In *Colloques Sainte-Beuve et Lamartine*, 8 Nov. 1968. Paris: A. Colin, 1970, pp. 86-101.

Czerny, Sigmond. *L'Esthétique de Louis-Claude de Saint-Martin*. Leopol, Warsaw: Ed. de la "Ksiaznica Polska T.N.S.W.," 1920.

Decottignies, Jean. *Prélude à Maldoror*. Paris: A. Colin, 1973.

Delaborde, Henri. *Ingres*. Paris: Plon, 1870.

Dowden, Edward. "French Aesthetics." In *Contemporary Review*, I (1866), 279-310.

Eggli, Edmond, and Martino, Pierre. *Le Débat romantique en France, 1813-1830*. Vol. I: *1813-1816* by E. Eggli. Paris: Les Belles Lettres, 1933.

Evans, David Owen. *Le Socialisme romantique: Pierre Leroux et ses contemporains*. Paris: Marcel Riviere et Cie, 1948.

Fabre, Jean. *André Chénier*. Connaissance des Lettres. Paris: Hatier-Boivin, 1955.

_____. "La Poésie et le poète selon André Chénier." In *Information Littéraire*, no. 3 (1966), pp. 99-105.

Fizaine, Jean-Claude. "Les Aspects mystiques du Romantisme." In *Romantisme*, 11 (1976), 4-14.

Folkierski, Wladyslaw. *Entre le classicisme et le romantisme.* Cracovie: Académie des Sciences et des Lettres; Paris: Champion, 1925.

Fontaine, André. *Les Doctrines d'art en France de Poussin à Diderot.* Paris: Laurens, 1909.

French Painting 1774-1830: The Age of Revolution. Detroit: Detroit Institute of Arts; New York: Metropolitan Museum of Art. In France: *De David à Delacroix.* Paris: Réunion des Musées Nationaux, 1974-1975.

Germain, François. *L'Imagination d'Alfred de Vigny.* Paris: Corti, 1961.

Gilman, Margaret. *The Idea of Poetry in France from Houdar de la Motte to Baudelaire.* Cambridge: Harvard University Press, 1958.

Gilson, Etienne. *Painting and Reality.* Bollingen Series XXXV/47. New York: Pantheon Books, 1957.

Gombrich, Ernst H. *Art and Illusion.* Bollingen Series XXXV/5. New York: Pantheon Books, 1960.

Grate, Pontus. *Deux critiques d'art à l'époque romantique: Gustave Planche et Théophile Thoré.* Stockholm: Almquist and Wiksell, 1959.

Guichard, Léon. *La Musique et les lettres du temps du romantisme.* Paris: Presses Universitaires de France, 1955.

Guitton, Edouard. *Jacques Delille (1738-1813) et le poème de la nature en France de 1750 à 1820.* Paris: Klincksieck, 1974.

Haskell, Francis; Levi, Anthony; and Shackleton, Robert, eds. *The Artist and the Writer in France.* Oxford: Clarendon Press, 1974.

Hautecoeur, Louis. *Littérature et peinture en France du 17e au 20e siècle.* Paris: Colin, 1942.

Henning, Ian Allan, *"L'Allemagne" de Madame de Staël et la polémique romantique.* Paris: Champion, 1929.

Holt, Elizabeth Gilmore, ed. *The Triumph of Art for the Public.* Garden City: Anchor Press/Doubleday, 1979.

Honour, Hugh. *Romanticism.* New York: Harper & Row, 1969.

Huyghe, Rene. *Delacroix.* Trans. Jonathan Griffin. New York: Harry N. Abrams, 1963.

_____. *L'Esthétique de l'individualisme à travers Delacroix et Baudelaire.* Oxford: Clarendon Press, 1955.

Iknayan, Marguerite. *The Idea of the Novel in France: The Critical Reaction 1815-1848.* Geneva: Droz; Paris: Minard, 1961.

Juden, Brian. "L'Esthétique: 'L'Harmonie immense qui dit tout.'" In *Romantisme*, no. 5 (1973), pp. 4-17.

_____. *Traditions orphiques et tendances mystiques dans le romantisme français (1800-1855).* Paris: Klincksieck, 1971.

Keyser, Eugénie de. *L'Occident romantique.* Geneva: Skira, 1965.

Kitchin, Joanna. *Un Journal "philosophique": La Décade 1794-1807.* Paris: Minard, Lettres Modernes, 1965.

Krestovsky, Lydie. *La Laideur dans l'art à travers les ages.* Paris: Eds. du Seuil, 1947.

Lee, Rensselaer, W. *"Ut pictura poesis:* The Humanist Theory of Painting." In *Art Bulletin,* 22 (1940), 197-269. Also published as a book; New York: Norton, 1967.

Le Gall, Béatrice. *L'Imaginaire chez Senancour.* 2 vols. Paris: Corti, 1966.

Lipschutz, Ilse Hempel. *Spanish Painting and the French Romantics.* Cambridge: Harvard University Press, 1972.

Lombard, Alfred. *L'Abbé Du Bos.* Paris: Hachette, 1913.

Maritain, Jacques. *Creative Intuition in Art and Poetry.* Bollingen Series XXXV/1. New York: Pantheon Books, 1953.

Marsan, Jules. *La Bataille romantique.* Paris: Hachette, 1912.

Matoré, Georges. "Les Notions d'art et d'artiste à l'epoque romantique." In *Revue des Sciences Humaines,* no. 62-63 (1951), pp. 120-36.

May, Gita. *Diderot et Baudelaire critiques d'art.* 2nd ed. Geneva: Droz, 1967.

Michaut, Gustave M.A. *Sainte-Beuve avant les "Lundis".* Fribourg: Librairie de l'Universite (B. Veith), 1903.

Michel, Arlette et Alain. "La Parole et la beauté chez Joubert, Jouffroy et Ballanche." In *Revue d'Histoire Littéraire de la France,* 80 (1980), 195-208.

Monchoux, André. "Madame de Staël interprète de Kant." In *Revue d'Histoire Littéraire de la France,* 66 (1966), 71-84.

Mongrédien, Jean. "La Théorie de l'imitation en musique au début du romantisme." In *Romantisme,* no. 8 (1974), pp. 86-91.

Montandon, Alain. "De la peinture romantique allemande." In *Romantisme,* no. 16 (1977), pp. 82-94.

Moreau, Pierre. "De la symbolique religieuse." In *Comparative Literature Studies,* 4 (1967), 5-16.

Münch, Marc-Mathieu. *La "Symbolique" de Friedrich Creuzer.* Paris: Ophrys, 1976.

Mustoxidi, T.M. *Histoire de l'esthétique française 1700-1900.* Paris: Champion, 1920.

Noske, Frits. *La Mélodie française de Berlioz à Duparc.* Amsterdam: North Holland Publishing Company, 1954.

Osborne, Harold. *Aesthetics and Art Theory.* New York: Dutton, 1970.

Panofsky, Erwin. *Idea: A Concept in Art Theory.* Trans. Joseph J.S. Peake. Columbia: University of South Carolina Press, 1968.

Pommier, Jean. *La Mystique de Baudelaire.* Paris: Belles Lettres, 1932.

Poulet, Georges. *Mesure de l'instant.* Paris: Plon, 1968.

Praz, Mario. *On Neoclassicism.* Trans. Angus Davidson. Evanston: Northwestern University Press, 1969.

Rosenthal, Léon. *L'Art et les artistes romantiques.* Paris: Le Goupy, 1928.

————. *La Peinture romantique.* Paris: L.-H. May, 1900.

Schneider, Rene. *L'Esthétique classique chez Quatremère de Quincy.* Paris: Hachette, 1910.

Scruton, Roger. *Art and Imagination*. London: Methuen, 1974.

Setbon, Raymond. *Libertés d'une écriture critique: Charles Nodier*. Geneva: Slatkine, 1979.

Shroder, Maurice Z. *Icarus: The Image of the Artist in French Romanticism*. Cambridge: Harvard University Press, 1961.

Souriau, Etienne. *La Correspondance des arts*. Paris: Flammarion, 1969.

Talbot, Emile J. "Stendhal, le beau et le laid: Autour de quelques problèmes esthétiques de l'époque romantique." In *Stendhal Club*, no. 20 (1978), pp. 205-15.

Teyssèdre, Bernard. *L'Esthétique de Hegel*. Paris: Presses Universitaires de France, 1958.

Todorov, Tzvetan. *Théories du symbole*. Paris: Eds. du Seuil, 1977.

Tronchon, Henri. "Une Science à ses débuts en France: L'Esthétique." In *La Revue du Mois*, 14 (1912), 37-64.

Unger, Esther. "An Aesthetic Discussion in the Early Nineteenth Century: The *Idéal*." In *Modern Language Quarterly*, 20 (1959), 355-59.

Venturi, Lionello. *History of Art Criticism*. Trans. Charles Marriott. New York: Dutton, 1936.

Viallaneix, Paul, *et al. Le Préromantisme: Hypothèque ou hypothèse?* Actes du Colloque à Clermont-Ferrand le 29-30 juin 1972. Paris: Klincksieck, 1975.

Viatte, Auguste. *Les Sources occultes du romantisme*. 2 vols. Paris: Champion, 1928.

_____. "Les Swedenborgiens en France de 1820 à 1830." In *Revue de Littérature Comparée*, 11 (1931), 416-50.

Ward, Patricia A. *Joseph Joubert and the Critical Tradition: Platonism and Romanticism*. Geneva: Droz, 1980.

Will, Frederic. *Flumen historicum: Victor Cousin's Aesthetic and Its Sources*. Chapel Hill: University of North Carolina Press, 1965.

_____. *Intelligible Beauty in Aesthetic Thought*. Tübingen: Max Niemeyer, 1958.

_____. "Winckelmann and Cousin: The Nature of Ideal Beauty." In *Symposium*, 10 (1956), 60-74.

Index

STANFORD FRENCH AND ITALIAN STUDIES

Editor: Alphonse Juilland